DIFFICULT HERITAGE AND IMMERSIVE EXPERIENCES

Difficult Heritage and Immersive Experiences examines the benefits involved in designing and employing immersive technologies to reconstruct difficult pasts at heritage sites around the world.

Presenting interdisciplinary case studies of heritage sites and museums from across a range of different contexts, the volume analyzes the ways in which various types of immersive technologies can help visitors to contextualize and negotiate difficult or sensitive heritage and traumatic pasts. Demonstrating that some of the most creative applications of immersive experiences appear in and at museums and heritage sites, the book showcases how immersive technologies offer the possibility of confronting and disputing presumptions and prejudices, triggering responses, delivering new knowledge, initiating dialogue and challenging pre-existing notions of collective identity. The book provides a conceptual, as well as a hands-on, approach to understanding the use of immersive technologies at sensitive sites around the globe.

Difficult Heritage and Immersive Experiences is essential reading for researchers and students who are interested in, or engaged in the study of, cultural heritage, memory, history, politics, dark tourism, design and digital media or immersive technologies. The book will also be of interest to museum and heritage practitioners.

Agiatis Benardou is Senior Research Associate at ATHENA Research Center in Athens, Greece, and Postdoctoral Fellow at the Department of Informatics, Athens University of Economics and Business.

Anna Maria Droumpouki is Research Associate at Ludwig-Maximilians-University München, Institute of Eastern and Southeastern European History.

DIFFICULT HERITAGE AND IMMERSIVE EXPERIENCES

Edited by
Agiatis Benardou and Anna Maria Droumpouki

Routledge
Taylor & Francis Group
LONDON AND NEW YORK

First published 2023
by Routledge
4 Park Square, Milton Park, Abingdon, Oxon OX14 4RN

and by Routledge
605 Third Avenue, New York, NY 10158

Routledge is an imprint of the Taylor & Francis Group, an informa business

British Library Cataloguing-in-Publication Data
A catalogue record for this book is available from the British Library

ISBN: 978-1-032-06085-9 (hbk)
ISBN: 978-1-032-06086-6 (pbk)
ISBN: 978-1-003-20065-9 (ebk)

DOI: 10.4324/9781003200659

Typeset in Bembo
by Deanta Global Publishing Services, Chennai, India

CONTENTS

FIGURES

CONTRIBUTORS

Georgios Artopoulos is Assistant Professor at the Cyprus Institute, where he works on immersive environments and digital simulation for the study of built heritage and the creative exploration of historical narratives. He leads the Virtual Environments Lab, where the spatial aspects of historic cities are explored through externally funded projects (under H2020, ENI-CBC-MED and Cyprus Research and Innovation Foundation frameworks), the DARIAH ERIC, and his role as Member of the Scientific Advisory Board of JPI Urban Europe, where he works on matters of sustainable and liveable cities and urban areas.

Agiatis Benardou is Postdoctoral Fellow at the Department of Informatics, Athens University of Economics and Business, and Senior Researcher at the Digital Curation Unit, ATHENA R.C. She has held posts as Research Associate at the Departments of Information Science and Critical Studies, University of Glasgow, and Visiting Scholar at the Department of Near Eastern Studies, University of California Berkeley. Agiatis has served as Teaching Fellow in Digital Curation at the Department of Media and Culture, Panteion University, and is co-ordinating the core course on Applications of Digital Methods in the Humanities at the MSc on Digital Methods in the Humanities, Department of Informatics, AUEB. Agiatis holds a PhD in Ancient History and Classical Archaeology from King's College London. As of January 2023 she will be Director of DARIAH-EU.

Erik Champion is Enterprise Fellow at UniSA, Emeritus Professor (and past UNESCO Chair) at Curtin University, Honorary Research Professor at Australian National University and Honorary Research Fellow at The University of Western Australia. He researches digital heritage, digital humanities and serious games. He wrote *Rethinking Virtual Places* (IUP, 2021), *Critical Gaming: Interactive History and Virtual Heritage* (Routledge, 2015) and *Organic Design in Twentieth-Century Nordic*

Architecture (Routledge, 2019). He edited *Virtual Heritage: A Guide* (Ubiquity Press, 2021) and *The Phenomenology of Real and Virtual Places* (Routledge, 2018) and co-edited *Cultural Heritage Infrastructures in Digital Humanities* (Routledge, 2017).

Tsong-Zung Chang (Johnson Chang) is independent curator, guest professor of China Academy of Art (Hangzhou), and director of Hanart TZ Gallery (Hong Kong). He has been active in curating Chinese exhibitions since the 1980s. Current active projects include Jia Li Hall, a series of research on Confucian rites and aesthetics; West Heavens, Sino-Indian exchange in art and social thought; Yaji Garden, which investigates Chinese aesthetic space and its culture of connoisseurship; and Inter-Asia School, which has organized "Inter-Asia Biennale Forums" at the Shanghai Biennial, Gwangju Biennial, Taipei Biennial and Kochi-Muziris Biennale.

Anna Maria Droumpouki is Research Associate at Ludwig-Maximilians-University München, Institute of Eastern and Southeastern European History. She holds a BA in History and Archaeology, an MA in Museology and a PhD in Contemporary Greek and European History (all from the University of Athens). She was Visiting Research Scholar at the Leibniz Institute for Jewish History and Culture – Simon Dubnow and Postdoctoral Fellow at the Research Centre for Modern History of Panteion University. She was the Scientific Coordinator of the Greek-German Project "Memories of the Occupation in Greece" at Free University Berlin (2016–2018).

Silvina Fernandez-Duque is Future Projects Manager at the United States Holocaust Memorial Museum. She explores the potential of emerging technologies in museums, researching and prototyping new experiences for visitors and learners, with a particular focus on difficult history. She received her BA in Art History from Williams College and MA in Architectural History from the University of Virginia.

Michael Haley Goldman became the Executive Director of New Hampshire Humanities in September 2021. New Hampshire Humanities is the independent, statewide nonprofit affiliate of the National Endowment for the Humanities and provides wide-ranging humanities programmes that connect people with ideas and each other through free public events, literature-based programmes, and grantmaking. Until 2021, he served as the United States Holocaust Memorial Museum's (USHMM) Director of Future Projects, combining techniques from museum studies, user experience, evaluation, and design thinking to create new experiences for museums and online audiences. Previously, he served as the USHMM's Director of Global Classroom and Evaluation from 2009 to 2014 and Director of the Benjamin and Vladka Meed Registry of Jewish Holocaust Survivors from 2006 to 2009.

Edward González-Tennant is Assistant Professor of Anthropology at the University of Texas Rio Grande Valley. He earned his PhD in 2011 from the University of Florida for original work on the 1923 Rosewood Massacre. His research focuses on the application of digital technologies in archaeology and history, a transdisciplinary approach combining geographic information systems (GIS), 3D modelling, geophysics and remote sensing. The use of these technologies allows Dr González-Tennant to investigate the legacies of racial violence in African American history, decolonization of collaborative archaeology in the Caribbean, the effects of ethnolinguistic differences on Chinese migration and modelling the impacts of storm surge and sea level rise on heritage resources in rural locations.

Lily Hibberd is an interdisciplinary artist, writer and academic based in France. Working across painting, video, performance, sound and installation art, her creative practice contends with frontiers of time and memory, past and present. Between 2016 and 2019, she led an Australian Research Council project on digital memory and immersive media at the University of New South Wales Sydney. She is the Founding Editor of the art writing publication, un Magazine, Adjunct Lecturer at UNSW Sydney and Associate Researcher at École polytechnique fédérale de Lausanne's (EPFL) Laboratory for Experimental Museology (eM+) and the Le Laboratoire de Recherche sur les Cultures Anglophones (LARCA) laboratory of the Université de Paris Cité.

Sarah Kenderdine is Researcher at the forefront of interactive and immersive experiences for galleries, libraries, archives and museums. She is Professor at EPFL, Switzerland, where she leads the Laboratory for Experimental Museology (eM+), exploring the convergence of cultural heritage, imaging technologies, immersive visualization, visual analytics, digital aesthetics and cultural (big) data. Sarah Kenderdine is also Director and Lead Curator of EPFL Pavilions, an art-science initiative blending experimental curatorship and contemporary aesthetics with open science, digital humanism and emerging technologies. In 2021 she was made Fellow of the British Academy.

Sharon Macdonald is Director of the Hermann von Helmholtz Centre for Cultural Techniques at the Humboldt University, Berlin. She has wide-ranging interests in questions of heritage. Current projects include "Making Differences: Transforming Museums and Heritage in the Twenty-First Century" (Alexander von Humboldt Foundation) and "Challenging Populist Truth-Making in Europe: the Role of Museums in a Digital 'Post-Truth' Society" (Volkswagen). Her publications include *Difficult Heritage: Negotiating the Nazi Past in Nuremberg and Beyond* and *Memorylands: Heritage and Identity in Europe Today*. She has co-authored *Heritage Futures* and edited *Doing Diversity in Museums and Heritage: A Berlin Ethnography*.

Eytan Mann is Architect and Interactive Designer working at the intersection of computational design and historiography. He is currently pursuing a PhD in Architecture at MTRL (Material Topology Research Lab) at the Technion Faculty of Architecture and Town Planning. In his work, he examines modes of transmedia storytelling by mixing archival material with digital modelling. Eytan holds a

Master of Science in Architecture Studies (SMArchS) from the MIT School of Architecture and Planning.

Georgios Papaioannou is Associate Professor at the Department of Informatics of the Athens University of Economics and Business and Head of the department's computer graphics group. His research is focused on real-time computer graphics algorithms, photorealistic rendering, illumination-driven scene optimization and shape analysis, with more than 85 publications in these areas. He has participated as principal investigator, research fellow and developer in many national, EU-funded and industrial research and development projects and has worked in the past as Software Engineer in virtual reality systems' development and production.

Sara Pitcairn is Prototype Developer and Researcher at the US Holocaust Memorial Museum, where she explores new technologies and techniques for engaging with Holocaust history. To evaluate the potential of these new approaches, she learns alongside museum audiences about what makes experiences accessible, engaging, relevant and meaningful. She received a BS in Mechanical Engineering from Yale University and an MA in Public History from American University.

Jeffrey Shaw has been a leading figure in new media art since its emergence from the performance, expanded cinema and installation paradigms of the 1960s to its present-day technology-informed and virtualized forms. Shaw was the founding director of the ZKM Institute for Visual Media Karlsruhe, co-founder and director the UNSW iCinema Center for Interactive Cinema Research, and the Dean of the School of Creative Media, City University of Hong Kong (CityU). His numerous awards include the Prix Ars Electronica Golden Nica for Visionary Pioneer of Media Art and ACM Siggraph Distinguished Artist Award for Lifetime Achievement in Digital Art. Shaw is currently Chair Professor at Academy of Visual Art, Baptist University Hong Kong, and Adjunct Professor at City University Hong Kong.

Aaron Sprecher is Associate Professor at the Technion Faculty of Architecture and Town Planning. He leads the Material Topology Research Laboratory at the Faculty of Architecture (https://mtrl.net.technion.ac.il/). In parallel, he is co-founder and partner of the award-winning practice Open Source Architecture (www.o-s-a.com), a collaborative research group that brings together international researchers in design, architecture, engineering and media research. His research and design work focuses on the synergy between information technologies, computational languages and automated architectural systems, examining how technology informs and generates innovative approaches to design processes. Aaron Sprecher co-edited *Architecture in Formation—On the Nature of Information in Digital Architecture* (2013, London: Routledge/Taylor and Francis) and *Instabilities and Potentialities* (2019, London: Routledge/Taylor and Francis).

ACKNOWLEDGEMENTS

This book was conceived during the first wave of the pandemic, in 2020. It was designed and largely synthesized in times of extreme insecurity and hard lockdowns. We would like to thank all contributors for responding so promptly during such peculiar times.

We would not have considered a publication on immersive experiences and difficult heritage had it not been for our Block 15 project team at the Department of Informatics, Athens University of Economics and Business: Panos Constantopoulos, Georgios Papaioannou, Dimitris Christopoulos, Giorgos Gousis, Yannis Ragos, Maria Ilvanidou, Vicky Dritsou and Spilios Spiliopoulos. They are all dear friends and companions, not just colleagues. Our debates on the details of the Block 15 immersive production were the seeds of many of the ideas discussed here. Not least, Georgios Monogioudis, our Block 15 Project Officer at the German Embassy in Athens, deserves our gratitude. We owe him, for his constant support, encouragement and constructive criticism.

We dedicate this book to our respective partners, Kostis Giannopoulos and Iason Chandrinos, who endured our mid-pandemic authoring and editing toils in the most loving ways possible.

DIFFICULT HERITAGE AND IMMERSIVE EXPERIENCES

Agiatis Benardou and Anna Maria Droumpouki

Difficult heritage

"Difficult Heritage", a term first coined by Sharon Macdonald, represents those "histories and pasts that do not easily fit with self-identities of the groups of whose pasts or histories they are part" (Macdonald 2009). The term refers to a historically significant past that remains embodied in sites, buildings, artworks, monuments and other artefacts, but which is difficult to reconcile with "a positive, self-affirming contemporary identity" (Macdonald 2009). It deals with unsettling histories rather than with those heroic or progressive histories with which museums and heritage sites have more traditionally been associated. In reality, and as noted by William Logan and Keir Reeves, "most societies have their scars of history resulting from involvement in war and civil unrest or adherence to belief systems based on intolerance, racial discrimination or ethnic hostilities" (Logan and Reeves 2009). Yet, past violence is often eschewed in favour of narratives that contribute to the creation and maintenance of social or national identities in a more positive, progressive, way. "Heritage" references materiality, intangibleness and durability over time and across value systems, a scope which underlines the inherent significance of material remains, including built space, in the reconstruction of the past.

Over the last decade, discourse has explored how contested or violent events have been remembered, misremembered or forgotten – and, as a corollary, how their physical traces have been preserved or not preserved, either consciously or unconsciously. Even decay as a product of negligence cannot be considered to be entirely unintentional.[1] Places of imprisonment and execution are sites of "Difficult Heritage" *par excellence*, although, as noted by Shu-Mei Huang and Hyun Kyung Lee, "prisons, as an architecture of punishment and imprisonment, are seldom seen as favored heritage buildings" (Huang and Lee 2020). Shu-Mei

DOI: 10.4324/9781003200659-1

Huang and Hyun Kyung Lee, in their study of post-colonial re-articulation of punishment and imprisonment as a tool to reframe contemporary society, utilize prisons within the East Asian heritagescape to focus on a regional history independent of the socio-political influences of a "global" heritage.

In her book *Memorylands*, Sharon Macdonald examines Europe's evolution as a "memoryland", a continent obsessed with the disappearance of collective memory and its preservation. Alongside widespread public agonizing over "cultural amnesia" – the loss of our foothold in the past, the disappearance of "eyewitnesses" to key events and the wane of inter-generational memory transition – there has been a corresponding urgency in both public and private memory work. Europe's rural- and urban-scapes have been gradually populated by the mnemonic products of this collective work – heritage sites, memorials, museums, plaques and art installations designed to preserve those histories that might otherwise be lost (Macdonald 2013).

Indeed, since the 1970s the commemoration and preservation of the "difficult past" has become a subject of increasing public attention. This public preoccupation, uniform in neither its presentation nor pace, has been termed the "European memory complex": A patterned repertoire of recollection and "past presencing" (Macdonald 2013). The publicly accessible past is embodied in buildings and places. It is acknowledged, processed and expressed through the experience of ruined buildings, monuments and commemorative rituals, mnemonic practices that are repeated, and adapted, across Europe. In the escalation of the European historical turn to memory, we have witnessed the emergence of a new dimension: The distinction of place through reference to historical narrative, whereby historical content is legitimized through exhibitions, memorial plaques and other modes of urban commemoration (Macdonald 2013). The recognized number of sites of "Difficult Heritage" has grown significantly from the latter half of the 20th century to date, particularly so those of atrocity, in line with a greater socio-cultural engagement with heritage in general (Macdonald 2009). Sites of historical trauma, internment, massacre and genocide are today regarded as "heritage sites", a far cry from their characterization even a generation ago (Logan and Reeves 2009).

Immersive experiences

Installation and new media artists have long created immersive experiences (mixed methods of virtual reality [VR], augmented reality [AR] or forms of perceptual and interactive use of technologies that blur the line between the physical and digital world, i.e., create a hybrid reality aiming at embracing all spheres of the user's attention), employing varying forms and levels of technology. Artists like Olafur Eliasson presented immersive work as early as 2003 at the Turbine Hall of Tate Modern, London: The Weather Project, as it was called, employed a semicircular screen, a ceiling of mirrors and artificial mist to create the illusion of a sun.[2] Since then, immersive art has evolved into a much-discussed field,[3] while museums are increasingly using immersion to enhance exhibition experiences. Just before the global pandemic, in early 2020, the Louvre offered audiences its very first immersive virtual reality experience to complement the Leonardo Da Vinci retrospective exhibition. "Mona Lisa: Beyond the Glass" effectively presented users with Leonardo's techniques in an informative and enjoyable way.[4] Unfortunately, no user experience report of the production is available.

Despite the opportunities afforded by immersion, there has been a lack of substantive evidence to evaluate current approaches and guide future developments, especially in difficult heritage sites. Particularly in Europe, immersion has not been employed widely in such sites. In Scotland alone, however, immersion is used in difficult heritage sites, with The Battle of Bannockburn Visitor Centre being the most prominent. In Bannockburn, the site of the 1314 AD battle considered to be Robert the Bruce's great victory, visitors of The Battle of Bannockburn Visitor Centre enter an interactive battle room followed by an exquisite and unique immersive heritage experience. Guided by a game master, visitors lead their own sections of either the Scottish or English armies, learn battle strategies and win or lose the Scottish Crown. The multi-award experience relies on a very simple yet clever concept: Visitors are allocated randomly to the Scottish or English armies, regardless of their age, nationality, political orientation. Immersed in the Bannockburn experience, a Scottish nationalist visitor may have to fight and win the battle for the English army. In times of Brexit and amidst talks about a new Scottish Independence Referendum, this is a true immersion in difficult heritage.

Needless to mention, the questions emerging are obvious and remain to be addressed convincingly enough: What do immersive experiences have to offer or add to the perception and memorialization of difficult heritage? Are immersive experiences the future of reconceptualizing, mediating and communicating sensitive or contested sites and their histories? Are they serving an educational purpose?

A study by Gad Yair (2014) showcased that, due to the trauma the Third Reich engendered, German memorials appear to be reluctant to advocate, direct or lead, thus shying away from manipulative educational strategies that they associate with the Third Reich. They intentionally avoid manipulating emotions or directing visitors to arrive at pre-determined moral conclusions and refrain from using expressive props to create authentic experiences. Yair argued that despite the many possibilities for introducing visitors to authentic and challenging exhibits and artefacts, German memorial sites and documentation avoided using emotive cues. Consequently, without a more challenging approach, these sites are unlikely to create key experiences with lasting effects on visitors' identities (Yair 2014). More recently, Marina Hassapopoulou's transdisciplinary work on the cognitive and affective demands emerging from immersion as a means of achieving innovative learning objectives such as critical thinking provides a new angle on our point of view of immersion as an innovative mode of education, inquiry and practice, both in terms of methodology and in terms of technology:

> The remix aesthetic, the productive distractions from predictable learning outcomes, as well as the "unfinished" and makeshift nature of these projects is something that I find adds value to this kind of process-oriented pedagogy because it remains in touch with the pre-institutionalized experimental ethos that prompted the formation of the digital humanities in the first place.
>
> *(Hassapopoulou 2018, 30)*

The case studies considered in the present volume illustrate how changes in practice in the field of "Difficult Heritage" reflect the transition from what M. J. Rymsza-Pawlowska describes as the *logic of preservation*, an understanding of history underwritten by material evidence and expressed by a sense of the past as monumental and spectacular, to the present experiential engagements with history (Rymsza-Pawlowska 2017).

Immersive engagement privileges an affective and experiential production of historical knowledge, pacing the subject within the past. In her chapter, Sharon Macdonald explores the effects and ethics of immersion in dangerous pasts. These are pasts that while widely and generally negatively evaluated in contemporary society are nevertheless – in part at least – glorified or viewed nostalgically by some. Through a discussion of examples of immersive heritage experiences about World War II history, including of Nazism, the chapter explores where the ethical limits of immersion lie. The consideration of immersion here is not restricted to digitally – or other technologically – induced immersion but also addresses forms such as reenactment. The potentially different effects of these are discussed. The chapter acknowledges arguments that immersion may allow for a sense of greater proximity to the past and thus potentially of empathy for certain historical persons or experiences, and that it might kindle desires for further reflection or learning, as well as that there may be a generational shift in the pedagogical effectiveness of certain forms of mediation. Primarily, however, it considers the risks of certain subject positioning – impersonation – and of a reduction of reflexivity that immersion may encourage. In conclusion it also reflects on possible strategies to reduce this.

George Artopoulos reflects on the capacity of practices of immersion for engaging inhabitants and occupants of historic neighbourhoods that are facing tensions, due to contested cultural heritage, in positive everyday experiences by means of interactive visualization of 3D spatial data. Practical aspects of this approach are presented through the analysis of interdisciplinary research activities developed in the context of European and international collaborations. These activities were conducted with the objective to contribute to the integration and socio-spatial cohesion of these "challenged by their history" sites that bear difficult pasts. The chapter raises theoretical considerations to provide a framework for this practice-led research about the fragmented, forgotten and most often threatened, built heritage of Nicosia, the last divided capital of Europe. The chapter questions whether sites, objects and their histories could belong simultaneously to (i.e., be shared by) more than one of the local communities, while at the same time these heritage sites are undergoing appropriation by those groups and individuals who practice their everyday cultural expressions. Also it reflects on the way that these spatial performances of appropriation can become associated with products of past human activities and ongoing place-making processes driven by the local stakeholders. It suggests this performative stage, that becomes accessible through VR-enabled immersion (Artopoulos and Smaniotto 2019), allows for the exploration of the role of place and built heritage in transforming shared identities as a contemporary spatio-cultural process of the city.

Moving from the material remnants of a divided city to intangible heritage, Sarah Kenderdine, Lily Hibberd, Jeffrey Shaw and Tsong-Zung Chang investigate the potential of immersive visualization for encompassing the affective new materialities of Remaking the Confucian Rites (RCR), a major reenactment project based on the "close reading" of *Book of Etiquettes and Rites Yili* 儀禮 compiled in the 2nd century CE by scholars and disciples of Confucius. *Yili* was a "performance manual" designed to empower individuals through self-cultivation in relation to family, state and cosmos. It was a core text in the Confucian canon for thousands of years until it was violently rejected by modernizers at the end of dynastic China, precipitating a breakdown in cultural transmission. Not only a philosophical concept, *li* or *li*-rites, in practice, comprise a belief system embedded in China's social structure and ancient laws. Despite the revival of Confucian aesthetics and heritage production, the everyday role of practiced Confucian rituals in community and family life remains marginalized. This chapter investigates the RCR project's unique use of multimedia approaches and immersive visualization for the dynamic recording of embodied acts and intangible cultural heritage forms. The chapter considers what immersive technologies can offer as novel modes for reenactment and the embodied transmission of tacit cultural knowledge through reperformable archives. To date, the documentation of these reenactments has relied on linear formats inadequate for both the historiography of the body and embodied transmission.

Edward González-Tennant discusses the role that digital technologies continue to play in revealing new truths about Rosewood, Florida, a majority African American community destroyed in 1923 during a week-long episode of violence commonly referred to as the Rosewood Massacre or Rosewood Race Riot. The multigenerational history of Rosewood as an African American community, not to mention the accumulated multigenerational wealth of its residents, was violently disrupted during this first week of 1923. The reconstruction of the contested historical experiences of Rosewood is possible with the help of digital technologies which provide a rapidly expanding toolkit for researching, interpreting and sharing difficult histories. Digital technologies in the form of geographic information systems (GIS) are key to understanding the spatial layout of the town prior to its destruction. Field research benefits from ground penetrating radar (GPR) and other technologies to unearth important aspects of the community's history. All of these combine via virtual world environments and documentary videos to support public outreach and conversations on racial reconciliation. Each step in this process is accompanied by unique challenges. A central goal of this research is to draw upon a mixed methods approach to historical scholarship while acknowledging the trauma associated with such events, which resonate in the present via structural and symbolic forms of violence. The research that Edward González-Tennant conducts is today more important than ever as he explores topics exploring the lingering effects of inequality and violence.

According to Erik Champion, the explosion in the development and communication of digital humanities has seen fascinating digital visualization projects. Some focus on slavery and massacre, such as the *Monroe and Florence Work Today* website, a database and mapping platform of lynching in America (plaintalkhistory.com/monroeandflorencework, Unknown), *Slave voyages* visualized by *SLADE* magazine (Kahn and Bouie 2015) and in Australia *the Colonial Frontier Massacres in Australia 1788-1930* map (Ryan 2019; Allam and Evershed 2019). Some focus on outright horror, while others use digital technology to convey contestation and issues of ambiguity. Despite the growth and spread of these digital humanities visualization projects, parallel and accessible examples in immersive virtual heritage are harder to find. Over the last three decades, immersive technologies (especially as "new" media) have embraced digital heritage to create showstopping instant experiences, but existing, durable examples of virtual heritage (virtual reality applied to cultural heritage) are relatively rare, and examples of difficult heritage far rarer. To review and address all these gaps, Erik Champion summarizes dilemmas in present research on immersion, presence and immersivity and covers recent developments in virtual, augmented and mixed reality technology by focusing on three case studies, three of Australia's most significant, tragic and horrifying heritage sites: Beacon Island (Batavia's Graveyard), Rottnest Island and Fremantle Prison. Inspired by UNESCO charters, indigenous manifestos and ethical design principles in digital humanities (Hepworth and Church 2018), he attempts to formulate a theoretical framework with criteria and guidelines to help immersive environment designers address the depiction or evocation of difficult pasts.

Eytan Mann and Aaron Sprecher in their chapter discuss the use of VR in the context of architecture's broader concerns. They argue that the general intellectual question of how VR can be used in the context of critical architectural research remains in its infancy and is, in fact, hampered precisely by the technology's general promise of simple, faithful realism. The case study of Wadi Salib, a neighbourhood in downtown Haifa in Israel, tells a painful story of violence and destruction during the early years of the founding of the state of Israel, and the narration of the difficult history of the site through VR serves as a medium that allows them to work between various epistemological registers. The authors provide a very useful theoretical background for critical historiography of contested places, and they discuss the use of VR as a medium for such historiography. They suggest a specific methodology to explore the use of VR for critical investigation of contested sites while overcoming some of the caveats of using such a medium in this context. To use computation and digital technologies for historiography can potentially underline opportunities as well as problems in the process. The project about Wadi Salib underlines the affordance of VR as a medium to introduce new participatory agency in the reading, writing and reconstruction of conflicted historical events.

Holocaust history represents a difficult past that challenges those who visit the United States Holocaust Memorial Museum (USHMM) in Washington, USA. Silvina Fernandez-Duque, Sara Pitcairn and Michael Haley Goldman discuss a virtual reality experience prototyped by the USHMM that brings together the ideas behind, and experience of, learning difficult history in an immersive environment. Empathy, perspective taking and imagination – while useful in pursuing many educational objectives – create complex challenges in teaching about traumatic events. By applying lessons from the history of immersion in museums to new experimentation in virtual worlds and techniques, the chapter proposes an approach to immersive experiences centred on perspective, role and engaged witnessing. In recent years, readily available and affordable virtual reality has launched hundreds of immersive museum experiences. But these experiences aren't new – museums and cultural heritage sites have long employed immersive techniques to interpret the past. For over 25 years, USHMM's permanent exhibition has offered visitors an immersive experience. The authors situate recent technological developments in immersion within this longer trajectory. Immersion has alternately been viewed with promise, scepticism and controversy. Longstanding debates about the benefits and dangers of immersion remain relevant today, especially for museums and heritage sites addressing difficult pasts. The authors question the goals of using immersion to interpret difficult pasts, including the history of the Holocaust and genocide. Drawing on examples from USHMM, the chapter defines key factors, such as one's perspective and role within an immersive environment, that influence how visitors understand and make meaning from unsettling histories. Further, it explores how immersive experiences can support affective learning and engaged witnessing as visitors grapple with difficult pasts.

Despite the fact that the German Occupation of Greece (1943–1944) has influenced public debates and inspired artistic displays and performances, the sites of memory and the materiality of World War II remain invisible. Agiatis Benardou, Anna Maria Droumpouki and George Papaioannou present in their chapter the project "Block 15. A Virtual Journey" that focuses on the infamous Block 15 of the Haidari Concentration Camp in West Athens, the largest and most notorious German concentration camp in wartime Greece, as a showcase of a largely neglected site of difficult heritage. In Greece immersive technologies have not been employed in historically contested sites. The project attempts to make Block 15 accessible to audiences and communities of diverse backgrounds through the use of immersive technologies. Through original scenarios based on primary and multimedia archival sources that are based on digital storytelling, the interactive, immersive virtual reality experience brings back to life the actual monument that is Block 15 and functions as a reminder of the horrors and torture inflicted by the Nazis on prisoners, in an attempt to reintroduce a historically and politically contested site to heterogeneous audiences, both in situ and in sites outside the concentration camp.

This book aims at revealing the benefits of the design and employment of immersive technologies in reconstructing difficult pasts by focusing on specific "difficult" heritage sites, which integrate innovation (both in terms of technologies employed and in the ways content is repurposed and presented) to sensitive concepts. The volume will revolve around the theoretical and applied ways in which immersive technologies can contextualize, shed light on and negotiate difficult or sensitive heritage and difficult, traumatic and/or ambiguous pasts which have been suppressed in various ways.

Through cases of primary research and implementation of immersive technologies on specific sites, we aim at showcasing how immersive technologies offer the possibility of illustrating unpleasant histories, confronting and disputing presumptions and prejudices, triggering responses, delivering new knowledge in novel educational ways, initiating dialogue and challenging preexisting notions of collective identity.

All of the topics (sites, concepts, events) discussed in this book remain pivotal in modern history and in the construction of national and cultural identities. The process of memorialization and remembrance through immersive experiences has also been a process of reshaping and re-interpreting perceptions of the historical and cultural past. The public landscape of cultural heritage is lined with monuments, sites and memorials accessible to visitors, who should experience, witness and become part of notions, which should under no circumstances be glorified. The present volume takes onboard the multi-perspectivity of the employment of immersion in difficult sites and notions, both in terms of the reconceptualization and meaning-making of the past, new custodial discourses and how these are perpetuated (or not) through the use of digital technologies.

The main challenge in this process has been to assess the universal humanistic narratives of collective culture through the development of experiences aimed at memorializing the victims, honouring the dead and preserving their memory. These experiences should also aim at creating a social and educational impact and at serving as reminders to future generations of the ideals of inclusion, diversity and democracy.

Notes

1 Indicatively: Amy L. Hubbell, Natsuko Akagawa, Sol Rojas-Lizana, Annie Pohlman (Eds.), *Places of Traumatic Memory. A Global Context*, Palgrave Macmillan, London 2020; William Logan, Keir Reeves, *Places of Pain and Shame: Dealing with 'Difficult Heritage'*, Routledge, London and New York 2009.

2 https://olafureliasson.net/archive/artwork/WEK101003/the-weather-project, last accessed 27.04.2022.

3 See *The New Yorker* (https://www.newyorker.com/news/letter-from-silicon-valley/the-rise-and-rise-of-immersive-art) and *The Guardian* (https://www.theguardian

.com/artanddesign/2022/apr/20/immersive-exhibitions-the-future-of-art-or-over-priced-theme-parks) for some of the most recent debates.

4 https://www.louvre.fr/en/what-s-on/life-at-the-museum/the-mona-lisa-in-virtual-reality-in-your-own-home, last accessed 27.04.2022.

Bibliography

Hassapopoulou, Marina, "From Distracted to Distributed Attention: Expanded Learning through Social Media, Augmented Reality, Remixing, and Activist Geocaching." *Digital Humanities Quarterly* 12, no. 2 (2018). http://www.digitalhumanities.org/dhq/vol/12/2/000386/000386.html.

Huang, Shu-Mei, Lee Hyun Kyung, *Heritage, Memory, and Punishment. Remembering Colonial Prisons in East Asia*, Routledge, Abingdon and New York 2020

Loga, William, Reeves Keir, *Places of Pain and Shame: Dealing with 'Difficult Heritage'*, Routledge, London and New York 2009

Macdonald, Sharon, *Difficult Heritage. Negotiating the Nazi Past in Nuremberg and Beyond*, Routledge, London and New York 2009

Macdonald, Sharon, *Memorylands. Heritage and Identity in Europe Today*, Routledge, London and New York 2013

Rymsza-Pawlowska, M.J., *History Comes Alive: Public History and Popular Culture in the 1970s*, University of North Carolina Press, Chapel Hill, North Carolina 2017

Yair, Gad, "Neutrality, Objectivity, and Dissociation: Cultural Trauma and Educational Messages in German Holocaust Memorial Sites and Documentation Centers." *Holocaust and Genocide Studies* 28, no. 3 (2014): 482–509

1

DIFFICULT HERITAGE AND IMMERSIVE EXPERIENCES

Immersion, impersonation and engagement in dangerous pasts – Limits, effects and ethics of immersive heritage experiences

Sharon Macdonald

In November 2017, a documentary showed on German TV, reporting on a proposed historically themed visitor experience, to be called *Reichspark*, that would focus on National Socialism (Böhmermann and Käßbohrer 2017).[1] Presented by the programme maker and television presenter Jan Böhmermann, the documentary included interviews with the CEO and Project Developer of HG Business Consulting, Raphael Gamper, about the fairly advanced plans for what he described as a "historically correct, responsible and family-friendly" "theme-park". Due to open summer 2023, it would be, he claimed, the largest such "living history" development concerning Germany's past.

As HG Business Consulting's slick PR film demonstrated through computer-generated graphics and smiling families, the park would offer a rich and interactive visitor experience across a range of historical events. Organized into four "experience areas" – Rememberland, Warland, Historyland and Old Berlin – many wishes would be catered for. Visitors not wanting to be "burdened with the controversial aspects of the German past", as CEO Gamper put, would be able to enjoy 25 themed gastronomic outlets, a petting zoo and a Black Forest village among other leisure offers. Much of the content, however, would be devoted to events from that "darker past", as it was referred to in the documentary. The violence of Kristallnacht would be represented in an immersive sound and light spectacle, and the Battle of Stalingrad could be experienced through virtual reality supplemented by feeling a chill of up to minus 20 degrees Celsius in "Europe's largest" visitor walk-in cooling facility. These were just some of the many and varied promised immersive "attractions", which, the documentary notes, even include a "lifelike" concentration camp that visitors will be able to enter. All of this will be built, according to the documentary, on a 52-hectare site just outside Berlin.

DOI: 10.4324/9781003200659-2

The documentary itself cast the making of the theme park within a wider context of the receding of memory of the Nazi past and Holocaust and the possible necessity to look to more immersive techniques in order to engage a new generation. As such, it also included reference to various other examples, such as video games. It also raised questions about the ethics of some of these. In the case of *Reichspark*, its CEO always responded robustly to any such questions, presenting his endeavour as fulfilling the morally important task of remembering this history and, thus, as inherently having an educational dimension. In response to a question about a planned ghost-train-style ride in which visitors can experience the bombing of Dresden, for example, he argued that it would enable children to realize how terrible the experience was, leading them, thus, to empathize with Grandma who still has nightmares about it. The underlying premise here was that immersion provides an affective charge that in itself leads to identification and empathy.

The show generated a good deal of online commentary, with many people expressing shock or disgust at the proposed "Nazi Park", as the presenter described it at one point (only to be corrected by the CEO: "We prefer to say 'historical themed visitor experience with an emphasis on National Socialism'") (see Zustra 2019). That the documentary was a spoof was not initially realized by many, not surprisingly given its skilful weaving together of fact and fiction. Real developments presented in the documentary include an Italian company producing a virtual reality experience of Auschwitz-Birkenau;[2] a former military prison in Latvia providing visitors with the experience of being reprimanded and incarcerated;[3] and the World War II re-enactment in Pickering, UK, discussed below. Meetings of the right-wing AfD (Alternative für Deutschland) party are shown in the documentary, and its members are interviewed. That an enterprising businessman would see the then rise in numbers of people voting for this party as a commercial opportunity seemed all too plausible.

In what follows, I offer some reflections on questions of mediating the national socialist past that the spoof documentary – or mockumentary – so engagingly raises. Such a programme is itself, of course, a mode of mediating the past – a point to which I will return. My main focus, however, is on considerations that the documentary often brilliantly raises about immersive and experiential modes of mediating the past, and about whether the passing of time and generation change perhaps make such modes not only more permissible but even necessary. In addressing these, I turn to a number of actual examples of immersion in what I call "dangerous pasts" – namely those that risk attracting people into extremist and especially xenophobic political positions – in order to highlight some of the issues and struggles involved.

Where to draw the limits?

The question of appropriate modes of mediation of difficult pasts, such as that of National Socialism, is one that is directly faced by those who manage sites associated with that history. In my book *Difficult Heritage: Negotiating the Nazi Past in Nuremberg and Beyond* (Macdonald 2009), I documented the various ways in which the former Nazi party rally grounds – the *Reichsparteitagsgelände* – in Nuremberg have been variously developed or partially demolished, as well as discussed, over the years. In many ways, the rally grounds could be seen as the original *Reichspark* and might even have been an ideal location for HG Business Consulting's venture. Constructed essentially as a backdrop for Leni Riefenstahl's propaganda films, and as a stage for the annual party rallies, the site consists of monumental buildings – mostly incomplete and now partially ruined – over some 58 hectares, almost exactly the same as the spoof proposed *Reichspark*, which, while the link is never stated, is surely no coincidence, and the model and layout of *Reichspark* certainly resembles the *Reichsparteitagsgelände*. It is worth noting here that the rallies themselves were a calculatedly immersive experience in which, as Hitler and his architect Albert Speer intended, the participant should react only viscerally and not through the reasoning brain, so compelling them all the more effectively into Nazi ideology (see Speer 1995; Macdonald 2005, 2009).

While there was never a proposal to develop the rally site into a historical theme park, various leisure ideas were mooted at various times, such as a proposal in the mid-1980s to turn one of the largest remaining buildings, the Congress Hall (which looks rather like the Roman Colosseum on which it was modelled), into a leisure and shopping centre. After serious consideration by the city council, this proposal was rejected after a group of concerned citizens actively campaigned against it. Elsewhere, however, decisions have been made differently. In Weimar, for example, parts of the *Gauforum* – a large SS Headquarters – have been turned into a shopping centre.

Turning such sites into leisure or shopping centres differs from the *Reichspark* proposals, however, in that they are essentially modes of forgetting the past. Although plaques or leaflets may remind us of their former use, history plays virtually no role in the sites' contemporary function. When it comes to representing the past in sites such as the Nazi party rally grounds, however, there are many potential considerations and differing positions, as can be seen from the deliberations over what to do with the Nuremberg party rally grounds. Especially significant was the opening in 2001 of a Documentation Centre. Even its name was a product of careful thought about how to avoid what was seen as a central problem of representing this particular history, namely that visitors might find it attractive and so, instead of acting as an educational warning about this atrocious past, it might instead lure them into admiration for it. At a site that was built precisely in order to generate emotional feelings of such admiration and attraction, this was seen by many of those charged with preparing the displays for the documentation centre as a particular risk.

As the name of the centre implies, its emphasis is on documentation, to which end it shows lots of historical photographs and other documents, such as architectural plans for the grounds, and newspaper articles. Nevertheless, it was recognized during its making that other modes of mediating the past – using more dramatic and even immersive techniques – were on the rise in relation to other historical events and periods. This gave rise to a good deal of discussion and some disagreement over what might be acceptable in the new Documentation Centre's displays. For the most part, the more documentary style wins out. Thus, a proposed more multimedia, multimodal exhibit showing the burning of the Reichstag was never realized but was instead replaced by a large photograph accompanied by a sound-track of burning and shouting. Numerous model Hitler busts – to show the manufacturing of a personality cult – are a relatively rare example in the exhibition of a 3D scenographic reconstruction, but this is hardly immersive in that its invitation is to invite the visitor to stand outside and view it. Even though the visitor is inside the actual building, then, they are constantly positioned outside the action – as a viewer not as a participant.

Here it is worth briefly revisiting what might be meant by "immersive". While Jenny Kidd (2018) helpfully describes it as "story-led, audience and participation centered, multimodal, multisensory and attuned to its environment", this seems to me to miss its most important quality, namely that of its attempt to engage the participant completely, to take them as fully as possible into another time and/or place. Such immersion entails a suspension of the usual reality and an invitation to not just gaze upon the past or elsewhere but to be *in it* (and see Dede 2009, discussed in the Conclusion section below). Just as being immersed in water means that one is entirely under the surface, being immersed in a heritage environment is to be totally within its reality. In practice, immersion may be only partial – semi-immersion – or a participant may move in and out of the immersive experience repeatedly in what we might call sporadic immersion. While immersed, however, they are not spectators or viewers standing outside the action or reality. Instead, they are within it and while we can use the term "participant" for this, it is important to note that this does not necessarily mean that they are "active" and contributing to the ongoing action as is often meant by participation in other contexts. Indeed, they may be quite passive within the immersive experience, even if they are physically moving. Rather, its very totality means that they may be taken over by the experience. This is in part the affective dimension of immersion that is mentioned by Kidd and others (e.g. Sterling 2019). But in some sense all experiences are affective. Characteristic here is that this is usually made especially compelling through the multisensory modalities and through the full-on-ness, or full-in-ness. In heritage experiences, this often also entails the enacting of "as if" being a person actually experiencing that time. This, I call "impersonation". It is these dimensions of immersive heritage experiences – the full-in-ness and suspension of an outside stance, and the impersonation – that can be particularly problematic in relation to what I call dangerous pasts.

Curatorial discussions and decisions during the making of the Documentation Centre showed struggles over just these issues. A major concern raised was that the use of sensorially compelling media might replicate Nazi tactics themselves. Exhibition-makers and the exhibition's academic advisory board expressed particular caution over anything that might constitute a form of emotional influencing. Documentation was, by contrast, seen as sticking more closely to facts and thus as less amenable to manipulation or to producing emotional (which were seen as non-rational) responses. Given that the content of the exhibition was necessarily highly selective and carefully designed – with much thought given to ensuring that visitors did not get the "wrong" perspective – even sticking carefully to facts was inevitably also within a chosen narrative and calibrated to a desired resulting visitor disposition. As in Handler and Gable's ethnographic study of Colonial Williamsburg (1997), however, the discourse of "the facts" – and in the Nuremberg case also of "documentation" – helped act as a proxy for a politicized and moralized framework governing what was shown. While in the Colonial Williamsburg case, that framework was problematically racialized, in that of Nuremberg what operated was a liberal progressive educational remit to ensure that the national socialist period was conveyed in a manner that was understood as helping to ensure that such atrocity could never recur.

Effective remembering

Yet whether such relatively "dry" documentary modes are indeed most effective for that end was questioned at the time of the centre's making and has also been since. In a conversation in 2013 with the then head of the Documentation Centre, Hans-Christian Täubrich, he mused over this question, especially in relation to what he saw as possibly changed visitors' expectations in light of what they would experience elsewhere, particularly for younger generations brought up on different media. There are now, he told me, immersive technologies in which it would be possible for visitors to experience being part of a crowd at a rally – they could stand amongst others chanting and cheering. "Would we do that? Should we do that?", he asked rhetorically.

In the past – at the time of the centre's making – he said that it was fairly clear to all of those involved with the exhibition's preparation that to do so would not be acceptable. It would have been seen as risky that a participant might feel too emotionally attracted to the experience. Whether that would really make them more likely to feel sympathy for National Socialism was something that he thought was probably overstated – there is little evidence one way or the other, he noted. Nevertheless, he found himself increasingly wondering, he said, whether we have now reached a time in which the situation has changed such that such techniques are maybe even necessary in order to maintain interest in this history. Giving people a sense of what it might have felt to be a "*Mitläufer*" – a participant (literally, one who goes along with) – and why they might have been attracted to Nazism could, he thought, be educationally important to convey. Moreover, he mused, a generation "brought up on video-games" was probably not only used to more exciting modes of presentation but was perhaps also more adept at evaluating these and not being as entranced as earlier generations might have been.

For newer generations, in other words, there may be a remediation, that is, a recalibration of media (as has been argued in other contexts by those such as Iliana Gershon 2010, and see Bolter and Grusin 1996) that would result in those media being perceived differently by the new generation. Specifically, Hans-Christian Täubrich's implication was that the use of game-like media might not be problematic for a younger generation in the way that it seemed to be for older ones. There was, he pointed out, little research available to enable a confident assessment of whether or not this is the case.[4] Although the amount of research has grown since then, there is no consensus, though the question remains important in relation to mediating such dangerous – but also vital-to-remember – pasts.

Hans-Christian Täubrich's reflections based on his own direct practical experience of running a site of Nazi perpetration have parallels in relation to other sites, including those of victimhood, and in academic literature. Historian Wulff Kansteiner has argued particularly strongly for considering the potential of a range of interactive and immersive media and overcoming what he calls "the Holocaust gaming taboo" (2017: 313).[5] As he writes:

> [I]t might be altogether unrealistic to expect that the kind of media that ushered in Holocaust memory 35 years ago, i.e. television, film, museums and memorials, could still provoke passionate feelings in audiences steeped in interactive digital culture and living at a point in time when the remembrance of the Final Solution transitions from the dynamic realm of communicative memory to the settled realm of cultural memory .... If Holocaust memory can be resurrected as an emotionally and politically relevant fixture of future memory culture it would have to be in the guide of immersive, simulative and possibly also counterfactual digital memory.
>
> *(Kansteiner 2017: 310)*

While Kansteiner is especially concerned with digital modes, their immersive and interactive capacities are at the forefront of the affordances that he sees as increasingly demanded by new generations. Yet, as he discusses, referencing many authors who express reservations about these media, it is the immersive and interactive capacities that pose especial ethical problems in relation to dangerous histories.

Immersion and experience

As scholars such as Alison Griffiths (2008) have argued, we should not forget that immersive experiences are not the preserve of new technologies. Cathedrals are just one of the examples that she gives of calculated multi-sensorial immersion. In relation to the mediation of the past more specifically, we can surely see castles, stately homes and sites of heritage more generally as at least partially immersive and experiential. The shift into being more fully so is usually seen when there is a fuller reconstruction of the past, such that glimpses outside the illusion are reduced and history is in some sense "brought to life" through either virtual reality or more traditional techniques such as actors in costumes.

"Living history" – a term that is used several times in relation to the fictive *Reichspark* – can be seen as one mode of this. It typically entails a re-enactment of the past either specifically for visitors (as at Colonial Williamsburg for example) or by amateur groups who exist now in many countries to "re-live" and experience particular events or periods. Sometimes criticized for being nostalgic – recreating preferred and sanitized versions of the past – such developments have also sometimes been seen as important ways for people to learn about and engage with the past and also to contemplate other possible modes of living in the present.[6]

While such living history may be innocuous enough, or even admirable, when it comes to, say, the re-enactment of peasant lifeways – so showing how it was possible to live more harmoniously with the natural environment – further questions are raised in relation to what I have here called dangerous pasts. The documentary about *Reichspark* includes one such example, from Pickering in North Yorkshire, where for 25 years there has been an annual acting out of WWII, organized by the local community, with local people dressing up in outfits of the time, running old motor vehicles and performing allocated roles in ways that they think people might have behaved at the time (Fox 2012). The re-enactment weekend has become a significant tourist attraction. It does not restrict itself, however, to the known facts but also dabbles imaginatively in "counter-history" – what might have been – a mode that Kansteiner (2017) suggests might also be necessary to rejuvenate historical interest. Thus in 2017, as the *Reichspark* documentary (accurately) depicted, the villagers were merrily playing out an imagined Nazi occupation, with stormtroopers in the streets shouting brusquely and acting out the beating up of civilians.

Probably not unconnected with the airing of the documentary, the North Yorkshire re-enactment weekend was at first banned in 2018 on grounds that it could "cause public offence" and then went ahead without the presence of any participants in German uniforms.[7] Comments objecting to the banning, like the following one in the *Daily Mail*, perhaps show better why it should be stopped than effectively making the case for its continuation: "I was hoping Brexit would see off this kind of pc [politically correct] nonsense. Are we soon going to pretend WWII never happened?"[8]

Immersion, as educational researcher Chris Dede puts it, "is the subjective experience that one is participating in a comprehensive, realistic experience" (2009: 66). While just how "total" that may be can vary, what is also involved, as he points out, is "a willing suspension of disbelief" (ibid.). In other words, participants need to switch off a certain criticality in order to "dive in" (to use another often-used metaphor). It is this that can make such approaches particularly risky in relation to dangerous pasts, as museologist Andrea Witcomb, drawing on ideas from historian Dominick La Capra (1998), has explored. Through contrasting examples, she argues that especially problematic are the formats that do not allow for any kind of "perspective from outside" (Witcomb 2013: 158). The risk is that while immersion may give visitors a sense of identification and empathy, there is no "unsettlement" or translation into language to prompt "critical thinking" (ibid.).

Here is where the imagined *Reichspark* would be so problematic. Not only would it allow immersion and an experience of the past; it would do so apparently without opportunities for more critical reflection or for wider contextualization. The experiential mode risks precisely turning each event into a specific "experience" – something in itself whose significance rests at an experiential level. Thus Kristallnacht, for example, is presented as noisy and scary but without mention of to whom violence was directed and within what wider politics and horror. The visitor can impersonate – and so easily indiscriminately – all manner of historical positions. As well as victims of terror, they can also be its perpetrators. And in the end, in the kind of visitor opportunity envisaged, it scarcely matters which or both, as long as they have "a good time".

Which histories are being mediated is important here too. Perhaps in some cases this is all very well. But in relation to difficult and dangerous pasts, it is all the more crucial to attend to the particular story or vision of history that is being narrated and to the subject positions that this and the media involved afford.

Conclusion

The questions raised in this chapter continue to be played out through many examples, including those relating to the Nazi past. One of these concerns proposals that were reported in news articles such as the following: "Wolf's Lair: Will Hitler HQ Makeover create a Nazi Theme Park?" (Peter 2019). This reported on plans to develop what in German is called the Wolfsschanze – a massive complex of bunkers and other buildings deep in a forest in Poland – into an attraction for more tourists (though already some 300,000 visit each year according to the article). The proposed makeover will include a reconstruction of von Stauffenberg's attempted assassination of Hitler, "including life-size 'symbolic figures depicting those present at the time'" according to a local spokesman. The article contains various comments such as the following: "critics argue that insensitive "attractions", such as amateurish re-enactments with people wearing Nazi uniforms, could turn it into a sort of ghoulish 'Disneyland'". In the fictive *Reichspark* too there was to have been a reconstruction of the Wolf's Lair and the von Stauffenberg assassination attempt – though to be followed by a family-friendly petting zoo to help allay visitors' possibly disturbed feelings. At the time of writing, the plans have not been realized, due in part to the COVID-19 pandemic. Neither, apparently, have they been totally shelved either.

Concerns about the development of the Wolf's Lair into a more immersive touristic experience repeat, in effect, worries that have been voiced over the years about other touristic developments of Nazi sites. The Berghof on Obersalzberg – Hitler's holiday retreat in the Bavarian Alps – is one such. The concerns are certainly not without justification. In recent years increasing numbers of right-wing Nazi sympathizers from Hungary and the Czech Republic have been arriving by coach at the spectacular mountain location (Boffey 2018). As the director of its new documentation centre has argued, however, the fact that there are now improved visitor facilities is probably not the reason for the increase – such pilgrims would come in any case. Moreover, having an educational centre that informs about the horrors of the Nazi past – that looks beyond and behind the glamorous surface of the mountain resort – surely does not play into the hands of such Fascist sympathizers.[9]

This leads then to the point that such sites can be important opportunities for mediating dangerous pasts in ways that show their horror and lessen the possibility of them becoming emotionally compelling attractions. It is not the media of mediation *per se* that cause the problems. Nevertheless, they have different affordances for, among other things, visitors' response in terms of degrees of suspension of disbelief, as well as potential engagement. Different modes of mediation variously encourage interaction with others or a more solitary experience, and this has implications for collective memory, as Wulff Kansteiner (2017), among others (e.g. Rigney 2015), has pointed out.[10] Whether we engage only with people who are physically present with us or also with those who we have never directly met, as is possible through social media, also shapes the kind of experience of the past and the ways in which it might be both remembered and related to critically or otherwise (Bareither 2021). That engagement with others might itself be contained within a shared immersion. But it can also be a significant mode of distancing, allowing for shared reflection that may even turn into collectively generated criticality.

These observations concur with the critical potential that some recent commentators suggest that immersive heritage experiences can offer (Kidd 2018; Sterling 2019; Swords et al. 2021). These have been written in part as corrections to an earlier tendency to dismiss immersive experiences as rather superficial and usually commercial forms of engagement. Yet, as Sterling points out, there can be a risk of also using the language of participation in ways that ignore its potential co-option by neo-liberal logics (2019: 107). A further risk, I have suggested, is that participation is so commonly associated with taking an active stance. Yet, in some forms of immersion the very suspension of reality, as Dede has noted, can lead to a less active engagement in criticality. Important, then, is further specification of the formats and content involved, and the kinds of subject positions afforded.

The immersive, experiential format of the theme park offers certain characteristic affordances. Being engaging and fun are part of its typical features. This is generally accompanied by bracketing out the political and contextual.[11] While maybe not inevitable, these seem to be from different cultural and touristic registers and bringing them together easily feels in itself discordant. This is one of the reasons for the disquiet that the very idea of *Reichspark* raises. Even so, in what is proposed, visitors are provided with little historical overview and sense of causes and connections but instead are given the equivalent of a set of Disneyland rides, grouped only into diverse "lands". Such a mode of mediation gives an illusion of experiencing something, but in its brevity and relative comfort – even if at minus 20 degrees – it is a long way from being anything like that which those living at the time would actually have felt. Perhaps most disturbing of all is how it turns such dangerous pasts into a game in which they are judged primarily not in terms of the damage – and lasting effects – that they caused but for their merits as fun on a jolly day out.

Let me here briefly also comment on the documentary – or mockumentary – itself. Does this also fall foul of some of the problems of the theme park that it conjures up? Namely, it is creating entertainment and even amusement out of a serious and dangerous history. Such a charge has been made for other screen products, such as the films *La Vita è Bella* (1997, Benigni), *Mein Führer* (2007, Levy) and *Er ist Wieder Da* (2015, Wnendt) (see Magilow 2020 for relevant discussion). Unlike these, however, the *Reichspark* documentary directly asks questions about the mode of relating to the past that it is presenting – indeed, it is centrally concerned to do so. Thus, it specifically raises questions about the nature of memory – doing so in part through its presenter's own obviously dubiously rosy memories of his grandfather, as well as with reference to right-wing politicians who claim that Germans should be allowed to be proud of their forefathers who fought for their country in WWII. When the presenter asks the CEO outright whether what he is doing is crossing ethical boundaries, the mockumentary lodges those very questions in the viewers' minds. As such, and together with its showing of the *Reichspark* plans as disturbing even while amusing, it works differently from those other comical counterfactual accounts of the Nazi past. It opens up rather than forecloses questions about what is being depicted. Moreover, it does so further by the very debate that it has generated – and the negative response to the prospect of such a theme park. Whether that will be enough to see off the prospect of such an enterprise, remains, however, to be seen.

Immersion is not a homogeneous experience. It takes a variety of forms. In some cases, it is entirely virtually or digitally enacted. While part of the claim of VR (virtual reality) is that it is indistinguishable from reality, at least while in the experience itself, it is nevertheless distinct from the actual embodied, three-dimensional and multi-sensorial experience of a theme park. This is not least on account of the very fact of our inevitable awareness of being in a particular kind of experience. In the case of the theme park, visitors must plan ahead and travel there by means of some kind of transport, probably along with a group of people who they already know. Then they will probably have queued to pick up tickets, perhaps passed through a gift shop or be aware that they will do so at the end of their visit. Even though they may sometimes be fully in the grip of undivided attention to the experience in which they are immersed, they are likely to become frequently aware of other visitors, including their companions, and to their actions and responses. These may appear minor or even banal differences from other kinds of immersive experiences and in practice the divisions are likely to be on a spectrum rather than qualitative. Nevertheless, these matter too, not least as they provide potential moments of movement in and out of immersion, and in and out of reflection and possibly even of critical engagement. How far that occurs requires more research, as it does in relation to more digital forms of immersion in difficult and dangerous pasts (cf. Kansteiner 2017). For this reason too, the current volume, bringing together studies of difficult pasts and immersive experiences, is especially welcome.

Acknowledgements

An earlier, shorter, version of this chapter was published as "Immersed in the Nazi past: Limits, risks and approaches in the mediation of dangerous histories", in Christoph Bareither and Ingrid Tomkowiak (eds) *Mediated Pasts, Popular Pleasures: Medien und Praktiken populärkulturellen Erinnerns,* Würzburg: Könighausen & Neumann. I thank Christoph Bareither and Ingrid Tomkowiak for inviting me to participate in the *Mediated Pasts* conference and thus encouraging me to give attention to the *Reichspark.* I also thank them and the publisher for permission to rework the chapter for publication here. I also thank Agiatis Bernadou and Anna Maria Droumpouki for their helpful comments. I am grateful to the Alexander von Humboldt Foundation for supporting my current research as well as my earlier research discussed here.

Notes

1 The documentary was titled *Unternehmen Reichspark,* which might be translated as "Enterprise Empire Park", with *Reich* (Empire) in this case referring to the National Socialist Third Reich. All quotations are my translations from the programme. Until 16.2.2018, the show was accessible through the *ZDF-Mediathek* and on *YouTube,* and at the time of writing is accessible through the platform https://www.dailymotion.com/ [accessed 05.07.2021].
2 http://www.101-percent.com/Works/Witness-Auschwitz (accessed 4.2.2022).
3 https://karostascietums.lv/en/ (accessed 4.2.2022).
4 This is part of a wider debate about the influence of different media forms, on which see, for example, Perse and Lambe 2016. More specifically in relation to the Holocaust, Kansteiner 2017 also points out the lack of consensus.
5 Others addressing this include Chapman and Linderoth 2015; Hayton 2015; Pfister 2016.
6 See, for example, Petra Tjitske Kalshoven's brilliant study of "Indianists" – Kalshoven 2012. The term itself may cover a range of formats. For discussion, see Tomann 2020.
7 See https://www.bbc.com/news/uk-england-york-north-yorkshire-45864398 (accessed 5.07.2021).
8 See https://www.dailymail.co.uk/news/article-5581617/Anger-villages-annual-Second-World-War-enactment-scrapped.html (31.08.2019).
9 See https://www.obersalzberg.de/home/ (31.08.2019).
10 So too do visitors' notions of what *kind* of site they are visiting, for example, whether they regard it as about a still relevant past or as more distant heritage. See Macdonald 2018.
11 Hayton's (2015) observation of the lack of reference to the Holocaust in many Nazi-themed video games is also instructive here.

References

Bareither, C. (2021). Difficult heritage and digital media: "selfie culture" and emotional practices at the memorial to the murdered Jews of Europe. *International Journal of Heritage Studies* 27 (1), 52–72.

Böhmermann, J. and Käßbohrer, P. (2017). Unternehmen Reichspark. In *Dokumentation (Neo Magazin Investigative)*. ZDFneo.

Boffey, D. (2018). What to do about Hitler's Berghof? *Museum Challenges Far Right Interest* (25.09.2018). https://www.theguardian.com/world/2018/sep/25/what-to-do-about-hitler-alpine-retreat. Accessed 31 August 2019.

Bolter, J. D. and Grusin, R. (1996). Remediation. *Configurations* 4 (3), 311–358.

Chapman, A. and Jonas Linderoth, A. (2015). Exploring the limits of play. A case study of representations of Nazism in games. In *The Dark Side of Game Play: Controversial Issues in Playful Environments*, edited by Torill Elvira Mortensen, Jonas Linderoth, and Ashley ML Brown. London: Routledge, 137–153.

Dede, C. (2009). Immersive interfaces for engagement and learning. *Science* 323 (5910), 66–69.

Fox, R. (2012). 11–13 October: Pickering war weekend 2013. https://www.hello-yorkshire.co.uk/blog/11-13-october-pickering-war-weekend-2013/. Accessed 31 August 2019.

Gershon, I. (2010). *The Break-Up 2.0: Disconnecting over New Media*. Ithaca: Cornell University Press.

Griffiths, A. (2008). *Shivers Down Your Spine. Cinema, Museums, and the Immersive View*. New York: Columbia University Press.

Handler, R. and Gable, E. (1997). *The New History in an Old Museum. Creating the Past at Colonial Williamsburg*. Durham: Duke University Press.

Jeff Hayton, J. (2015). Beyond good and evil: Nazis and the supernatural in video games. In *Revisiting the "Nazi Occult:" Histories, Realities, Legacies*, edited by M. Monica Black and E. Eric Kurlander. Rochester: Camden House, 248–269.

Kalshoven, P. T. (2012). *Crafting 'the Indian'. Knowledge, Desire and Play in Indianist Reenactment*. Oxford: Berghahn.

Kansteiner, W. (2017). Transnational holocaust memory, digital culture and the end of reception studies. In *The Twentieth Century in European Memory. Transcultural Mediation and Reception*, edited by Barbara Törnqvist-Plewa and Tea Sindbaeck Andersen. Leiden: Brill, 305–343.

Kidd, J. (2018). 'Immersive' heritage encounters. *Museum Review* 3 (1) https://themuseumreviewjournal.wordpress.com/2018/04/16/tmr_vol3no1_kidd/.

La Capra, D. (1998). *History and Memory after Auschwitz*. Ithaca: Cornell University Press.

Macdonald, S. (2005). Enchantment and its dilemmas: The museum as a ritual site. In *Science, Magic and Religion. The Ritual Processes of Museum Magic*, edited by M. Bouquet and N. Porto. Oxford: Berghahn, 209–227.

Macdonald, S. (2009). *Difficult Heritage. Negotiating the Nazi Past in Nuremberg and Beyond*. London / New York: Routledge.

Macdonald, S. (2018). Endorsement effects and warning potentials. Architecture from totalitarian eras as heritage. In *Architecture as Propaganda in Twentieth-Century Totalitarian Regimes. History and Heritage*, edited by H. Hökerberg. Florence: Polistampa, 261–287.

Magilow, D. H. (2020). Contemporary Holocaust film beyond mimetic imperatives. In Gigliotti, S. and Earl, H. (eds) *A Companion to the Holocaust*. New York: Wiley.

Perse, Elizabeth M. and Jennifer Lambe, J. (2016). *Media Effects and Society* (2nd Ed.). New York: Routledge.

Peter, L. (2019). Wolf's Lair. Will Hitler HQ makeover create a Nazi theme park? (31.07.2019). https://www.bbc.co.uk/news/world-europe-49111787. Accessed 31 August 2019.

Pfister, Eugen. (2016). Das Unspielbare spielen – Imaginationen des Holocaust in Digitalen Spielen. *Zeitgeschichte* 4 (2016), 250–263.

Rigney, A. (2015). Cultural memory studies: Mediation, narrative and the aesthetic. In Tota, A. L. and Hagen, T. (eds) *Routledge International Handbook of Memory Studies*. London: Routledge.

Speer, A. (1995). *Inside the Third Reich*, trans. R. and C. Winston. London: Phoenix.

Sterling, C. (2019). Designing 'critical' heritage experiences: Immersion, enchantment and autonomy' *Archaeology International* 22 (1), 100–113.

Swords, J., Nally, C., Rogage, K., Watson, R., Charlton, J. and Kirk, D. (2021). Colliding epistemologies, productive tensions and usable pasts in the generation of heritage-led immersive experiences' *International Journal of Heritage Studies* 27 (2), 186–99.

Tomann, Juliane, (18.5.2020) Living history, Version: 1.0. In *Docupedia-Zeitgeschichte*.

Witcomb, A. (2013). Using immersive and interactive approaches to interpreting traumatic experiences for tourists: Potentials and limitations. In *Heritage and Tourism: Place, Encounter, Engagement*, edited by R. Staiff. London: Routledge, 152–170.

Zustra, A. (2019). „Reichspark"-Fake. So täuscht Böhmermann die Zuschauer mit einem Nazi-Park (17.11.2017). https://www.t-online.de/unterhaltung/tv/id_82725166/boehmermann-taeuscht-die-zuschauer-mit-einem-nazi-park.html. Accessed 31 August 2019.

2

REFLECTIVE EXPERIENCES WITH IMMERSIVE HERITAGE

Erik Champion

Introduction

In this chapter I will examine difficult and dark heritage. Others have articulated the overlap and potential different connotations and spheres of influence of dark heritage and difficult heritage (Thomas et al. 2019). For the sake of expediency, I will not attempt to distinguish between difficult heritage and dark heritage (a term imported from dark tourism) as I am particularly interested in the difficult interaction aspects of communicating dark heritage due to the technical challenges of virtual heritage, gaps or immaturity in virtual heritage as a distinct scholarly field, and the still to be fully explored role and impact of virtual heritage as an immersive and interactive medium capable of coaxing, encouraging and affording reflectivity.

Virtual heritage: False dichotomies

Simply defined, virtual heritage does not appear to be problematic. Virtual heritage is virtual reality (VR) applied to cultural heritage. This raises three questions relevant to difficult heritage. Firstly, virtual heritage implies the virtual heritage object *is* heritage, (or, perhaps, that it pretends to be heritage). Which heritage values are meant to be conveyed, what is to be learnt and how this helps the further preservation of the objects or practices simulated are questions seldom answered in "virtual heritage" academic publications. While the virtual can provide a filter to the difficult, difficult heritage raises the further challenge of how the heritage aspects should be preserved and presented because of or despite the dark or difficult heritage elements.

Secondly, virtual heritage implies there is a non-virtual heritage, (and by extension, virtual is purely digital). Virtual predates and overarches the digital,

DOI: 10.4324/9781003200659-3

and heritage itself is arguably virtual. For the object is more than an object, it contains clues to higher realms, invisible associations with a higher realm (an ideal cultural vision) as well as emotive connotations arriving from personal associations and identity.

Thirdly, virtual heritage has often been considered a container of tangible heritage objects that signify intangible heritage by force of presentation, or by an authorial narrative (usually via text, potentially via voice-overs triggered by where the participant is navigating or positioning themselves).

Intangible heritage is seldom virtual heritage

UNESCO (n.d.) described intangible heritage as "oral traditions, performing arts, social practices, rituals, festive events, knowledge and practices concerning nature and the universe or the knowledge and skills to produce traditional crafts", and they defined four important attributes of intangible heritage:

- *Traditional* ("*traditional, contemporary and living at the same time* … practices in which diverse cultural groups take part").
- *Inclusive* ("share expressions of intangible cultural heritage that are similar to those practised by others").
- *Representative* ("thrives on its basis in communities and depends on those whose knowledge of traditions, skills and customs are passed on to the rest of the community, from generation to generation, or to other communities").
- *Community-based* ("intangible cultural heritage can only be heritage when it is recognized as such by the communities, groups or individuals that create, maintain and transmit it – without their recognition, nobody else can decide for them that a given expression or practice is their heritage").

For immersive technologies to include these defining aspects of intangible heritage, we need to work out four elements: Via tradition, the simulation of long-term but slowly changing processes handed down in some way, inclusive suggests a variety of practices that can be compared or even collated, representative implies practices can be conducted rightly or wrongly (and can be judged), while community based indicates a range of roles and actors. Very few virtual heritage projects have one or more of these defining aspects. Why?

The UNESCO fourfold factors take a very optimistic approach to intangible heritage; their factors are participatory, democratic and representative. I am not convinced this encapsulates all intangible heritages, but also these factors lead more to the reception of intangible heritage as a benevolent product. However, there are important considerations within the description: Heritage must be maintained and passed on; it can change and include diverse practices, but it must provide self-recognition. This means that virtual heritage is only an approximation of heritage (in many cases) because strangers not "locals" may experience it, or the "owners" may no longer be with us or may not be able to communicate the full value or meaning. They may have also lost the inclination or capacity to recognize, maintain or pass on the heritage themselves.

Virtual heritage issues

The overall reason is straightforward: Virtual heritage has issues. In 2019 Champion and Rahaman (2019) surveyed academic conferences on virtual heritage and found a worrying lack of reference to actual 3D models, that were archived or otherwise accessible, and still in working or otherwise usable condition. In 2020 we surveyed 12 commercial and 8 non-commercial 3D hosting platforms such as Sketchfab, MyMiniFactory, TurboSquid, Europeana, EPOCH, CyARK and Smithsonian (Champion and Rahaman 2020) and found that they were focused on presentation rather than preservation and did not offer many features suitable for cultural heritage research, education and specialized dissemination.

A second issue is the role, participation and future rights of the shareholders of the cultural heritage that was digitalized and incorporated into virtual heritage projects. While there are charters and manifestos for working with and respecting indigenous communities, and charters for professional and appropriate 3D heritage, there are few specific policies and requirements for indigenous-related 3D digital heritage.

These two central issues result in a dilemma as to how the content should best be presented, preserved and updated, and the issue is confounded with frequent uncertainty or a lack of planning as to where or how the data should be experienced, hosted and cared for. Difficult pasts do not ameliorate these issues, how difficult heritage can be and should be viewed and experienced by different parts of society may not even be predicated on whether the audience is indigenous or not, and different indigenous societies may have protocols for different levels of access and control by their own members. Such a concern led to the development of Mukurtu (Christen, Merrill and Wynne 2017), a database for providing different levels of access to cultural data depending on the related cultural protocol. I do not however know of an equivalent in virtual heritage practice, let alone virtual heritage of difficult pasts.

Issues concerning troubling content, contentious stories, differing cultural protocols and non-consensus as to veracity, authenticity or ownership lead us to the question of appropriate immersion and interaction.

All of the above factors can contribute to phenomena leading to the next observation: Virtual heritage projects are very difficult to get off the ground. There are reservations about funding, a lack of detailed evaluation, hesitation on the durability and trainability of technology and a lack of tools that can demonstrate the significant, meaningful and educational experience for people to comprehend before the project is completed. So, virtual heritage can prove difficult to initiate before we even get to the difficult part of difficult heritage content.

Given the above, how do the inherent problems of virtual heritage as a field and practice affect the depiction of and immersion into difficult heritage situations using virtual reality technology? In the next section I wish to give three examples of failed projects and a successful one, as well as ways in which questions and aspects of difficult heritage can be workshopped.

Case studies

Australian heritage sites: Horror, imprisonment and neglect

Three of Australia's most significant, tragic and horrifying heritage sites are in Western Australia. Beacon Island (Batavia's Graveyard), Rottnest Island and Fremantle Prison embody the challenges facing Australian heritage sites: They are remote and under-visited, popular but forgotten or not fully documented and digitalized. In order to encourage richer and more meaningful cultural tourist experiences, interactive virtual and augmented experiences could leverage their fascinating but terrifying histories to more engagingly but also more empathically be understood and appreciated by remote, online or on-site visitors. However, researching and designing interactive experiences for them is fraught with difficulty, and I will expound on these issues in this section and then expand to explain how they relate to worldwide virtual heritage experiences.

While history is more than ghosts of the past, sometimes they are exactly ghosts of the past, and these ghosts are both sensational and eye catching, and difficult to communicate appropriately. Horrific historic details raise technical and ethical problems. Augmenting dark heritage sites of imprisonment and murder with augmented reality (AR) or recreating them in virtual reality raises their own problems but are also affected by problems besetting virtual heritage in general. However, the difficulties of creating moving but also appropriate immersive difficult heritage experiences are pre-empted not only by the inherent challenges of virtual heritage but also by problems facing researchers and institutes to secure funding for their deployment.

"The Batavia Shipwreck is the craziest Australian horror story you've never heard of" was the headline of the 2018 Australian Special Broadcasting Services (SBS) article by Maria Lewis (2018). In 1629 the Batavia ran aground in the Wallaby Group of islands, nearly 90 kilometres from Geraldton. Also known today as Batavia's Graveyard, of the 316 that survived the wreck, well over 100 men women and children were killed by Batavia's merchant Jeronimus Cornelisz and his henchmen in a reign of terror and murder eventually overturned by returning soldiers who were in turn saved by the captain returning from Java on a rescue ship. Harrowing accounts of the tragedy were written down by Commander Francisco Pelsaert at the time and only recently digitalized.

During the two months, the commander was absent, having taken one of the longboats to seek help (and ending up in Indonesia), Cornelisz committed acts of imprisonment, murder, torture and sexual enslavement, famously retold in the 1966 book *Islands of Angry Ghosts* by Hugh Edwards, one of the parties to discover the wreck (Edwards 1966). In 2019 Edwards declared the Batavia to be Australia's "most significant shipwreck" (Poulsen 2019).

The Batavia's destination was Indonesia, and it carried silver coins, ancient Roman art owned by the painter Rubens and a giant gateway designed for the Batavia fort (Jakarta). The original wreck can be dived today, skeletons of the shipwreck survivors, who were killed over several months of terror by Jeronimus Cornelisz in 1629, are still found on Beacon Island. Parts of the original Batavia and a copy of the gateway (portal) are at Geraldton Museum and WA Shipwrecks Museum in Fremantle. Actor Russell Crowe signed a contract to film the story in 2016 (now lapsed). Today Beacon Island is an archaeological site; a full-scale replica of the Batavia vessel, built with traditional methods and materials, is a tourist attraction at the Bataviawerf (Batavia Wharf) in Lelystad, the Netherlands. While in Australia, very recently, the Western Australian state government announced plans to reopen Beacon Island to the public.

Via an Australian Research Council grant "Shipwrecks of the Roaring Forties: A Maritime Archaeological Reassessment of Some of Australia's Earliest Shipwrecks", the University of Western Australia, WA Museum and their partners took extensive digital photography of the island and a digital elevation model. The University of Western Australia Honorary Research Fellow Mr Paul Bourke created a Unity environment of Beacon Island with the modern fishing huts (Bourke 2015), and Curtin University refined the 3D environment as a lower-resolution Beacon Virtua to run on a desktop PC or inside smartphones and inside VR headsets (Woods et al. 2019). A Curtin University honours thesis by Adam Greenfield evaluated an early version of the walk-through VR environment and found major usability issues.

In 2020 I proposed to develop a collaborative mixed reality (two or more play different parties on the excavated Beacon Island. Participants interpret the local clues to uncover treasure and other remains) evaluated against a PC-based sandbox (open) digital desktop 3D interactive environment, in partnership with WA Museum/Geraldton Museum. The application would track which elements of dark heritage the participants decided to filter, remove or focus on. I suggested that mixed reality, along with different media presentations of horror, could allow participants and guides to filter and personalize the more horrific elements of the story. The group of islands is very remote, and perhaps I should have made more effort to explain the scattered and hard-to-visualize geographical and historical aspects of this dark and troubling history. Having experienced touring the Geraldton Museum exhibition with and without a guide (Figure 2.1), I feel the challenge to surround the remaining artefacts with atmospheric texture is still a great opportunity waiting to be developed. Ironically, the developer of the advanced but expensive technology I proposed for part of this application contacted me while I was writing this chapter.

The second site proposed to be included was Rottnest Island, and in particular, Rottnest Island Prison. Today Rottnest Island is home to holidaymakers and

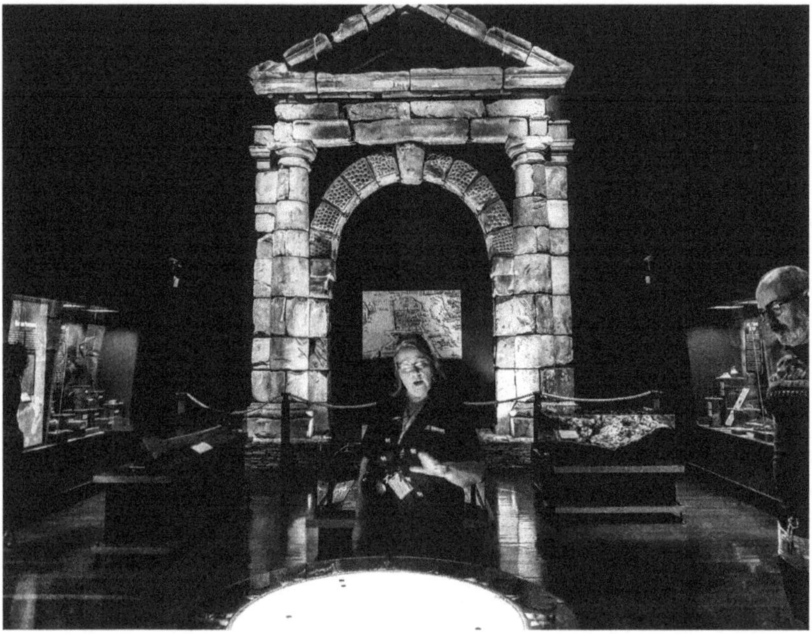

FIGURE 2.1 A museum guide explains the rich, tortured, history of the Batavia.

day-trippers eager to photograph quokkas, and the prison is part of a hotel, its past ignored or missed by most. Rottnest Island Prison was established in 1838 as "Australia's first and only mass segregation of Aboriginal people in a racially determined prison" (Stasiuk 2015). Closing in 1931, Rottnest Island Prison has since been described as a forgotten element of a modern playground (Stasiuk and Hibberd 2017) while few people visiting Rottnest Island on holidays are aware of its dark past. Remarkably, the prison also became a wartime internment camp during World War I when German and Austrian-Hungarian soldiers shared the prison but not a language (Ludewig 2019).

Although there has been recent and commendable development of Aboriginal memorialization rituals at the second prison (Rottnest Island Authority 2020), many tourists who used the remaining edifice as the primary accommodation are still unaware of its dark and troubling past, the influenza and death that overtook so many of the 4,000 men and boys crowded into tiny cells without windows, heating or furniture. In the words of Rangi Hirini, "many people don't know the island has the record of being the location of the largest deaths in custody gravesite in the [Australian] nation" (Hirini 2018). Dr Glen Stasiuk wrote, "Despite its significance, its role as the first and longest operating Australian Aboriginal prison site remains hidden beneath national forgetting" (Stasiuk 2015). Yet there is archival evidence of the brutality – the State Library of WA has released shocking photos of prisoners in neck chains (which I have not asked to be included here, but you can view on their website: https://slwa.wa.gov.au/).

Add to this horror the symbolic significance of the island. To the Whadjuk Noongar people, Rottnest Island is Wadjemup, a "place across the water where the spirits are". For them, the island is part of the journey of the spirit as it departs a dying person. To be incarcerated in such a place of transition between life and death would be harrowing for them in terms of location alone. Today the burial ground is considered "the largest deaths in custody site in Australia and the largest known burial ground of Aboriginal people" (Melville 2016). Rottnest Island is also a resting place for the departed, for the local people, so incarceration for them on that island may well have been extra horrifying. To add to the challenge of respectful and appropriate visualization of this traumatic history, to name or display photographs of deceased people can recall and disturb their spirit (Australian Institute of Aboriginal and Torres Strait Islander Studies 2007).

My proposal for this second site was to provide panoramic digital environments pre-tour and then on-site AR experiences via tourists' smartphones with an emphasis on audio rather than visual information. I suggested we evaluate which elements are too traumatic or preferred by the tourists and determine whether events from an indigenous perspective could be handled sensitively and appropriately via immersive technology. This project raised the most clear-cut opposition (from one reviewer in particular) that the local community must be involved, even though I had the support of the Rottnest Island Authority (RIA) and local expert and indigenous scholar Dr Glen Stasiuk, as well as other local historians.

The criticism raised difficult issues for me. Firstly, the RIA was in the process of developing cultural protocols with the indigenous shareholders, which I agreed to follow, and they would be responsible for the ethical approval and management of community input. I felt that bypassing the RIA and asking the overall community to agree before I had secured the funding was unethical, but obviously the reviewer disagreed (and they ignored the budget component set aside for community focus groups, given directly to the participants as thanks for their time and input). I am still wrestling with this issue of contacting multiple parties before applying for grants, and how best to work with and for indigenous communities as a researcher.

Secondly, although there is no equivalent immersive experience, and there are great challenges in providing specialist devices to an offshore island with no permanent inhabitants (apart from workers for the tourist shops), it seems difficult to convince reviewers of the importance of communicating the dark heritage of Rottnest amongst the sunshine and cute marsupials. As part of the larger grant application with the other proposed sites mentioned below, this proposal was not funded.

The third site proposed was Fremantle Prison, with the support of Fremantle Prison. Built in 1859 and in use until 1991, Fremantle Prison is a Convict

Heritage World Heritage Site and until COVID, a highly successful guided tourist destination, famous (or infamous) for its hangings, floggings, daring escapes and riots. The organization running Fremantle Prison as a highly successful heritage tourism site is seeking to increase their online heritage experience and prepare for future potential physical lockdowns (due to the current pandemic), but staff have expressed reticence in deploying VR as it can break down, requires specialist care and interferes with the human guides. My proposal here was to develop magic-lens-type AR clues and directional sound to evaluate whether guided mystery clues or completely free AR-audio tours can best explain further previous inhabitations and traumatic scenes of prison history. Ideally the resulting evaluation data could help determine" whether smartphones provide a sense of previous "placeness" and convey the situated sense of helplessness and terror.

Digital technology can provide augmented and online experiences, but as Fremantle Prison Heritage Conservation Manager Luke Donegan has explained to me, virtual, augmented and mixed reality technologies are too often expensive, obtrusive and difficult to maintain (personal email, April 2018). I also noted that there is no free Wi-Fi at the site, and the thick walls of the prison might block phone signals.

Fremantle Prison contained normal and "dark" cells to punish prisoners (four condemned prisoners were also hanged there). The content-based challenge is to immerse the visitor in layered, incomplete and contested historical or archaeological information of remote and long-past tragedy (Batavia-Beacon Island), allow visitors to filter but also recognize alternate cultural sensitivities to incarceration (Rottnest Island Prison) and provide practical, accessible experiences that augment rather than impede a guided experience (Fremantle Prison). In consultation with the interpretation officer, no indigenous prisoner stories were to be incorporated, but this project was not funded.

Reviewers are often dismissive of museum feedback that museumgoers do not like downloading phone apps including museum AR apps, even though this has been reported, the news isn't in academic publications and therefore discounted. Grant reviewers also seem unaware of the new formats that can provide extended reality (XR) applications that work in the web browsers (of phones, tablets and computers) and do not require an application download and automatically tailor the 3D environment to the capability of the device running it.

The second and third proposed projects I consider to be a lesson in applying consumer-level technology for practical implementations, but reviewers of academic grant applications are often unimpressed, for they expect that any exciting and innovative research requires the deployment of new, powerful but previously untested technology. A solution might be to elaborate on the challenges of matching technology, practicality and the contextual demands of the cultural heritage *in context*, but this might indicate the research is too risky to fund.

Australian wartime wreckages: Sydney-Kormoran

On a more successful note, we are currently developing and evaluating virtual heritage museum projects. In cooperation with two museums (the Western Australian Museum and Australia's National Maritime Museum), we are developing a photogrammetry-derived project to design and evaluate virtual heritage experiences of the HMAS Kormoran and the HSK-8 Sydney.

The HMAS Kormoran and the HSK-8 Sydney sank after battling and sinking each other on November 19, 1941, 22 kilometres apart, 290 kilometres off the West Australian coast. While the majority of the Germans of the German auxiliary cruiser Kormoran were eventually rescued (80 died), the 645 Australians on the Sydney never returned to shore, and the sinking of the Sydney remains "Australia's worst naval disaster ... Mystery surrounding aspects of the battle resulted in anguish and disbelief that is still evident in the Australian community" (Department of Agriculture 2011). The German commander stated where the ships sank, but he was not believed. Collating witness accounts, theories and archaeological evidence, the eventually found wrecks corroborated where the German commander said they sank, (2,500 metres under the sea in the Indian Ocean) and became evidence in a 2009 Commission.

I am currently co-supervising a PhD student who will evaluate virtual heritage experiences, expectations and alternatives in communicating the impact and engagement of the complex but riveting story, and hopefully this research will distinguish between focus groups of the general public, museum curators and archaeologists and descendants of the lost sailors. Although I have supervised two PhD students on recent difficult or dark heritage projects, I have not found a great deal of attention on how these issues can be tackled in virtual heritage research. I suggest that overlapping concepts of presence, and immersion and affect in telepresence studies, dark tourism and tourist studies (and in related museum and heritage studies), as well as museum evaluation studies in computer–human interaction studies, could be better collated and assessed, but the original data, of audiences, museums, interaction design and the digital projects themselves, need to be better preserved and outlined. I still feel that we are reinventing the wheel, particularly in interaction design, and we are not helped by the start-stop of expensive but impressive immersive technology showcases.

Workshopping contested and difficult heritage

Rather than wait on expensive ongoing research projects, I have endeavoured to approach some of these challenges collaboratively, by inviting heritage students and practitioners to workshop how they would design games as immersive experiences themselves. I have delivered workshops on game design and gamification of history and heritage in Italy (Figure 2.2), Qatar, Finland, Australia and Easter Island (Rapa Nui).

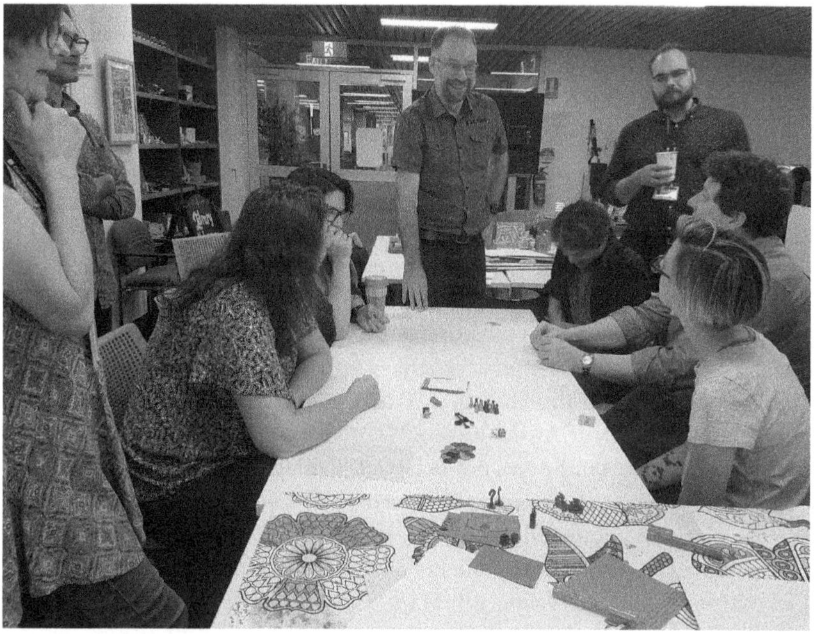

FIGURE 2.2 Workshop participants at Curtin University library discuss a boardgame prototype that uses strategy mechanics to reveal and reflect on colonialism.

Gamification

How can gamification help present difficult heritage contents? Will gamification trivialize or mask the cultural significance and potential social trauma of these sites? With an emphasis on games as engaging challenges that act as learning environments, in these workshops I have proposed that vague and contested information can be meaningfully incorporated as part of the game and that heritage issues may be more impactful if the audience is drawn into the design challenges. In other words, the unfinished, complex issues of heritage can be approximated by the challenges of the game itself and deeper learning can be achieved by inviting the audience in as co-designer.

The procedural rhetoric of games can also be captured and reversed in those moments when the player realizes that their subconscious attitudes and behaviours are no longer adequate (or perhaps never were), and I call the underpinning mechanics of the games that bring players to these points of realization, reflective mechanics (but there may well be a better term). The point is, complex and finished and authoritative immersive content does not always necessarily create impactful and profound moments of reflection. Sometimes even paper prototypes can convey the elements of engagement, challenge and reward. And if these prototypes cannot be played, that may well indicate some issues with the eventual immersive technology before much money is spent.

Real-world games are more than systems; they are imaginative frames of references that challenge, hinder, create risks and provide rewards and goal-based activities, and their laws (not set rules) are negotiated in real time and re-created by imagination and groups of people, competitively and collaboratively.

While games are engaging challenges and addiction machines, one is either in a reflective place or in a game's dynamic magic circle. Gamification tends to focus more on the rules and rewards of the system than on the exploration, creativity and imagination of the player.

Rather than turning heritage content into playful challenges, that are clearly, simply rewarded, the player may be rewarded with more creative options to explore or reconfigure. More advanced games offer different strategies and learning modes and so are powerful devices to provide different ways of experiencing and filtering difficult heritage content. An issue is of course that inside the magic circle of gameplay, the real-world trauma and horror of the simulated event might be trivialized or not be taken seriously. Moving from *playing a game* to *participating in a serious, complicitly respected immersive ritual* is a goal I think worthy of pursuit.

Framing and foreshadowing affect

Because games involve levels, stages and transitions, game design can help focus on the narrative stages required to prepare participants for dark or difficult heritage content. Martini and Buda (2020) have described how affective places can frame and foreshadow dark tourism:

> Successful places of dark tourism are deliberately built so that material remains, narratives, and reproductions of tragic events are assembled in a coherent, powerful way that creates an atmosphere in which affects are perceivable.

Narratives can be framed as spatial narratives, and dramatic or difficult encounters can be foreshadowed. Foreshadowing is a literary device used to give an indication or hint of what is to come later in the story. As pointed out by various researchers (Pagano et al. 2020), when immersive heritage involves process-driven experiences, difficult heritage elements can be foreshadowed, both developing a sense of drama and allowing participants time or options to prepare or modify the severity of difficult heritage, how it is presented or choose options to seek or avoid it. Foreshadowing can also create a sense of unease, prompting the participant to reflect on the situation, and their choices or options.

Aphasia

Ann Laura Stoler (2011) has described aphasia (in terms of French colonial history, but also in other cultures and periods) as "a difficulty in retrieving both conceptual and lexical vocabularies and, most important, a difficulty in comprehending what is spoken", and she applied it to aspects of problematic history. Because games, and by extension, interactive immersive virtual environments, restrict the initial interaction of the player or participant, there exists the opportunity to allow the player to discover this vague and amorphous barrier and unfold its secrets or at least attempt to circumnavigate it.

Solutions

Improved scholarly research

I suggest there are many resources and tools still worthy of investigation to solidify a more scholarly approach: For example, literature surveys and collection of case studies and technologies and methods, and collated datasets and results with shared and standardized procedures and methods (across virtual heritage, VR/MR cases, critical heritage) helping us towards useful data and extrapolatable results.

Improved documentation

A model by itself does not reveal the scholarly methods, the process, the design decisions or the provenance of the tangible and intangible heritage source material. Documentation of the process, intentions, data and of the paradata is required (Stone and Ojika 2000) (as recommended in the London Charter [Denard 2016] as well as shareholder involvement from the culture from which the content was derived and simulated). Copyright information and ownership of media and memories are further difficult issues. Ideally, in the research output of digital heritage projects, information on the ethical research administrative processes that the researchers undertook is included. There is also the matter of the designer's intentions and the user's experience.

Designers and researchers can provide information and guidance on where and when and how the material was expected to be used, and observations of the project as evaluated by and for different audiences. Following on from my quick discussion of valuable elements of game design, I suggest we can better leverage the process-visualization and multimodal capabilities of immersive technologies along with the inherent challenges of engaging gameplay to support different learning styles and types of audiences.

Fragmentation and phantasmagoria

In terms of design, flexible, reconfiguring interaction that caters to its audience could be deployed, providing attention to non-visual media and stimuli institutions where visual media may create trauma. As reported by Galani and Kidd (2019), empathic engagement with heritage sites is difficult, but Jenny Kidd (2019) has suggested that "embodied and tangible digital heritage encounters can be created from loose fragments and in outdoor environments that might themselves be considered challenging" even if it raises important ethical issues.

Essential questions

In workshops discussing the risks and potentials for game design ideas and themes for virtual heritage I have emphasized the importance of understanding what are the culturally significant elements of the site or heritage practice, the specific ways digital immersive technology can bring forward these culturally significant elements, and how games (but less frequently) in virtual heritage projects increase in complexity of challenge to engage, frustrate and ultimately reward the player. Yes, games can be learning environments, but applying games to virtual heritage projects also requires culturally situated meaningful learning. Others (Katifori et al. 2019) have researched the importance of essential questions in developing dark heritage projects, but unfortunately virtual heritage designs seldom begin with these central, fundamental questions.

Critical and reflective interaction

Others (Haddad 2016) have argued digital heritage, and virtual heritage by extension, could be more reflective, and provocative, even for the questionable group labelled "digital natives". How could interaction design strategies help provoke, coax and encourage a reconsideration of beliefs, habits and behaviours? The immersive experience design could:

1. Show the player the consequences of their actions.
2. Take away agency (interactive control) from the player to show differing levels of control and authority.
3. Take away the certainty of results gained from the decisions taken to convey contestation of historical knowledge.
4. Allow for diminishing or expanding counterfactual results or ending gameplay if actions are taken not based on cultural appropriate strategies or behaviours.
5. Change the sensory feedback to indicate changes in emotion or importance.
6. Swap or reverse the character controlled or the role played in the game to convey different levels of power or authority.
7. Allow the player to begin to influence other players to show the coercive power of certain authority figures in history.
8. Provide a more singular, phenomenological experience rather than a generic experience that sweepingly explains how everyone is affected.
9. Provide a commentary on historical consequents via a narrator beyond or parallel to the gameplay.

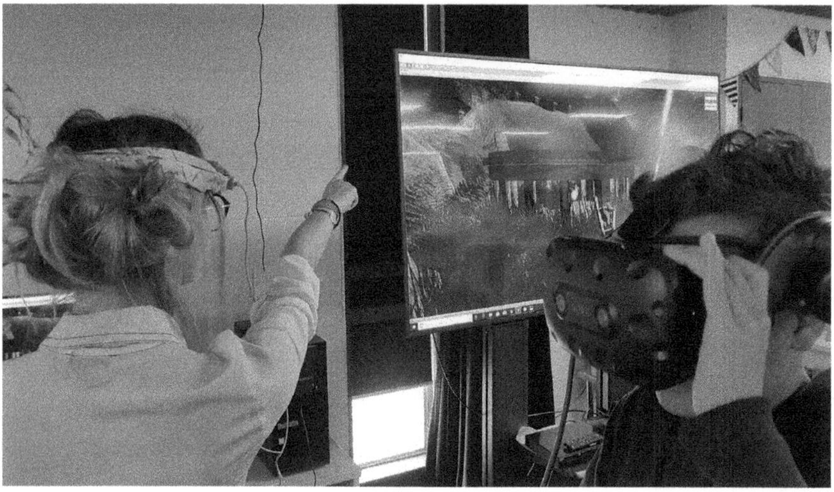

FIGURE 2.3 Two participants with different views and different forms of immersive technology must collaborate to coordinate their avatar or to view the same cultural or historical milieu (content by intern student: Agathe Limouzy).

10. Using mixed reality or augmented reality provides different perspectives of the past that can only be blended successfully if players or participants learn to see what the other is seeing or otherwise experiencing (Figure 2.3).

Conclusion

At the risk of being provocative, Australia's record on preserving and communicating heritage is suspect (Gregory and Paterson 2015; Cooke and Hayward-Jackson 2018; Australian Institute for the Conservation of Cultural Material 2020; Wahlquist and Allam 2020). There are reasons for this, apart from the vast distances, Australia has many hidden stories and from a Western perspective lacks the centuries-old preservation institutions of other nations. Sadly, millennia-old traditions of indigenous heritage as performance and art do exist in Australia but defy simplistic attempts to visualize and fully understand them via digital displays and collections – they must be performed and experienced to be understood.

And I have suggested there are many opportunities for difficult virtual heritage research, in terms of shareholder consent and participation, in resolving technical challenges, providing clearer definitions of immersion suitable for history and heritage, developing a wider and richer range of multimodal approaches, resolving best practices for guided and non-guided heritage tours, considering the importance of immersive literacy of designers and the audience (two sides of the same coin) and improving the potential for critical thinking arising from immersive experiences. Such research requires the development of and access to larger international research data and examples.

That said, given Australia's unique, contested, lost and forgotten histories, immersive technologies offer significant potential, but not just in terms of international agreements and protocols. Various modes of extended reality (AR, VR and MR) need to be compared and evaluated in context. And by context I do not only mean geographical borders but also institutional and site-specific borders. There are evaluation frameworks for experiencing interactive and immersive pieces, sites and environments in museums, but these surveys, frameworks and technologies will also need to be evaluated beyond museum contexts for a pressing market factor is the technology that can scale from consumer-level phones to the near-future certain appeal of virtual reality headsets.

Can these modes of digital intervention augment the experience, improve the understanding of others and allow visitors to filter difficult heritage more appropriately? How do we allow digital technology to provide both focused and reflective spaces where people have time to reflect and discuss potentially traumatic scenes? (Akagawa 2020).

Here there are two aspects to the element of "place" in dark tourism, and by extension, to dark heritage. As noted by Martini and Buda (2020), "Space is affectively saturated and tourists in dark places make sense of difficult and often contested places".

This means to develop affective space, we require the design or modification of environments that allow for (p. 685) "the fluid, relations amongst their bodies, emotions, affects, thoughts, social, cultural, and spatial interactions". But spaces also must allow for reflection after or during the affective experience. Choreographing active spaces of experience and reflective places for contemplating and reconsidering requires expertise in the spatial narrative.

In terms of cultural tourism for dark and difficult heritage sites, can we deploy pre-tour visualizations to gauge increased interest more effectively in physical visits to the sites? Such questions wait to be answered, due to the silos of scholarly disciplines and the pressing logistics and practical needs of digital design projects, where time meant to evaluate is often hindered or even swallowed up by pressing needs to modify, resolve and change the technology. Partly, the technology is often overtly visual, does not allow for participatory feedback and does not cover a wider sensory array of stimuli and affordances.

Cultural heritage and individual memories rely on multimodal and multisensorial information (Liu and Lan 2021). While it is understandable that early virtual reality technology was vision focused, with many of the pioneers also experts in computer vision, the development of biofeedback, wearable computing and new sensory interfaces will hopefully allow us to convey more than just the image and increase emotional impact and engagement through a multitude of senses with a wider and ideally reconfigurable learning affordances.

But a further issue that may not be obvious to many is the important but often lacking use of *reflective mechanics*. Game mechanics are well known, studied and discussed, but confusion reigns as to their relation to game logic, gamer understanding of the "rules" and their relation to the core gameplay. For the moment, if I could loosely describe them as the essential parts of the game that decide on how to move the game along, from one stage (or level) to another, then we could distinguish game mechanics per se from the player's understanding of what is happening. For virtual heritage, reflective mechanics might then describe the processes and affordances by which a player is led to appreciate or become self-aware of steps or perspectives that prevent them from underlying other situated cultural perspectives.

I believe this is an important concept for virtual heritage: We are not merely presenting 3D models, images, sounds etc., but trying to convey the culturally situated agency that gives value and meaning to those media objects as living heritage. Allowing for reflective meaning-making and meaning-consideration suggests a need for spatial repose and consideration of altered embodiment (Waterton 2014; Micieli-Voutsinas and Person 2020).

But with difficult *virtual* heritage, we encounter a further challenge: Do we wish to communicate the difficulty of the simulated situated past to ourselves or the difficulty of that past as experienced and felt by others *from that past*?

References

Akagawa, Natsuko. 2020. "'Difficult Heritage', Silent Witnesses: Dismembering Traumatic Memories, Narratives and Emotions of Firebombing in Japan." In *Places of Traumatic Memory*, 37–59. Cham: Springer.

Australian Institute for the Conservation of Cultural Material. June 2020 2020. *Statement by the Australian Institute for the Conservation of Cultural Material on the destruction of the Pilbara Caves.* https://aiccm.org.au/wp-content/uploads/2020/06/AICCM-Statement-on-Destruction-of-Pilbara-Caves.pdf.

Australian Institute of Aboriginal and Torres Strait Islander Studies. 2007. "AIATSIS Pathways: Guide to the AIATSIS Thesauri (Sensitivity Message)." http://www1.aiatsis.gov.au/SensitivityNotice.asp.

Bourke, Paul. 2015. "Beacon Island Virtua: A Digital 3D Representation." In Australian Archaeological Association 2015 Conference, Fremantle, Western Australia, 2–4 December. http://australianarchaeology.com/conference/aaa2015/.

Champion, Erik, and Hafizur Rahaman. 2019. "3D Digital Heritage Models as Sustainable Scholarly Resources." *Sustainability* 11 (8): 1–8. http://www.mdpi.com/2071-1050/11/8/2425.

———. 2020. "Survey of 3D Digital Heritage Repositories and Platforms." *The Virtual Archaeology Review (VAR).* https://doi.org/10.4995/var.2020.13226. https://polipapers.upv.es/index.php/var/article/view/13226.

Christen, Kimberly, Alex Merrill, and Michael Wynne. 2017. "A Community of Relations: Mukurtu hubs and spokes." *D-Lib Magazine* 23 (5/6). https://doi.org/10.1045/may2017-christen. https://www.dlib.org/dlib/may17/christen/05christen.html.

Cooke, Glen, and Iva Hayward-Jackson. 2018. Waking up to Wadjemup. *Office of the Register of Indigenous Corporations*. Accessed 19 November 2020.

Denard, Hugh. 2016. "A New Introduction to the London Charter." In *Paradata and Transparency in Virtual Heritage*, 83–98. London: Routledge.

Department of Agriculture, Water and the Environment. 2011. "National Heritage Places - HMAS Sydney II and the HSK Kormoran Shipwreck Sites." *Environment* (blog). https://www.environment.gov.au/heritage/places/national/sydney-kormoran.

Edwards, H. 1966. *Islands of Angry Ghosts*. New York: William Morrow.

Galani, Areti, and Jenny Kidd. 2019. "Evaluating Digital Cultural Heritage "In the Wild" The Case For Reflexivity." *Journal on Computing and Cultural Heritage (JOCCH)* 12 (1): 1–15.

Gregory, Kate, and Alistair Paterson. 2015. "Commemorating the colonial Pilbara: beyond memorials into difficult history." *National Identities* 17 (2): 137–153.

Haddad, Naif A. 2016. "Multimedia and Cultural Heritage: A Discussion for the Community Involved in Children's Heritage Edutainment and Serious Games in the 21st Century." *Virtual Archaeology Review* 7 (14): 61–73.

Hirini, Rangi. 2018. *Western Australia Promotes Rottnest Island as One of Their Major Tourist's Destinations, However Many People Don't Know the Island Has the Record of Being the Location of the Largest Deaths in Custody Gravesite in the Nation*. SBS. https://www.sbs.com.au/nitv/article/tourists-to-be-kicked-out-of-holiday-accommodation-built-on-aboriginal-burial-ground/udhd2vgl0

Katifori, Akrivi, KM Restrepo Lopez, Klaoudia Marsella, Dimitra Petousi, Manos Karvounis, Vassilis Kourtis, Maria Roussou, and Yannis Ioannidis. 2019. "Approaching "Dark Heritage" through Essential Questions: an Interactive Digital Storytelling Museum Experience." *MW19* | Boston. https://mw19.mwconf.org/paper/approaching-dark-heritage-through-essential-questions-an-interactive-digital-storytelling-experience-for-the-university-of-athens-criminology-museum/

Kidd, Jenny. 2019. "With New Eyes I See: Embodiment, Empathy and Silence in Digital Heritage Interpretation." *International Journal of Heritage Studies* 25 (1): 54–66.

Lewis, Maria. 2018. The Batavia Shipwreck is the craziest Australian horror story you've never heard of *The Guardian*. Accessed 14 November 2020.

Liu, Peng, and Lan Lan. 2021. "Museum as Multisensorial Site: Story Co-making and the Affective Interrelationship Between Museum Visitors, Heritage Space, and Digital Storytelling." *Museum Management and Curatorship* 36 (4): 403–426.

Ludewig, Alexandra. 2019. *War Time on Wadjemup: A Social History of the Rottnest Island Internment Camp*. Perth, Australia: UWA Publishing.

Martini, Annaclaudia, and Dorina Maria Buda. 2020. "Dark Tourism and Affect: Framing Places of Death and Disaster." *Current Issues in Tourism* 23 (6): 679–692. https://doi.org/10.1080/13683500.2018.1518972

Melville, Kirsti. 2016. Rottnest Island: Black Prison to White Playground. *ABC Radio National*. Accessed 18 November 2020.

Micieli-Voutsinas, Jacque, and Angela M Person. 2020. *Affective Architectures: More-than-representational Geographies of Heritage*. London: Routledge.

Pagano, Alfonsina, Augusto Palombini, Guido Bozzelli, Maurizio De Nino, Ivana Cerato, and Stefano Ricciardi. 2020. Arkaevision VR Game: User Experience Research Between Real and Virtual Paestum. *Applied Sciences* 10 (9): 3182. https://doi.org/10.3390/app10093182.

Poulsen, A. 2019. Hunting for wrecks and bones: islands reveal their secrets. *Midwest Times*. Accessed 24 September 2021.

Rottnest Island Authority. 2020. "Aboriginal Culture and History of Wadjemup/Rottnest Island." [website]. Last Modified unknown. Accessed 20 October 2020. https://rottnestisland.com/the-island/about-the-island/our-history/aboriginal-history.

Stasiuk, Glen. 2015. *Wadjemup: Rottnest Island as Black Prison and White Playground*. Thesis. Perth, Australia: Murdoch University.

Stasiuk, Glen, and Lily Hibberd. 2017. "Rottnest or Wadjemup: Tourism and the Forgetting of Aboriginal Incarceration and the Pre-colonial History of Rottnest Island." In *The Palgrave Handbook of Prison Tourism*, 191–215. Cham: Springer.

Stoler, Ann Laura. 2011. "Colonial Aphasia: Race and Disabled Histories in France." *Public Culture* 23 (1): 121–156.

Stone, Robert, and Takeo Ojika. 2000. "Virtual heritage: what next?" *IEEE Multimedia* 7 (2): 73–74.

Thomas, Suzie, Vesa-Pekka Herva, Oula Seitsonen, and Eerika Koskinen-Koivisto. 2019. "Dark Heritage." In *Encyclopedia of Global Archaeology*, 1–11. Cham: Springer International Publishing.

UNESCO. n.d. What Is Intangible Cultural Heritage?. UNESCO. Accessed 7 March 2022. https://ich.unesco.org/en/what-is-intangible-heritage-00003.

Wahlquist, Calla, and Lorena Allam. 2020. Rio Tinto Blew up Juukan Gorge Rock Shelters 'to Access Higher Volumes of High-grade Ore'. *The Guardian*. Accessed 18 November 2020.

Waterton, Emma. 2014. A More-than-representational Understanding of Heritage? The "Past" and the Politics of Affect." *Geography Compass* 8 (11): 823–833. https://doi.org/10.1111/gec3.12182.

Woods, A., N. Oliver, P. Bourke, J. Green, and A. Paterson. 2019. Beacon Virtua: A Virtual Reality Simulation Detailing the Recent and Shipwreck History of Beacon Island, Western Australia. *3D Recording and Interpretation for Maritime Archaeology*, edited by J. K. McCarthy, J. Benjamin, T. Winton and W. van Duivenvoorde, 197–210. Cham: Springer.

3

REMAKING CONFUCIAN RITES

Reenactment, immersive visualization and the revitalization of the marginalized cosmological body

Sarah Kenderdine, Lily Hibberd, Jeffrey Shaw and Tsong-Zung Chang

Introduction

Compiled in the 2nd century CE by scholars and disciples of Confucius, the *Book of Etiquettes and Rites, Yili* 儀禮 documents the ritual mastery of the early Confucians in the constant expression and visible performance of *li* 禮.[1] The *Yili* is a performance manual designed to empower the self-cultivation of the ritual ethics of the body and social behaviour in relation to cosmos, state and family.[2] A crucial text in the Confucian canon for thousands of years, modernizers at the end of dynastic China violently prohibited its use. To perform any one of the *Yili* rites could result in imprisonment or death, compounding cultural repression, loss of know-how and ultimately to the rupture in the cultural transmission of Confucian Rites (Billioud and Thoraval 2015). The contemporary activation of the Confucian ritual body requires reconciliation with difficult pasts, which pivot on conflicting paradigms of ideology, morality, family and the collective body because of their forceful marginalization over more than a century. Also known as *li*, or *li*-rites, the renewed cosmology of the body is arguably crucial to understanding modern China, yet a range of persistent difficult pasts, from the loss of embodied knowledge to the fear of punishment, could be the reason that recent revivals of Confucian aesthetics as part of official Chinese heritage reconstruction have yet to inspire everyday practices of Confucian rituals in community and family life.

The revitalization of the Confucian Rites arises from a "difficult past" that can be situated within the theoretical framework and concept of difficult heritage. Emanating from the earlier notion of dissonant heritage, which first surfaced in the 1990s, it was Sharon MacDonald's work in the 2000s that formalized difficult heritage as part of wide-ranging critiques of historical interpretation and heritage practices as well as sociological, ethical and human rights questions

DOI: 10.4324/9781003200659-4

about postcolonial and post-conflict societies (see Lehrer, Milton and Patterson 2011; Logan and Reeves 2009; Macdonald 2009; Tunbridge and Ashworth 1996). The Confucian Rites are an inherently corporeal knowledge and a particularly difficult form of heritage in two regards. First, they must be performed in order to exist. The transmission of Confucian Rites, like martial arts practice, requires a performed person-to-person exchange that hinges on a novice's imitation of an expert's movements (Chan et al. 2011; Komura et al. 2006). While the *Yili* offers a level of guidance, its contents are only fully understood when performed, hence the need to revive transmission through live embodied acts. Second, this tacit knowledge is even more difficult to reconstruct because of the contemporary Chinese politics of heritage within and beyond China, with the paradoxical forms of Confucianism in China at the centre of its contested or difficult heritage.

This chapter investigates the reconciliation of this difficult past through the work of the Remaking of Confucian Rites (RCR) project, the most significant reenactment endeavour to date to contend with this historical material and its cultural life. The RCR project is specifically grounded in the reconstruction of the *Yili* « 儀禮 » (*Book of Etiquette and Rites*), which collates basic performance instructions for 17 of Confucius's rituals, originally recorded by disciples in the 5th century BCE. Apart from these notes, all other aspects of the ritual performance have notably been lost. To address this gap and in order to reconstitute the text's historical practice, RCR undertakes close reading and philological study, specifically to restore lost contextual information through other surviving literature or studies on the original language and meaning of that literature. The outcome of this process is a detailed script for contemporary performance of the Rites. RCR's scholars also embed their findings within technological innovations that archive embodied knowledge systems. Just as importantly, RCR is developing new approaches to immersive visualization that can effectively encompass the performed aesthetic, cultural, affective and mnemonic dimensions of ritual heritage. In this chapter, we delineate the role of immersive and interactive technologies for the twofold documentation of the reenactment of the Confucian Rites and their novel transmission as reperformable archives in a knowledge system and database that can be re-inscribed based on practice over time. As such, rather than restoring the past as it was, RCR is providing a foundation for the revitalization of social, ethical and contemporary practices of the Confucian Rites. As the project generates a contemporary forms of transmission of the Chinese cosmological body, it contends with the difficult past of this body's marginalization during the Communist Revolution from the mid-20th century.

The Confucian cosmology of the body and its difficult past

Confucian Rites, teachings and texts were at the core of China's ideological, social and civil curriculum for almost 2,000 years. Though the teachings were recorded, the rites that Confucius consecrated were not archived in his lifetime. The *Lunyu* « 儀禮 » (*The Analects of Confucius*) are the earliest version of these documents, dated to the 4th century BCE, which followers and disciples generated and arranged based on Confucian sayings and dialogues with his disciples.[3]

The concept of *li* 禮 is at the core of the Confucian theory of ethics. As a cosmological attitude and form of training, *li* instils in a person the perpetual awareness of the wholistic connectedness of all living and inanimate things. Though the word *li* can be literally translated as "ritual", the term has more complex interpretations that resist succinct definition. For instance, *li* is a cosmology that refers to order and wholistic relations. The Confucian ideology of *li* ritual performance, or "*li*-rites", aims to cultivate ethical character in three ways: through the organization of social and political institutions, in ceremonies and rites to honour familial elders and ancestors as well as authorities and deities, and in everyday behaviour and etiquette. Above and beyond ritual acts and the reenactment of shared values, the *li*-rites has the greater intent of fostering the core value of *ren* (仁), encompassing virtue, humanity, humaneness, goodness, benevolence and love (see *Lunyu* « 論語 », *Analects*, 6:30; Do-Dinh 1969, 107).

Twentieth-century modern China's political upheaval and social shifts caused a major decline in Confucian tradition, ritual practice and the cosmology of *li*. The 1900 sacking of Beijing was the precursor for comprehensive political change led by the multinational military coalition of the Eight-Nation Alliance (*baguo lianjun* "八國聯軍" in Chinese). When the civil service examination of Confucian classics was terminated in 1904, the ideological system was also forced to change. The revolution of the National Republic, which began in 1911, radically transformed China's dynastic political system to shift the country's cultural emphasis away from Confucian learning.

The year 1949 inaugurated an era that would devastate Confucianism when the People's Republic of China banned almost all practices associated with traditional culture and made Marxism-Leninism its official ideology along with the social and economic campaign of the "Great Leap Forward". The Cultural Revolution from 1966 to 1971 had the aggressive objective to modernize China. During this time traditional rituals and Confucianism were denounced as a form of "feudal ethics", *fengjian lijiao* 封建禮教 in Chinese (Louie 1980, 1986; Zhang and Schwartz 1997). Once foundational to Chinese culture, Confucian social relations and rituals were not only considered backward but were also criminalized. As a result, the trifold artform, performance and aesthetic lineage of the Chinese cosmological body, which had been communicated over thousands of years through Confucian ritual practices, was successfully suppressed and dissociated from all forms of cultural and social transmission (Billioud and Thoraval 2015).

Certain contemporary scholars claim that Confucianism was never eradicated but remains intact in the Chinese body and mind, some of whom consider that *li* is pivotal to understanding modern China (Billioud 2007; Billioud and Thoraval 2015; Leng and Salzman 2016; Peng 2017; Peng and Liu 2017; Tu 1985; Wu

2014). *Li* in practice, or *li*-rites, provides the grounds for the claim of its continuity as a ritual code of conduct and awareness because it is not a philosophical concept but a belief system integral to the social structure and ancient laws of China. Because they are at the root of China's civilization, the *li*-rites are fundamental to the RCR's reconstruction of the Confucian Rites and cultural paradigms on which they depend, which is the reason that Remaking Confucian Rites project intends to restore these rites as a living ceremony.

Difficult heritage, reenactment and intangible cultural heritage in China

China has significantly embraced the revival of Confucian Rites as part of its recent return to tradition. It was also one of the first countries to espouse the legitimization of UNESCO's cultural heritage register in the 1970s.[4] Even earlier, from 1950, China was already implementing conservation measures at historical sites. UNESCO's universal heritage values not only bolstered this effort but also fostered the revitalization of "national studies" (*guoxue* 國學). When the UNESCO Convention for the Safeguarding of the Intangible Heritage (ICH) was inaugurated in 2003 (UNESCO 2003), it provided a means to recognize and register forms of non-material heritage, such as dance, music, craft, storytelling or ritual practice. In addition to their formulation as performance repositories, expressions of ICH remain vitally linked to people because they can only be perpetuated through acts of social transmission (Taylor 2003; 2016).

ICH is a significant discourse in contemporary post-socialist China that has produced Chinese perspectives on ICH as well as its culturally specific theorization and interpretation (Gao 2014; Kuah and Liu 2017; Maags and Svensson 2018; You 2015; Zhu 2014). Chinese authorities have listed 42 ICH elements (UNESCO n.d.) since the ratification of the UNESCO Convention on Intangible Cultural Heritage in 2004 and have introduced the term "*feiyi* 非遺" as an abbreviation of the three words in Chinese for "intangible cultural heritage" to advance its burgeoning cultural heritage enterprise. In some quarters, however, the role of ICH in China is contested. Wu (2012), for instance, purports that ICH has been used to augment the nationalistic heritage policies of the Chinese Communist Party. The work of Chinese scholars whose focus on a local standpoint of ICH has also been criticized for mainly being directed at securing recognition for overtly traditional practices (You 2015). Similarly, other Chinese ICH experts argue that subjective dimensions of intangible cultural heritage, such as "identity, creativity, pride, memory, feeling, belief, sociable needs", have largely been excluded from the "authentic" ICH paradigms authorized by the Chinese state, which tend to prioritize material forms (Su 2018, 923. See also Gao 2014). Nonetheless, Yu (2015) highlights how active "vernacular" practices have remained vital for the ongoing transmission of Chinese ritual life.

Irrespective of the politics of heritage, the unbroken transmission of ICH in the present requires forms of mediation between performers and audiences, of which reenactment is an important form that has been gaining increasing attention worldwide. In the mainstream, reenactment is regarded as an amateur or community-led re-staging of past events, such as historical rites or battle scenes, some of which have nonetheless been repeated for thousands of years, like seasonal rituals, or ancient rites of passage, passion plays and pageants (Agnew 2004; Schneider 2011). In populist iterations, according to Agnew (2004, 327–328), historical reenactment favours "high-concept themes – Vikings, medieval knights, pyramid builders, pirates and mutineers, cowboys and Indians, explorers, slaves, pilgrims, and soldiers". Other kinds of reenactments alternatively reprise lost arts of performance, including martial arts practices, or more conceptual endeavours like the reperformance or appropriation of live art works (see relevant chapters in Agnew, Lamb and Tomann 2020, and Schneider 2011). Though not all these forms are presented before an audience, reenactment is often witnessed by non-actors, providing wider populations with direct encounters with history and the aesthetic, social, economic, political and epistemological function of the historical past, in contrast to static objects or sites as vessels of historical transmission.

In reconnecting communities with physical action, reenactment can also enliven embodied knowledge systems (Daugbjerg, Eisner and Knudsen 2014). Because performers and audiences can review, revisit, re-do and rebuild the performative repertoire by engaging in the active reception, learning, recording and transmission of knowledge, reenactment has become medium both of heritage production and of academic research (Jae-Phil et al. 2011; Mulhe 2020; Ten Brink and Oppenheimer 2012; Waterton and Watson 2013). Yet, as Bénichou underscores (2017: para. 15), popular historical and academic reenactment can be considered fundamentally "contradictory regimes" that should not be equated. While many academics have shunned mainstream, touristic and amateur reenactment as legitimate historical forms worthy of study, it is nonetheless gaining legitimacy in the domains of social science and humanities (Agnew 2004, 327–330). Interdisciplinary scholars across sports, science, history and the arts have deployed reenactment in analytic scientific processes that seek to understand and reconstruct human performance using authentically reconstructed settings, costumes and tools, most prominently in the case of martial arts (Cognot, Jaquet and Sorenson 2015). Pertinent to this chapter, ritual studies scholarship has also embraced reenactment as an important method of scholarship and analytical tool (Dreschke 2020).

Reenactment has its own cultural lineages in China. During the second half of the 20th century, for instance, reenactment was a prevalent feature of Chinese documentary films promoting Communist Party narratives (Qian 2013). China has seen the popular rise of historical military, ritual and martial arts reenactment, which is thriving in amateur contexts as well at Chinese state-sponsored culture parks and historic sites re-staging historic battles and other events (Bowman 2016; Li 2020). Confucian rituals have been reenacted as well; though, by many accounts, these revivalist events so far seem to have been conducted on a symbolic level rather than through deep spiritual engagement or in the common, everyday activities of ordinary Chinese people (Hammond and Richey 2015; Maags and Svensson 2018, You 2015; Zhu 2014). Adding to the challenge of understanding this contemporary situation, reenactment in China has yet to be extensively theorized (Jaurès 2012; Zhang 2021). In tandem with the renewal of Confucianism in China, historical reenactment has nonetheless been a vital instrument in the state-sponsored Chinese heritage paradigm, which has made Classical Studies into a venerated topic across cultural, political and academic contexts, and vitally supported research projects such as Remaking Confucian Rites.

Remaking Confucian Rites: Revitalizing the *Li-rites* through immersive and interactive technologies

Led by Peng Lin, Tsinghua University Professor in the Centre of Ritual Studies, Beijing, Remaking Confucian Rites is the most prominent project to revive the Confucian Rites to date, pivoting on the renewed study of the *Yili* « 儀禮 » (*Book of Etiquette and Rites*). Originating in records from the 5th century BCE, the *Yili* provides instructions for rituals and behaviour for conducting 17 ceremonies, including seminal events such as capping, marriage, mourning, sacrificial offerings, archery competitions, banquets, official visits and court audiences (see Yucai and Habberstad 2014). Presented as a manual, the *Yili* mainly features performance instructions, such as the appropriate gestures for greeting visitors, when and how to curtsey, how to drink or make a toast, the correct arrangement of banquet seating and the timing of musical accompaniment. These technical details have proven to be vital in the reconstruction of the Rites.

Peng and his team of scholars have undertaken an extended and meticulous analysis of the *Yili*, entailing a word-by-word examination in a collective reading and close study system to painstakingly reconstruct the 17 ritual ceremonies of the *Yili*. Notably, of the *Five Confucian Classics* the *Yili* is the text that is the least understood, though it once underpinned China's ancient civilization. This is because the original significance of its rich embedding in material culture and performative customs were lost a long time also and, prior to Peng's studies, there was little known historical documentation of the Rites (Morgan 2017). For example, the book of *Yili* shows ground plans but there are no elevations or exterior renderings of the temple compound in which the ceremony is supposed to take place, and there are a few other historical records that describe the architecture. Fortunately, Peng has been able to locate other technical manuals as well as fiction and poetry describing rituals surviving from the dynasties of Han (206 BCE–220 CE), Song (960–1279 CE), Yuan (1271–1368 CE), Ming (1368–1644 CE) and Qing (1644–1912 CE). Cross-referencing these primary literary, musical and archaeological sources against the *Yili* has enabled the wholistic reassembly of the material and aesthetic context of the Confucian Rites. Reconstruction processes have also included the analysis of archaeological materials for fabricating replica objects, from drinking vessels, tools and weapons, elaborate costumes and musical instruments through to the presence of live animals like geese and horses.

The barriers facing the revival of Confucian Rites were pointed out by contemporary Chinese artist and curator Li Zhenhua when he asked in 2017, "who is going to perform [the *Yili*] … who will transfer its inner meaning? How can we travel there to 2000 years ago?"[5] While aiming to authenticate all aspects of this contextual research, RCR does not intend to reinstate the past per se, but rather to revive and reunite the core cosmology of the *li*-rites with the Chinese social body of today. Nor does the RCR aim to restore ritual forms as they were practised up to 1911, but to revitalize them as they were preserved in the *Yili*.

Peng's close reading of the *Yili* is not only a pursuit of scholarly detail but also has the practical outcome of a movement-by-movement script for the reenactment of each Rite, with reconstructed props, musical and movement notes. The script further provides scenographic information for the Rites' professional cinematic documentation, the scope of which has been augmented through the application of new media arts approaches along with immersive and interactive programs specifically designed for the RCR project.

Following more than 35 years of research and study, in 2012 Peng began to reenact a series of Rites with 30 elite actors from the Beijing Opera, who performed the ceremonies alongside amateur players. The reconstruction and digital recording of these rites were undertaken in collaboration with Hong Kong art curator Tsong-Zung Chang and Director of the Jia Li Hall foundation, along with Professor Jeffrey Shaw from City University Hong Kong's Centre for Applied Computing and Interactive Media (ACIM) (now at the Academy of Visual Art, Baptist University Hong Kong) and Professor Sarah Kenderdine of the Laboratory of Experimental Museology (eM+) at École Polytechnique Fédérale de Lausanne (EPFL), Switzerland. To date, three complete Rites have been filmed in Hong Kong, Taiwan, and China (the capping, marriage and archery ceremonies). Recorded over several months at professional cinema quality and the highest levels of cinematic aesthetic excellence, the resulting documentation has already been included in major exhibitions including the 2015 Royal Opening of the China Exchange London, as part of the *Body of Confucius* curated by Tsong-Zung Chang and Shiming Gao for *Beyond the Globe* at the Eighth Triennial U3 Ljubljana, Slovenia in 2016 (Figure 3.1) and at the USA's Art Institute Chicago exhibition *Mirroring China's Past: Emperors and Their Bronzes* in 2018.[6]

Intensive research on immersive technologies and architectures for embodied knowledge transmission has additionally been critical to the RCR project. While single-channel video recordings are an important means to capture the performance of the Rites, they comprise an inherently linear format that cannot fully convey the performance of these rituals or their evolution over time and through space. Since the early 1990s, however, new forms of performance documentation have arisen at the nexus of domains of media arts, gaming and immersive technologies that are more apt to convey the bodily practices inherent

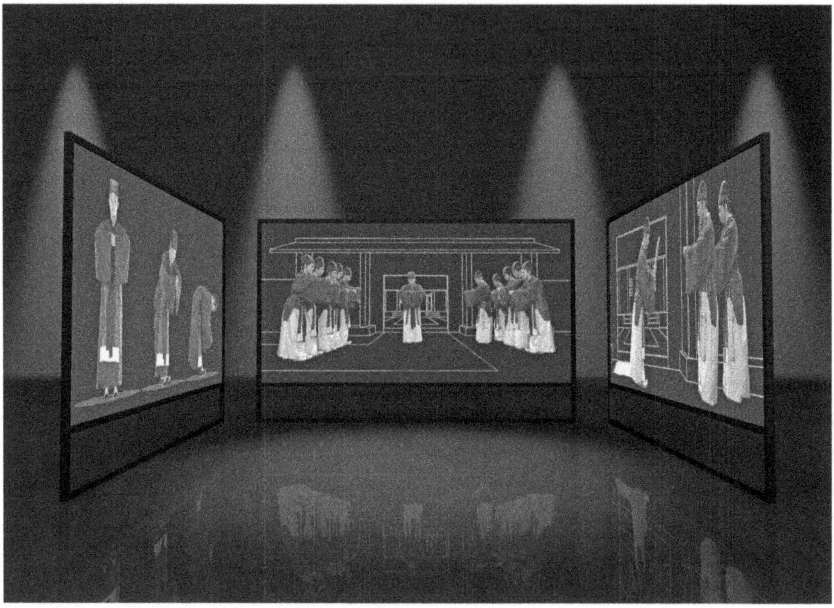

FIGURE 3.1 Remaking Confucian Rights, "Three-screen installation of the capping ceremony", Eighth Triennial of Contemporary Art, Ljubljana, Slovenia, 2016. Image: Paul Nichola. Courtesy of Remaking Confucian Rights project.

to ritual practices. Furthermore, these innovations have provided the basis for the pioneering works of two of the co-authors of this chapter, Jeffrey Shaw and Sarah Kenderdine.[7] Over the past two decades, these and other innovations advancing digital technologies have become a significant apparatus for the transmission of embodied cultural knowledge. These technologies are even more important for what are known as "reperformable archives", in which a recording is not only stored as a static repository but can also be annotated, re-inscribed or updated each time a new performance is completed or when relevant new knowledge is acquired. To illustrate these possibilities, the following pages detail the immersive technologies and methodologies developed to document the "Rites of the Provincial Archery Competition", which has additionally resulted in a database and reperformable archive for study, teaching and transmission.

The digital documentation of the "Rites of the Provincial Archery Competition" crucially takes place within a close-to-full-scale set of the original ritual temple compound described in the *Yili*, which was constructed in a sound studio in Beijing. All the temple architecture and the landscaping with real grass and dirt followed a protocol of strict historical accuracy, in keeping with RCR's larger reconstitution effort, using academically justified interpretations of physical elements, from architecture, lighting, clothing and equipment to actor behaviour, movement and musical performance.

For certain scenographic elements, however, cinematic green screen methods were used to allow the entire surrounding environment and scenery of the temple complex to be digitally completed in post-production, including the roof, sky and distant grove of fruit trees (Figure 3.2). Advanced digitization and video recording technologies were used, including 4k–8k videography featuring multiple points of view, as well as static, mobile and dolly shots, close-up, medium and long shots, aerial views and high-speed videography, to make a comprehensive and complete record of the Provincial Archery Competition. State-of-the-art 3D imaging was additionally employed through panoramic 3D and 360-degree photography as well as spherical 360-degree videography. A 270-degree cylindrical panorama was also captured on the north side of the set using a custom 360-cylinder rig built by the ACIM team from City University Hong Kong.

Because the focus of the shoot was on the ritual performance and movement of the actors, photorealistic representation of the location was not the main priority of the recordings. As the camera followed a specific performer to focus on their actions while the ceremony unfolded, motion tracking was a critical component in the integration of the visual effects. Motion tracking importantly maintained the synchronization of live-action and computer-generated imagery (CGI) elements while the camera rolled across the set. Within the larger RCR project, however, the comprehensive high-fidelity digital recording of the Provincial Archery ceremony was a first and basic stratum of documentation.

Remaking Confucian Rites has additionally sought to establish an operative embodied expression of Confucian intangible cultural heritage as a core objective for present and future iterations and performance. To this end, the project has harnessed some of the latest contemporary tools and technologies specifically applied or adapted to embodied expressions, such as interactivity, immersive

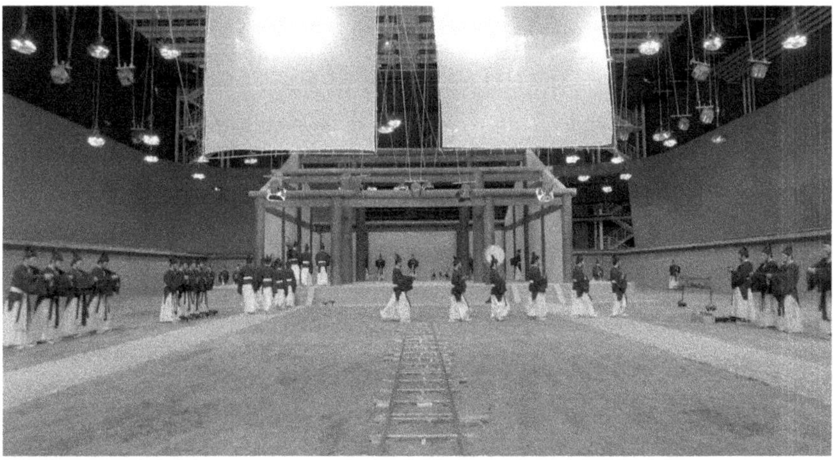

FIGURE 3.2 Set and green screen solutions for the Rite of Archery, 2018: Remaking Confucian Rites. Image courtesy of Remaking Confucian Rights project.

visualization, virtual reality, augmented reality, artificial intelligence and deep learning. Furthermore, as a repetitious and precise endeavour, the Confucian ritual order is ideally suited to computational modelling. Finally, the project offers its collaborators novel opportunities for research in embodied transmission through interoperable and reusable archive technologies of immersive interactive system design.

With the input of ACIM and EPFL's eM+ as leading research laboratories in the domain, RCR has benefitted from the digital encoding of its performed and embodied reenactment in a range of technological capture processes, from green screen video capture, key frame pose extraction, motion capture, animation, photogrammetry and conventional 3D modelling, as well as a wide range of photography and video formats. Of these, the motion capture record of movement over time has provided the most advanced documentation of expressive corporeal action in spatial/temporal modelling for the project. This is because motion capture produces datasets with unprecedented levels of detail that are particularly adept for documenting reenacted heritage. It also provides a continuous topological model that allows for easier retainment of the affective or sensory qualities of movement. Increasingly visible in action cinema production, the technique is moreover being adopted for the transmission of other forms of performed cultural heritage, such as dance and martial arts (Channon and Jennings 2014; Chao et al. 2018; Kelly 2015; Whalen-Bridge and Farrer 2011). Extending into the educational context of both these disciplines, motion capture data is being used as a basic teaching aid that can serve as a prosthesis or replacement transmitter of social and practical knowledge when masters or teachers are unavailable (Kenderdine and Shaw 2017, 2018).

According to Professor Peng, the originating sources supporting RCR's research no longer convey the original intention of Confucius to contemporary audiences.[8] Furthermore, the new methods and technologies being developed for the project are likely the only viable method for the future community and public transmission of *Yili* as well as for the groundwork reenactment research, which cannot be derived from textual studies alone. For example, the temple reconstruction for the Provincial Archery ceremony filmset provided the first-ever platform to reperform ritual acts with human bodies and objects in a wholistic and realistically scaled emplacement. Motion capture recordings have permitted a level of close analysis that has in turn resolved academic disputes about the performance of the Rites, which text-based study was unable to accomplish. Working with ACIM and eM+ engineers and animators, Peng's team has furthermore produced a digital animation of ritual movement within a virtual three-dimensional or panoramic space, onto which annotated layers of past rituals have been scripted to create an active informatic system of embodied knowledge.[9] This database is the basis for the RCR's ongoing and in-depth endeavour to compare movement and performance with historical information. It also permits the RCR team to harmonize the macro data with minute ritual acts, enabling scholars and practitioners to mine what project collaborator and co-author of this article Tsong-Zung Chang calls the "molecular structure" of the *li*-rites.[10]

The question of how to ascribe meaning to ritual motion and act in a way that is observable and decipherable for novice viewers poses a key challenge for the embodied archives of the RCR project. There are several contexts that the project draws on for its innovation. Firstly, dating back millennia, the recording of movement in performance manuals has a long history in China across martial arts and other ritual practices, of which the *Yili* is just one example. Meanwhile, since modern times, choreographers, dancers and directors of performance have established systems of notation and the semantic transcription of movement that can be said to meld with the mind of the performer (deLahunta and Barnard 2018). The predominant notation and analytic systems used in Western performance contexts are Labanotation or Laban (1947) and Benesh (1977). These systems have provided the foundations to develop sophisticated aesthetic and movement transcription techniques, among them William Forsyth's 1999 interactive DVD project *Improvisation Technologies* (which this chapter's co-author Jeffrey Shaw played a large role in developing). Such methods have been redeployed in the decades since to create software programs for the "aesthetic transcription" of choreographic and other forms of embodied or performed cultural knowledge (Brown et al. 2003; Kenderdine 2016; Kenderdine and Shaw 2009). The most successful aspect of these computationally driven systems has been to use them as annotation tools to transcribe abstract and aesthetic physical action into a legible and communicable visual and textual language and thus automatically determine and transmit the meaning of movements.

Yet another foundation for the RCR's innovation lies in the Hong Kong Martial Arts Living Archive (HKMALA), for which sophisticated transcriptions of expressive embodied motion have been realized to dynamically visualize the aesthetic and spatial-temporal dimensions underlying the movements of kung fu masters through colour and motion graphics (Kenderdine and Shaw 2017, 2018). Drawing on this work, the RCR interface allows the aesthetic features of one performer to be correlated or combined with others in its visual transcription by using annotated and real-time visualization layers (Figure 3.3). Beyond *a priori* motion analysis, the annotation of ritual reenactment has great potential for the scholarship of ritual performance and Confucian *li*-rites as it enables the reflexive scholarly re-reading of manuscripts and amendment of interpretations.

For Professor Peng, the application of computational modelling and interactive archive technologies to the RCR project is already bringing the *Yili* to life as a re-performable ritual database.[11] For instance, as part of the digital reconstruction embodied ritual practice, the RCR team has already realized 600 ritual diagrams to construct a wholistic 3D space. As described above, during the Rites of the Provincial Archery Competition performance the actors' movements in the real space were documented using motion capture and tracked in 3D. This information was used to create a database of animations for scholarly purposes that the RCR has been populating with annotations of past rituals. The RCR

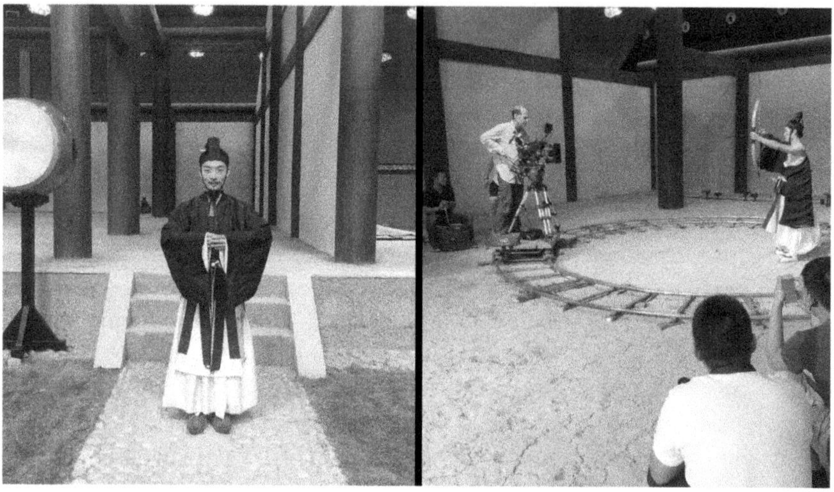

FIGURE 3.3 Multimodal recordings and annotation of the capping ceremony: Remaking Confucian Rites. Image courtesy of Remaking Confucian Rights project.

team is continuously exploiting this active database to test hypotheses drawn from its historical and philological work, which involves reconstituting the text's historical practice through other literature or the language of that literature, subsequently comparing this with the performance of the ritual acts to then make deductions to identify and correct previously unsolvable problems.

In harnessing the different documentary methodologies we have outlined so far, the RCR intends to create a database of descriptive and narrative assets, which can be used to create an array of presentation platforms for diverse exhibition, performance, scholarly or public contexts. Early outcomes of this effort include archival recordings of the entire real-time rendering of the Archery Ceremony (around 12 hours). Sequences have also been edited as linear single-screen documentary movies (from 10 to 120 minutes), for online, television and cinema viewing or multi-screen installations for exhibition, including a three-screen installation, *The Confucian Body: Rite of Archery*, produced for the EPFL Pavilions' exhibition, "Deep Fakes: Art and Its Double", curated by Sarah Kenderdine in 2021.[12]

To offer an affective compression of the real-time duration of the original performance, displays of the performance providing multiple viewpoints are being created. Fully immersive contexts are also envisaged for the project data to place spectators in virtual reality environments and multi-dimensional experiences that enhance the forms of embodied cognition required to understand ritual performance (Stefaniak 2014). For example, the panoramic photography and videography captured in the recording of the Rites of the Provincial Archery Competition provide the basis for a mixed reality immersive and interactive experience. Viewed on a head-mounted display (HMD), spectators can see, explore and participate in the Ritual Archery performance, or experience the event within a 360-degree surround video projection that makes them feel they are present and moving around in the same space as the archers at one-to-one scale.

The construction of an entire temple and exterior environment as a "virtual world" and 3D set has been the basis for another unique iteration of the Archery ritual performance, which appears as a realistic scene that the participant inhabits and freely navigates through an HMD interface. Mobile video panels suspended within the 3D scene display video recordings of Archery rituals. The panels appear and disappear, synchronized with the temporal and narrative flow of the original video recordings and are spatially positioned with respect to the original camera point of view in the temple on set. The panels additionally move in tandem with any camera movements, such as in a dolly shot (Figure 3.4). Finally, viewers are free to navigate synchronous real-time recordings between different points of view, from full, medium, close-up, panoramic or aerial perspectives of the Rites of the Provincial Archery Competition.

Such a virtual environment merges the kind of interactive virtual world found in computer games in a form of mixed reality with a hybrid mode of cinematic moving images. For one, it is designed to offer many levels of interactive freedom so that spectators can reposition themselves in the environment or focus their attention on details as they access other layers, such as analytical data. A viewer may simply opt to observe screened events from a distance or wander and follow the videos through the surrounding space. If desired, they can also approach and "enter" any one of these video panels at any time, at which point their field of view will be filled by the video recording. Still, at any time, the viewer can step

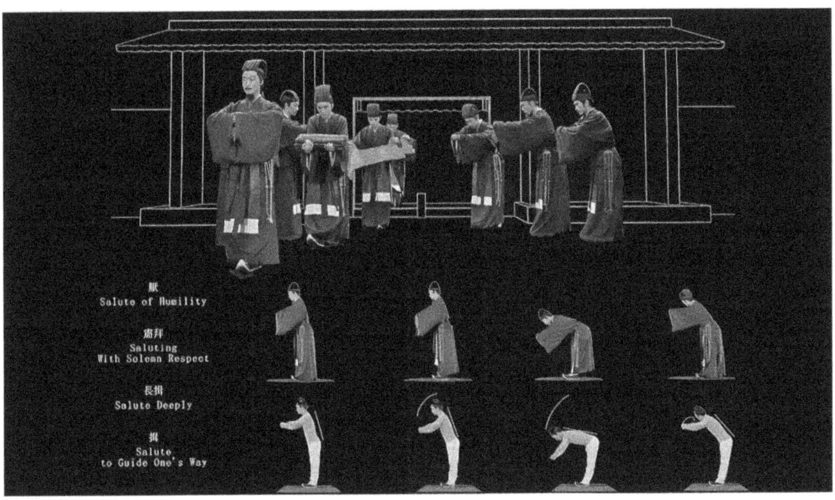

FIGURE 3.4 Beijing-based studio set, capturing the Rite of Archery, 2018: Remaking Confucian Rites. Image courtesy of Remaking Confucian Rights project.

back out of the full-screen video to return to the virtual set. Most significantly, the temporal and spatial dualities presented to spectators in this 3D virtual set mirror those of Confucian ritual practitioners and their embodied states that conjoin mind and body, and Cosmos and Earth.

Conclusion

After a century of radical politics attended by the violent destruction and denial of its own traditions, China is situated at a turning point of a future that nonetheless remains entangled in its historical past. In RCR collaborator Tsong-Zung Chang's words, it is time to excavate China's "deep history" to reconnect with the roots of its aesthetic sensibility and grasp the structure of its moral being.[13] Today, the revival of the Confucian Rites is regarded as a key to unlock this past. But, as a marginalized example of cultural heritage with thousands of years of associated embodied knowledge and social practice is enormously difficult, and requires overcoming compound challenges across scholarly, societal, political and artistic contexts. The Remaking Confucian Rites project faces the particularly onerous situation of its repositories and the transmitters of its knowledge being cut off from practising, performing and thus knowing how to transmit their customs.

Apart from the complexities of appropriate visual display, these archives must be accurately elicited, reconstructed reenacted, recorded and eventually encoded. Yet, unseen, behind the public presentation of civilization through objects, architectures, and scenographies are archives of embodied experience. Supporting the excavation of these archives are recent computational advances in data science and graphics modelling, which have been successfully applied to material cultural heritage, including 3D scanning, and displays using immersive and interactive technologies to enliven immutable objects online and in museums. RCR's epic undertaking to record, encode and display the tacit contents of the Confucian Rites archive provides the first possible means for the renewed transmission of the Rites through presence and immersion within Confucian ritual knowledge systems. Bringing together traditional documentary modes with the power of novel interactive multimedia editing is enabling the entire RCR digital archive to be presented in immersive modes as well as to be interactively explored and remade again. Coupling reenactment with the power of computational modelling is, moreover, key to revitalizing the *li*-rites embedded in the Rites and the modern Confucian body. As such, RCR's reconstruction offers a means to assimilate the rapid changes that have taken place in Chinese people's sensibilities in terms of the physical body and could become a future conduit to reconcile the *li*-rites in Chinese corporeality.

Confucian Classics Manuscripts

Lunyu «論語» (*Analects of Confucius*) 公元前480年 – 公元前350年。

Yili «儀禮 » (*Book of Etiquette and Rites*) (汉) 郑玄注、(唐) 贾公彦疏 «仪礼注疏» 五十卷，«文渊阁四库全书 » 本；«十三经注疏 » 本，中华书局,1957年。Han, Zheng Xuan and Tang, Jia Gongyan. 1957. *Yili zhushu*, 50 volumes, Zhonghua Book Company.

Notes

1 This text originates in the writings of Confucian disciples from the 5th century BCE, much of which was lost. The version called *Yili* was compiled by 2nd century CE scholar Zheng Xuan (127–200 CE) and provided the material for subsequent editions and scholarship (Boltz 1993, 240). For an English translation of the *Yili*, see Steele 1917.
2 Rites or rituals are defined as formal or performed ceremonial acts that evolve from long secular tradition or sacred orders. See Bell 1997 and Schechner 1993.
3 For the English translation of *The Analects of Confucius*, see Legge 1861.
4 The "Convention Concerning the Protection of the World Cultural and Natural Heritage" was adopted by the General Conference of UNESCO on November 16, 1972. See https://web.archive.org/web/20200526200434/https://whc.unesco.org/en/convention/. As of February 2022, China has 56 World Heritage Listed properties, ranking second only Italy, which has 58 sites. See https://whc.unesco.org/en/statesparties/cn.
5 Li Zhenhua, speaking on a panel with Jeffrey Shaw at "Deep Time Machine II: Jeffrey Shaw's Screening of the Remaking of Confucius Rites". *Potential Spaces Conference*, 2017, ZKM, Karlsruhe. Retrieved on 17 February 2022 from: https://www.youtube.com/watch?v=ry2leciY58Q.
6 Tsong-Zung Chang and Shiming Gao, "*Re-making the Confucian Rites – Capping Ceremony*", 2016. Retrieved on 22 January 2022 from: http://www.mg-lj.si/en/exhibitions/1717/u3-the-body-of-confucius/. *Mirroring China's Past: Emperors and Their Bronzes*, Art Institute Chicago, USA, 25 February – 13 May 2018. Retrieved on 17 January 2022 from: https://www.artic.edu/exhibitions/2681/mirroring-chinas-past-emperors-and-their-bronzes.
7 See https://sarahkenderdine.info and https://www.jeffreyshawcompendium.com/.
8 Peng Lin, "Practice gives deeper understandings than theoretical readings. Why is the reenactment of Confucian Rites critical?" 纸上得来终觉浅——为何《仪礼》需要做复原研究. *Guang Ming Daily* December 12, 2020, p. 15. Retrieved on 22 December 2021 from: https://epaper.gmw.cn/gmrb/html/2020-12/16/nw.D110000gmrb_20201216_2-15.htm.
9 Peng, *Guang Ming Daily,* 2020.
10 Tsong-Zung Chang speaking on conference panel "Deep Time Machine II: Jeffrey Shaw's Screening of the Remaking of Confucius Rites", *Potential Spaces Conference*, 2017 at ZKM, Karlsruhe, Germany. Retrieved on 22 December 2021 from: https://www.youtube.com/watch?v=ry2leciY58Q.
11 Peng, *Guang Ming Daily,* 2020.
12 The Confucian Body: Rite of Archery. See https://epfl-pavilions.ch/archive/deep-fakes-confucian-rites
13 Tsong-Zung Chang, "Deep Time Machine II", 2017. Retrieved on 22 December 2021 from: https://www.youtube.com/watch?v=ry2leciY58Q.

References

Agnew, Vanessa. 2004. 'Introduction: What Is Reenactment?'. *Criticism* 46 (3): 2. Retrieved on 17 February 2022 from http://digitalcommons.wayne.edu/criticism/vol46/iss3/2

———————, Jonathan Lamb and Juliane Tomann, eds. 2020. *The Routledge Handbook of Reenactment Studies*. London: Routledge. https://doi.org/10.4324/9780429445637.

Bell, Catherine. 1997. *Ritual: Perspectives and Dimensions*. New York: Oxford University Press.

Benesh, Rudolf. 1977. *Reading Dance. The Birth of Choreology*. London: Souvenir Press.

Bénichou, Anne. 2017. 'Introduction: Le reenactment ou le répertoire en régime intermédial.' *Intermédialités* 28 (29). https://doi.org/10.7202/1041075.

Billioud, Sébastien. 2007. 'Confucianism, 'Cultural Tradition' and Official Discourses in China at the Start of the New Century.' *China Perspectives* 2: 50–65.

——— and Joel Thoraval. 2015. *The Sage and the People. The Confucian Revival in China*. Oxford and New York: Oxford University Press.

Boltz, William G. 1993. 'I-li.' In *Early Chinese Texts. A Bibliographical Guide*, edited by Michael Loewe, 234–244, Berkeley: Society for the Study of Early China.

Bowman, Paul. 2016. 'Making Martial Arts History Matter.' *The International Journal of the History of Sport* 33 (9): 915–933. https://doi.org/10.1080/09523367.2016.1212842.

Brown, Neil, Dennis Del Favero, Jeffrey Shaw, and Peter Weibel. 2003. 'Interactive Narrative as a Multi-temporal Agency.' In *Future Cinema. The Cinematic Imaginary After Film*, edited by Jeffrey Shaw and Peter Weibel, 312–315. Cambridge, MA: MIT Press.

Chan, Jacky C. P., Howard Leung, Jeff K. T. Tang and Taku Komura. 2011. 'A Virtual Reality Dance Training System Using Motion Capture Technology.' *IEEE Transactions on Learning Technologies* 4 (2): 187–195.

Channon, Alex, and George Jennings. 2014. 'Exploring Embodiment Through Martial Arts and Combat Sports: A Review of Empirical Research.' *Sport in Society: Cultures, Commerce, Media, Politics* 17 (6): 773–789. https://doi.org/10.1080/17430437.2014.882906.

Chao, Hing, Matt Delbridge, Sarah Kenderdine, Lydia Nicholson, and Jeffrey Shaw. 2018. 'Kapturing IKung Fu: Future Proofing the Hong Kong Martial Arts Living Archive.' In *Digital Echoes: Spaces for Intangible and Performance-based Cultural Heritage*, edited by Sarah Whatley, Rosamaria K. Cisneros and Amalia Sabiescu, 249–264. London: Palgrave Macmillan.

Cognot, Fabrice, Daniel Jaquet and Claus Frederik Sorenson. 2015. 'Historical European Martial Art: A Crossroad between Academic Research, Safeguarding Intangible Heritage and Martial Sport Practices.' *Acta Periodica Duellatorum* 3: 5–35. Doi: https://doi.org/10.1515/apd-2015-0001.

Daugbjerg, Mads, Rivka Syd Eisner, and Britta Timm Knudsen. 2014. 'Re-Enacting the Past: Vivifying Heritage 'Again'.' *International Journal of Heritage Studies* 20 (7/8): 681–87. https:/doi.org/10.1080/13527258.2014.939426.

deLahunta, Scott, and Philip Barnard. 2018. 'Seeing the 'Choreographic Mind': Three Analytic Lenses Developed to Probe and Notate Creative Processes in Dance.' In *The Neurocognition of Dance: Mind, Movement and Motor Skills*, 2nd edition, edited by Bettina Bläsing, Martin Puttke, and Thomas Schack, 88–11. London: Taylor and Francis.

Do-Dinh, Pierre. 1969. *Confucius and Chinese Humanism*. New York: Funk and Wagnalls.

Dreschke, Anja. 2020. 'Ritual'. In Vanessa Agnew, Jonathan Lamb and Juliane Tomann, eds. *The Routledge Handbook of Reenactment Studies*, 202–205. London: Routledge.

Forsythe, William. 1999. *Improvisation Technologies. A Tool for the Analytical Dance Eye*. (CD-ROM). Germany: Produced at ZKM Karlsruhe.

Gao, Bingzhong. 2014. 'How Does Superstition Become Intangible Cultural Heritage in Postsocialist China?' *Positions* 22 (3): 551–572.

Hammond, Kenneth J., and Jeffrey L. Richey. 2015. *The Sage Returns: Confucian Revival in Contemporary China*. Albany, New York: State University of New York Press.

Jae-Phil, Lee, Choi Suk-Kyung, Lee Chae-Won, Cho Eun-Jung and Lee Han-Seung. 2011. *Guidebook for the Documentation of Intangible Cultural* Heritage. Daejeon, Korea: National Research Institute of Cultural Heritage.

Jaurès, Anne. 2012. 'Le tourisme rouge en Chine: véritable engouement ou carte forcée ?' *Monde chinois* 29 (1): 88–101.

Hamilton, Kelly. 2015. 'Mapping Motion II: Motion Capture and the Visualisation of Dance.' *Proceedings of the Conference on Electronic Visualisation and the Arts*, 46–55. Retrieved on 17 February 2022 from: https://doi.org/10.14236/ewic/eva2015.5.

Kenderdine, Sarah. 2016. 'Embodiment, Entanglement and Immersion in Digital Cultural Heritage.' In *A New Companion to Digital Humanities*, edited by Susan Schreibman, Ray Siemens, and John Unsworth, 22–41. John Wiley and Sons.

———. and Jeffrey Shaw. 2009. 'New Media in situ: The Re-socialisation of Public Space.' *International Journal of Arts and Technology* 2 (4): 258–276. https://doi.org/10.1504/IJART.2009.029235.

———. 2017. 'Archives in Motion. Motion as Meaning.' In *Museum and Archive on the Move: Changing Cultural Institutions in the Digital Era*, edited by Oliver Grau. Berlin: De Gruyter, 211–233. https://doi.org/10.1515/9783110529630-014.

-----. 2018. 'The Museological Re-enactment of Lingnan Hung Kuen'. In *Lingnan Hung Kuen Across the Century: Kung Fu Narratives in Cinema and Community*, edited by Hing Chao, 137–159. Hong Kong: City University of Hong Kong Press.

Komura, Taku, Beta Lam, Rynson W. H. Lau and Howard Leung. 2006. 'e-Learning Martial Arts.' In *Lecture Notes in Computer Science*, 239–248. Heidelberg: Springer.

Kuah, Khun Eng, and Zhaohui Liu. 2017. *Intangible Cultural Heritage in Contemporary China: The Participation of Local Communities*. London: Routledge.

Laban, Rudolf. 1947. *La Maîtrise du Movement Essai*. Paris: Actes Sud. Trans. 1994. J. Challet-Haas and M. Bastien. London: Macdonald and Evans.

Legge, James. 1861. English translation of 'The Analects of Confucius (480–350 BC)'. In *The Chinese Classics*, Vol. 1 (reprinted 1893). Oxford: Clarendon Press.

Lehrer, Erica, Cynthia Milton and Monica Patterson. 2011. *Curating Difficult Heritage: Violent Pasts in Public Places*. London: Palgrave Macmillan.

Leng, Lu, and Michael Salzman. 2016. 'The Renaissance of Confucianism in Contemporary China from the Perspective of Terror Management Theory.' *Sociology and Anthropology* 4 (2): 52–58. https://doi.org/10.13189/sa.2016.040202.

Liu, Yucai and Luke Habberstad. 2014. 'The Life of a Text: A Brief History of the *Liji* (*Rites Records*) and its Transmission.' *Journal of Chinese Literature and Culture* 1 (1/2): 289–308. https://www.muse.jhu.edu/article/565263.

Logan, William, and Kier Reeves. 2009. 'Introduction.' In William Logan and Kier Reeves (eds), *Places of Pain and Shame: Dealing with 'Difficult Heritage'*, 1–14. New York: Routledge.

Louie, K. 1980. *Critiques of Confucius in Contemporary China*. New York: St. Martin's Press.

———. 1986. *Inheriting Tradition: Interpretations of the Classical Philosophers in Communist China*. Oxford: Oxford University Press.

Maags, Christina, and Marina Svensson. 2018. *Chinese Heritage in the Making: Experiences, Negotiations and Contestations*. Amsterdam: Amsterdam University Press.

Macdonald, Sharon. 2009. *Difficult Heritage. Negotiating the Nazi Past in Nuremberg and Beyond*, London: Routledge.

Morgan, Daniel P. 2017. 'Calling out Zheng Xuan (127–200 CE) at the Crossroads of Ritual, Maths, Sport and Classical Commentary.' In Commentaries on Mathematical

Texts in a Comparative Perspective, Aug 2017, Berlin, Germany. Retrieved from: https://halshs.archives-ouvertes.fr/halshs-01490864.
Mulhe, Maria. 2020. 'Mediality.' In *The Routledge Handbook of Reenactment Studies*, edited by Vanessa Agnew, Jonathan Lamb and Juliane Tomann, 133–137. London: Routledge.
Peng, Lin. 2017. 'The Implication of Moralization in Confucian Life Etiquette' «儒家人生礼仪中的教化意涵 ». *Journal of Guangxi University*, 3.
——— and Liu, Junya. 2017. *Ritual, Music and Ethos of Culture in Ancient China (English only)*. Beijing: China Renmin University Press.
Qian, Ying. 2003. 'Crossing the Same River Twice: Reenactment and the Founding of PRC Documentary Cinema.' In Carlos Rojas and Eileen Cheng-Yin Chow, eds., *The Oxford Handbook of Chinese Cinemas*, 590–609. Oxford: Oxford University Press.
Schneider, Rebecca. 2011. *Performing Remains. Art and War in times of Theatrical Reenactment*. New York: Routledge.
Schechner, Richard. 1993. *The Future of Ritual. Writing on Culture and Performance*. London: Routledge.
Steele, John. 1917. *The I-Li or Book of Etiquette and Ceremonial*. London: Probsthain.
Stefaniak, Jill. 2014. 'Immersive Simulation: The Replication of Environments to Practice Problem Solving.' In *Curriculum Models for the 21st Century: Using Learning Technologies in Higher Education*, edited by Maree Gosper and Dirk Ifenthaler, 313–324. New York: Springer.
Su, Junjie. 2018. 'Conceptualising the Subjective Authenticity of Intangible Cultural Heritage.' *International Journal of Heritage Studies* 2 (9): 919–937. https://doi.org/10.1080/13527258.2018.1428662.
Taylor, Diana. 2003. *The Archive and the Repertoire. Performing Cultural Memory in the Americas*. Durham: Duke University Press.
———————. 2016. 'Saving the 'Live? Re-Performance and Intangible Cultural Heritage.' *Études Anglaises* 69 (2): 149–161. Retrieved on 20 January 2022 from: https://www.cairn.info/revue-etudes-anglaises-2016-2-page-149.htm.
Ten Brink, Joram, and Joshua Oppenheimer. 2012. *Killer Images. Documentary Film, Memory and the Performance of Violence*. New York: Wallflower Press.
Tu, Wei-Ming. 1985. *Confucian Thought: Selfhood as Creative Transformation*. Albany: Suny Press; State University of New York Press.
Tunbridge, John, and Gregory Ashworth. 1996. *Dissonant Heritage. The Management of the Past as a Resource in Conflict*. Chichester: John Wiley and Sons.
UNESCO. 2003. (2016 edition) 'Convention for the Safeguarding of the Intangible Heritage'. Retrieved from: https://ich.unesco.org/en/convention
UNESCO. n.d. 'China and the 2003 Convention.' Retrieved from: https://ich.unesco.org/en/state/china-CN
Waterton, Emma, and Steve Watson. 2013. 'Framing Theory: Towards a Critical Imagination in Heritage Studies.' *International Journal of Heritage Studies* 19 (6): 546–561.
Whalen-Bridge, John, and Douglas S. Farrer. 2011. 'Martial Arts, Transnationalism and Embodied Knowledge.' In *Martial Arts as Embodied Knowledge: Asian Traditions in a Transnational World*. Albany: Suny Press.
Wu, Zongjie. 2012. 'Transdisciplinary and Cross-Cultural Turn of Critical Discourse Studies: A Case of Remaking Chinese Cultural Heritage Discourse', *Journal of Guangdong University of Foreign Studies* 06, unpaginated.
Wu, Shufang. 2014. 'The Revival of Confucianism and the CCP's Struggle for Cultural Leadership: A Content Analysis of the People's Daily, 2000–2009.' *Journal*

of Contemporary China 23 (89): 971–991. https://doi.org/10.1080/10670564.2014.882624.

You, Ziying. 2015. 'Shifting Actors and Power Relations: Contentious Local Responses to the Safeguarding of Intangible Cultural Heritage in Contemporary China.' *Journal of Folklore Research* 52 (2/3): 253–268. https://doi.org/10.2979/JFOLKRESE.52.2-3.253.

Yu, Hua. 2015. 'A Vernacular Way of 'Safeguarding' Intangible Heritage: The Fall and Rise of Rituals in Gouliang Miao Village.' *International Journal of Heritage Studies* 21 (10): 1016–1035. https://doi.org/10.1080/13527258.2015.1048813.

Zhang, Y. 2021. 'Historical Explanation and Historical Re-enactment: Reshaping the Image ofDuke Zhuang in the First Year ofDuke Yin's Time (722 BC)' (Chinese) *Journal of Shanxi University (Philosophy and Social Science Edition)*, 15 January, unpaginated.

Zhang, Tong, and Barry Schwartz. 1997. 'Confucius and the Cultural Revolution: A Study in Collective Memory.' *International Journal of Politics, Culture and Society* 11 (2): 197–202.

Zhu, Y. 2014. 'Cultural Effects of Authenticity: Contested Heritage Practices in China', *International Journal of Heritage Studies* 21. doi: 10.1080/13527258.2014.991935.

4

THE ROLE OF DIGITAL TECHNOLOGIES IN UNEARTHING THE ROSEWOOD MASSACRE

Edward González-Tennant

Introduction

Digital technologies provide a rapidly expanding toolkit for documenting, interpreting and sharing difficult histories. The application of these tools also represents one of the most powerful methods for archaeologists working to name and confront historical legacies of inequality and racial violence. Unfortunately, the use of digital tools to investigate such histories remains rare, and when applied they are often not used to their full possibility. There exists enormous potential for exploring digital archaeology as it relates to places with painful histories, sites where injustice haunts the historical record (González-Tennant 2013; Morgan and Eve 2012; Nieves 2009; Rose 2016). Perhaps one of the reasons digital archaeologists do not explore these histories is the focus on monumental and/or prehistoric places most commonly explored by these practitioners, which often neglects local and difficult forms of heritage. This is not a critique or attempt to diminish the importance of work taking place at prehistoric and monumental sites, but rather to highlight the need that work with local, small and difficult histories requires a unique approach. This chapter discusses one such approach, an inherently transdisciplinary project exploring the tragic story of Rosewood, Florida, a majority African American community destroyed in 1923 during a week-long episode of violence commonly referred to as the Rosewood Massacre or Rosewood Race Riot (González-Tennant 2018).

Conducting research on the difficult history of African American experiences has taken on new meaning as Black Lives Matter (BLM) and similar movements remind us that events like the 1923 Rosewood Massacre echo across time and space. Confronting these histories and their legacies remains a central project of Black Studies scholarship, particularly the political commitment to demonstrating how shamefully common such events were in 19th and 20th century

DOI: 10.4324/9781003200659-5

America (Ifill 2007). Archaeologists who engage in this research must develop ways of theorizing the multidimensionality of violence revealed by such events. Interpreting the destruction of Rosewood, and the hundreds of similar African American settlements that no longer exist, demands a thorough understanding of and engagement with changing patterns of interpersonal, structural and symbolic violence. Interpersonal violence refers to face-to-face physical harm, such as the race riots and lynching events used to terrorize disenfranchised communities. Structural violence focuses on the construction of social structures to marginalize entire communities based on culturally constructed ideologies (e.g., race). Redlining (the practice by real estate agents and bank officials of demarcating neighbourhoods as off-limits to minority buyers), gerrymandering and other forms of segregation continually demonstrate how elites manipulate society through various economic and political means for these immoral ends. Symbolic violence refers to the violence of disturbing thoughts supporting unequal cultural and social beliefs. This is the fear and insecurity produced in the psyches of both perpetrator and victim. Early Hollywood cinema and the infusing of eugenics-based perspectives in state health regimes remain important examples with shameful echoes today. The changing patterns and intersections of these three forms of violence are clearly visible to those undertaking this research.

Regarding episodes of racial violence like the Rosewood Massacre, interpersonal violence represents the primary way racial elites in the USA halted minority participation, at least until the early 20th century. Over the past century, structural and symbolic forms surpass the earlier preference for interpersonal violence, coinciding with the global rise in state terror (Sluka 1999). Emerging state apparatuses continue to support unfair incarceration rates and the disproportionate use of the death penalty among African American communities. Increasingly robust structural and symbolic systems restricting minority access to education, economic advancement and political representation became normalized. Of course, interpersonal violence remains common, especially in its targeting of minority individuals and communities for everyday acts of violence. These include everything from bullying, the use of racial slurs and the use of police to restrict African Americans from enjoying simple pleasures like walking in a park. Unlike a century or more ago, interpersonal violence is typically resorted to and/or supported by elites and their allies (e.g., constituents) when structural and symbolic means are seen as failing. For instance, when crimes associated with impoverished minority communities are overreported by media outlets, and the crimes of the wealthy and powerful downplayed, or even publicly paraded as a way of ideologically separating "us" from "them" in public discourse.

Conducting the sort of research discussed in this chapter is more important now than ever. As a historical archaeology project, researching and sharing Rosewood's story reveals the deeply interconnected historical roots of modern social inequality. Perhaps more importantly, it involves creative experimentation with ways for translating this scholarly information into public knowledge. Digital archaeologists occupy a unique and potentially very powerful role in helping guide public conversations on a range of topics exploring the lingering effects of inequality and violence. This chapter examines these topics by exploring digital archaeology work in Rosewood and its neighbouring communities. This research begins with a robust geographic information system (GIS), reconstructing the spatial layout of Rosewood and its environs prior to 1923. This guides archaeological work to verifying the GIS, which aids in managing these cultural heritage resources. These management practices include new solutions for virtual reconstructing sites so users can virtually visit sites via immersive online platforms (e.g., Sketchfab). This also provides new historical data answering questions asked by descendants and the public.

Brief history of Rosewood

The former site of Rosewood is located nine miles from the Gulf of Mexico in Levy County, Florida (Figure 4.1). Although the town was never incorporated, business directories and historical maps describe a small settlement in the area as early as the 1850s. The town remained difficult to reach and sparsely populated prior to the American Civil War (1861–1865). Following the completion of Florida's first cross-state railroad, and the resumption of rail travel after the Civil War, Rosewood experienced rapid economic and population growth. This

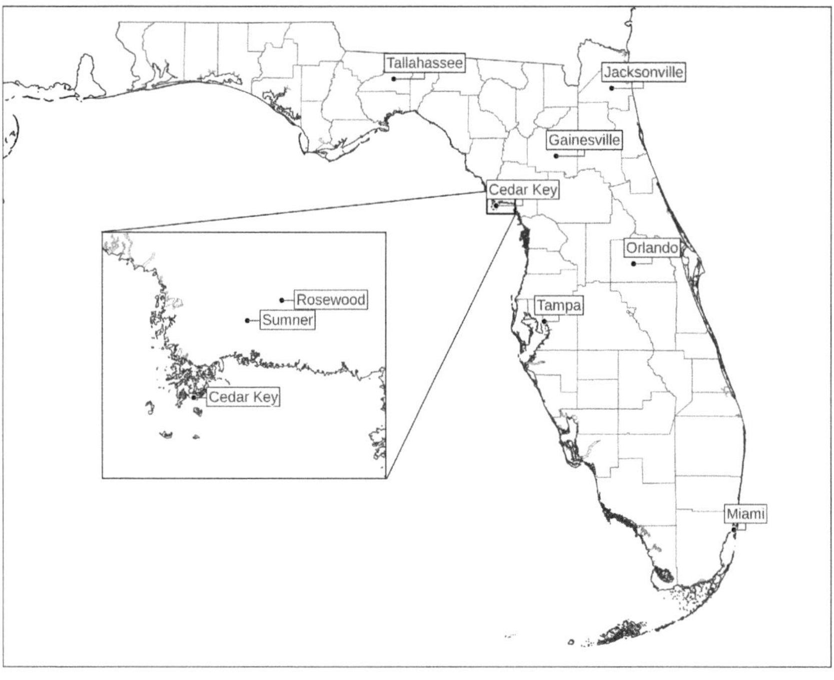

FIGURE 4.1 Locations mentioned in the text. Image by author.

growth was further fuelled by the area's abundant natural resources. Rosewood was initially settled by a small group of White landowners in the 1850s, with initial African American property purchases following the Civil War. These earlier settlers were either sympathetic to Black advancement, or eager to sell their properties as the natural resources quickly dwindled, or both. These developments transformed Rosewood into a majority African American community during the 1890s. Rosewood's Black families built a resilient, mixed economy in response to the previous over-reliance on timber. Although technically a renewable resource, the over-cutting of timber could impact local communities for a generation as the pine trees grew to maturity. This forced Rosewood's African American families to adapt. In addition to eventually operating smaller-scale sawmills and turpentine stills, Rosewood's Black residents also worked in market gardens, raised livestock, hunted wild game and worked in various support roles for neighbouring communities. The next test for Rosewood's economy arrived in the 1910s with the construction of the Cummer and Sons Lumber Company sawmill in Sumner, located approximately two miles to the southwest of Rosewood. Sumner quickly emerged as a company town. Its population was more equally divided between Black and White workers, and their families. Over time, many Rosewood residents also began working at the sawmill or in the service industry for Sumner families (e.g., laundresses) during this time (Jones 1997). Rosewood's mixed economy and a history of Black land ownership allowed African Americans to survive such challenges. Although growth slowed in Rosewood, it did not cease. By 1920, the Black community boasted three churches, a masonic hall, a privately funded school and a mix of house styles associated with the town's different economic classes (Jones et al. 1993).

The multigenerational history of Rosewood as an African American community, including the accumulated multigenerational wealth of its residents, was violently disrupted during the first week of 1923. This event, more accurately understood as a week-long episode of sustained violence would eventually conclude with the complete destruction of all Black-owned structures and the violent displacement of Rosewood's African American community. This event was part of a larger history of anti-Black violence in Florida. Only one month earlier a group of White men lynched three Black men in nearby Perry, Florida. The White mob then descended upon Perry's Black neighbourhood and proceeded to burn several homes. Local newspapers ran inflammatory accounts of this event for weeks (Jones et al. 1993).

On the morning of Monday, January 1, 1923, while James Taylor was at work as a foreman of the local sawmill, his wife, Fannie, claimed a Black man entered their Sumner home and attacked her. The event was witnessed by Sarah Carrier and her granddaughter Philomena, residents of Rosewood who worked as laundresses for the Taylor family. The Carriers' account of the attack was considerably different, implicating a White man in the attack at the Taylor home. Sarah Carrier indicated not only that the assailant was a White man, but that he and Fannie Taylor were having an affair, and Taylor sustained her injuries when the man became outraged for an unknown reason (Jones et al. 1993). Taylor's decision to resort to the easy and all-too-common lie of a Black assailant prompted swift action from local Whites, including Levy County Sheriff Robert Walker, who quickly organized a posse. The posse borrowed bloodhounds from a nearby convict labour camp. The bloodhounds led the growing posse towards Rosewood. They first encountered Aaron Carrier on the road between the two communities. Carrier was an African American resident of Rosewood known to many Whites for his refusal to bow to White prejudice. Sheriff Walker, noting this reputation, placed Carrier in protective custody. The posse continued to grow with reinforcements, becoming little more than a mob, which moved towards Rosewood and the home of long-time resident Sam Carter (Jones et al. 1993). The mob interrogated Carter. They hung him by his neck from a tree, but he only admitted to taking a White individual out of the area, corroborating the account of Sarah and Philomena Carrier. Dissatisfied with Carter's answers, members of the mob eventually shot him multiple times and hung his corpse from a tree where it was discovered the next day (Dye 1996). Carter became the first fatality of the events of that first week of 1923 (Jones et al. 1993). Although Carter's murder was investigated weeks later, a six-man jury found that Carter had been "shot by unknown party [or parties]" (Jones et al. 1993: 38).

No further deaths occurred for nearly three days. On January 4th, a group of Whites returned to Rosewood to investigate unconfirmed reports of Black men taking refuge with some of Rosewood's families. It is likely these rumours did not exist, and several Whites were discontent with the events of Monday, which they must have viewed as anticlimactic. This time, the White men targeted the Carrier home, where two White individuals, Henry Andrews and C. P. "Poly" Wilkerson, approached the house's porch. They then attempted to force their way into the house. When these attempts were unsuccessful, the men attempted to burn the house. Several members of the Carrier family defended themselves, including firing shots at the Whites. Members of the White mob returned fire, and a large gun battle commenced for several hours. The two White men were both struck by bullets and would later die of their injuries (Jones et al. 1993).

The battle continued into the early hours of Friday. Word eventually reached neighbouring communities. Whites began to arrive in greater and greater numbers, including many Klu Klux Klan members from their New Year festivities in nearby Gainesville, Florida. The White mob left for a few hours, and then only to replenish ammunition or care for the wounded White men. African Americans fled their homes, with dozens taking refuge in the surrounding swamps. The White mob returned and began the systematic burning of homes. They also burned at least two churches. The mob reportedly found the bodies of Sylvester Carrier and his mother Sarah Carrier upon entering the now empty Carrier house, both victims of deadly gunshots from the previous night (Jones et al. 1993). Lexie Gordon, an elderly Black widow, was also shot as she fled her burning home on Friday (Jones et al. 1993). She became the sixth recorded death in Rosewood after Sam Carter, Sylvester Carrier, Sarah Carrier, Henry Andrews and C. P. "Poly" Wilkerson. The seventh death is attributed to the riot that took place when Mingo Williams was shot in the head by Whites as they drove through nearby Bronson on their way to Rosewood. Two White brothers from Cedar Key took a train to Rosewood in the early morning hours on Saturday. The brothers John and William Bryce rescued African American women and children. They were too nervous to evacuate men as they feared White vigilantes would kill everyone if they found Black men on the train. They evacuated survivors to towns east of Rosewood, where descendants live to this day, in places like Archer and Gainesville. Other residents fled the violence in other ways, some walking 15 or more miles through the cold winter temperatures to reach communities like Gulf Hammock or Otter Creek.

James Carrier, brother of Sylvester and son of Sarah, returned from hiding to bury his family members. A White mob appeared and captured him in Rosewood's cemetery as he completed his solemn task. The mob lynched him after they forced him to dig his own grave next to his brother and mother (Jones et al. 1993). On Sunday, a White mob returned to Rosewood. They burned any remaining African American buildings. African Americans never returned to the area. In total, six African Americans and two Whites lost their lives during the week. A handful of local Whites purchased the properties at rates far below fair market and in several cases sold them at a considerable profit within months or years (González-Tennant 2018). The event remains one of the largest forced displacements of an African American community in US history. Even so, Rosewood's destruction was not an isolated event, but one of the dozens of race riots between the years 1917 and 1923 alone, and hundreds that have occurred over the past century.

Residents of Rosewood, those who survived long enough, and their descendants waited seven decades for any semblance of justice. While a State Grand Jury convened in February 1923, no convictions were made, and the records have been lost (or more likely intentionally removed from the county courthouse). Rosewood lingered at the edges of memory for decades. Survivors and descendants, aided by historical researchers, journalists and lawyers successfully lobbied the State of Florida for compensation, resulting in a landmark 1994 decision to pay compensation to survivors and descendants (D'Orso 1996). The state commissioned an official report as part of its investigation (Jones et al. 1993). Several of the scholars who worked on the report went on to publish peer-reviewed articles on the subject (Dye 1996; Colburn 1997; Jones 1997). A popular book written by a sports journalist centres on the 1994 State of Florida decision (D'Orso 1996), and much of this research was later adapted into a 1997 film directed by John Singleton.

The history and destruction of Rosewood continue to linger at the edges of collective memory. This is largely due to intentional acts of erasure and obfuscation by local Whites (i.e., removal of maps and grand jury records from local archives) and America's larger culture of silence regarding the treatment of minorities who question progressive, nationalist narratives of the nation.

Rosewood's destruction echoes larger developments, and other work has more deeply explored the connections between past interpersonal violence and modern social inequality (González-Tennant 2018). Other important questions remain, particularly among locals in Levy County and Rosewood descendants. These seemingly simple questions can prove difficult to answer. For instance, many descendants are aware of the general location of Rosewood but desire greater specificity regarding the location of their ancestor's homes. Other questions centre on the location of the victims' graves. Digital archaeology has proved vital to addressing these and other questions.

Early digital archaeology in Rosewood

Research leading to the Rosewood Heritage and virtual reality (VR) Project began in 2005. This was conceived of as a specifically *digital* archaeology project from its creation. Preliminary goals concentrated on using a mix of GIS, digital storytelling and virtual world environments to address three interrelated topics. First, the reconstruction of the spatial layout of the town prior to its destruction. Second, the exploration of emerging and creative ways of sharing this and other research with as wide an audience as possible. Third, the demonstration of how interpersonal violence like race riots transformed into structural forms of violence across the 20th century. Intertwining these three goals, the first two generated through conversations with descendants and the third representing a scholarly interest, represents a central aspect of keeping this research public facing and engaged (González-Tennant 2014). The methodological requirements of this involved a transdisciplinary approach embracing historical archaeology's focus on artefacts, documents and oral history (Deetz 1996). It also necessitated a transdisciplinary approach combining GIS, 3D modelling, digital storytelling and the construction of a virtual world environment. I decided early in the project to personally undertake this work, answering an increasingly recognized need for archaeologists to undertake this work in addition to our traditional methods (Morgan 2009).

These efforts were immediately complicated by the fact that the area of Rosewood remains privately owned. The extra time involved in contacting landowners, most of whom were either disinterested or actively hostile to such work, proved disheartening. While a handful of landowners have been receptive, most have declined because of personal reasons, or in some cases, because they believe such work does little else than "open old wounds". Partly in response to this reluctance, but also to better select areas for potential investigation, it became necessary to predict which modern properties might hold historical resources associated with 1923 and before. The methodology for reconstructing this information centred on a massive GIS project. The general method for this work involves the following steps: (1) identify appropriate property records, (2) translate metes-and-bounds information into a GIS file, (3) identify owners of properties in relevant census records, (4) associate this data to the GIS record and (5) overlay this information on other forms of data including aerial photographs, LiDAR (a type of 3D laser scanning that produces accurate measurements of the ground's surface) and historical maps to precisely locate structures. These steps were repeated for hundreds of properties across a 50-year period (1870–1930), providing an accurate spatial layout of Rosewood through time. As of 2021 excavations by the author and his students at a dozen different properties have validated the predictive potentials of this approach and continue to guide archaeological work.

In addition to guiding excavations, the computer mapping project provides the raw material for a virtual reconstruction of Rosewood as it existed prior to its destruction. This involved five broad steps. The first focused on gathering appropriate historical data (the GIS). Next, blocking out the entire community, or creating a rough 3D version of the landscape with simple objects representing the location of structures and other objects. The third step involves adding details to these blocks and transforming them into realistic 3D models of complex structures. The fourth step involves texturing each model. The fifth and final step involves selecting a method for sharing the virtual reconstruction (Figure 4.2). Increasingly, this is accomplished through the construction of a virtual world environment with software typically used for the creation of video games (referred to as game engines). In the case of the Rosewood virtual world environment, the Unity (https://unity.com/) game engine was used to construct and share the virtual world environment. The act of virtually reconstructing historical structures in this part of Florida is complicated by the ephemeral nature of the buildings. For instance, buildings were typically placed on footings, meaning no foundations existed to be discovered through traditional archaeological investigations or the use of remote sensing technologies like LiDAR. As such, the

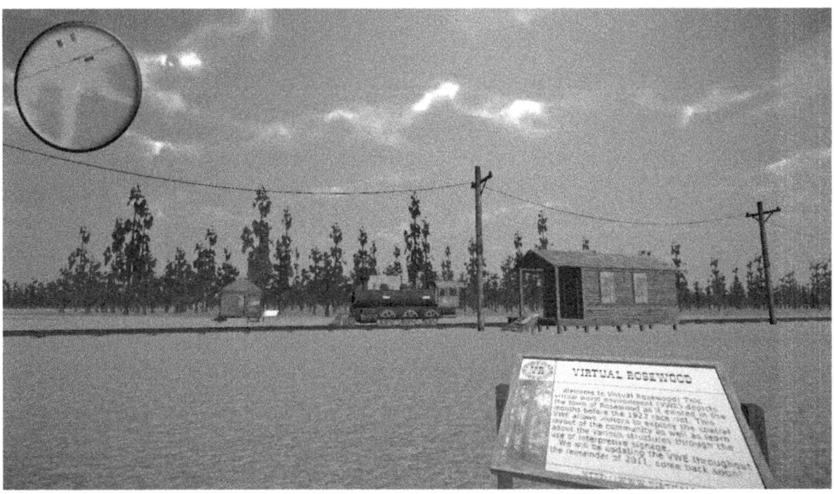

FIGURE 4.2 Initial Rosewood virtual world environment (2010). Image by author.

conjectural nature of reconstructing these buildings was also informed through a detailed review of the area's architectural history. For a deeper explanation of these steps as applied to multiple sites, please refer to González-Tennant and González-Tennant (2016).

Since the initial virtual world environment went live in 2010, updates have taken advantage of additional interactive potentials. This includes scripting interactive locations in the virtual world where users access and collect notes explaining the historical data, interpretive decisions and biographical details of each location. The inclusion of narrative notes combining census records, property deed information, oral history excerpts and so on provides additional details regarding the local landscape, design decisions of individual structures and the experiences of survivors in the decades after 1923. A demo of the updated virtual world, now referred to by the title *Rosewood: An Interactive History* (Figure 4.3), is available for free online at www.virtualrosewood.com.

Many of the data informing the virtual world environment also support digital storytelling outputs, particularly a series of oral histories with survivors and descendants (these and other supporting documents are available to download at www.virtualrosewood.com, including transcripts of oral histories, census records and other data discussed throughout this chapter). Digital storytelling provides a third approach to addressing the project's goals. Digital storytelling traces its roots to a series of workshops in Los Angeles during the 1990s (Lambert 2009). It offers an inexpensive and accessible method for sharing historical research (Earley-Spadoni 2017) that investigates the lives of those "without history" (Deagan 1982; Wolf 1982). The use of digital storytelling in Rosewood initially produced a 26-minute digital documentary in consultation with members of the descendant community. The video was designed for use in educational tours to

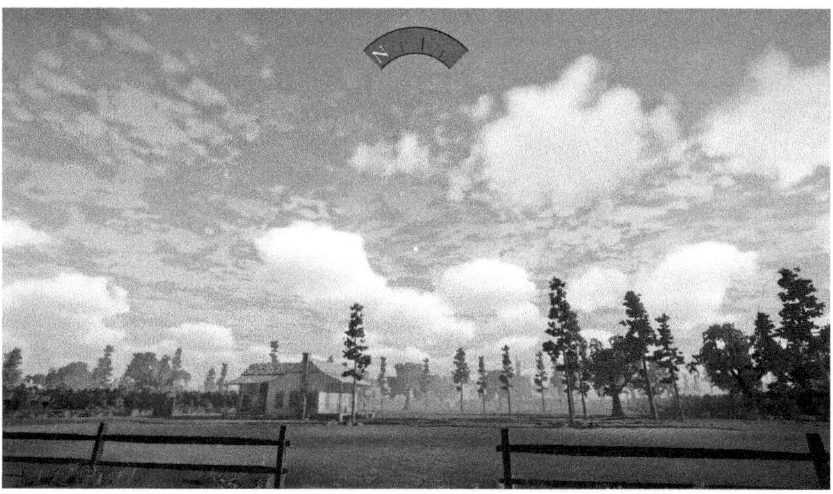

FIGURE 4.3 Screenshot from *Rosewood: An Interactive History*. Image by author.

the area surrounding Rosewood. The first half begins with an overview of the development and destruction of Rosewood before moving into a short description of the digital archaeology research. The second half centres on interviews with two Rosewood survivors, Mary Hall Daniels and Robie Mortin. Mortin and Daniels, who have both passed since interviews with them in 2009, serve as living representatives of Rosewood. Their lives continue the story of Rosewood beyond the town's destruction, demonstrating how a displaced community survived in a racially hostile American society. Their personal experiences tie the history of Rosewood to larger African American experiences.

Additional documentaries are nearing completion. A Florida Division of Historical Resources Small Matching Grant (2018–2019) funded additional archaeological and filming work in 2019. Initially delayed by COVID, a final series of interviews with descendants are currently ongoing. These and other aspects will likely be edited into one or more additional digital documentaries. While plans are yet finalized, this may include a series of YouTube videos discussing how digital archaeology provides unique approaches and perspectives regarding racial violence in the past. A longer documentary will seek to combine footage of fieldwork and interviews into a longer documentary, in an attempt to create a more engaged video than the traditional "talking head" approach common to modern documentaries, which can reduce the emotional impact of such traditional approaches (Aufderheide 2007).

The above research began at a time when many of the tools associated with digital archaeology were still emerging (mid-2000s). Researching Rosewood's past continues to benefit from advances in computing power, high-speed Internet access and free and open-source software, all of which have greatly expanded in the past 15 years. This includes shifting geospatial work to QGIS (https://qgis.org/), the world's leading open-source GIS software. LiDAR continues to inform efforts and is now processed and analyzed using a mix of CloudCompare (https://cloudcompare.org) and QGIS. Although I continue to use AgiSoft Metashape (https://www.agisoft.com/) for some of the photogrammetry work, this is increasingly replaced with Meshroom (https://alicevision.org/). All 3D modelling, including translation of photogrammetry models into low-poly, lightweight meshes – a process referred to as retopology – is completed with Blender (https://blender.org/). There are many benefits to these advances for the work in Rosewood. Perhaps most significant is an increased ability to quickly share large 3D and geospatial datasets via the Internet. The following section discusses how recent research combines a mix of data into shareable, interactive and immersive content delivered via the web. The author maintains a series of free tutorials regarding this work at www.youtube.com/anthroyeti.

Building the virtual Rosewood cemetery

Archaeological research in Rosewood continues, although large-scale work is likely completed unless new landowners emerge, willing to allow work on their properties. The recent grant from the Florida Division of Historical Resources funded the most recent large-scale investigation, during the summer months of 2018 and 2019. This included traditional archaeological work (e.g., shovel testing, excavation) at several privately owned sites. Results were consistent with the GIS work, again demonstrating its efficacy as a predictive model. Additional fieldwork benefitted from new digital approaches, combined in unique ways at each of the nine sites investigated during this grant. This section discusses work at a single site, the Rosewood Cemetery and how digital and virtual technologies allow archaeologists to translate complex data into public knowledge in interactive and immersive ways.

Work began with mapping visible surface features at the site. This was accomplished with a total digital station (TDS). After clearing the site of vegetation, the author and a small field crew mapped all visible features. These included visible graves, grave markers and other features. Graves without markers were identified by their east-west orientation, rough arrangements in north-south rows and longer than wide individual dimensions. Surface mapping identified 11 grave depressions in addition to three marked graves for a total of 14 visible graves. Benchmarks used for the TDS mapping were assigned real-world coordinates with an Emlid RTK GNSS unit (Hill et al. 2019), allowing the total station data to be projected into real-world coordinates (Figure 4.4).

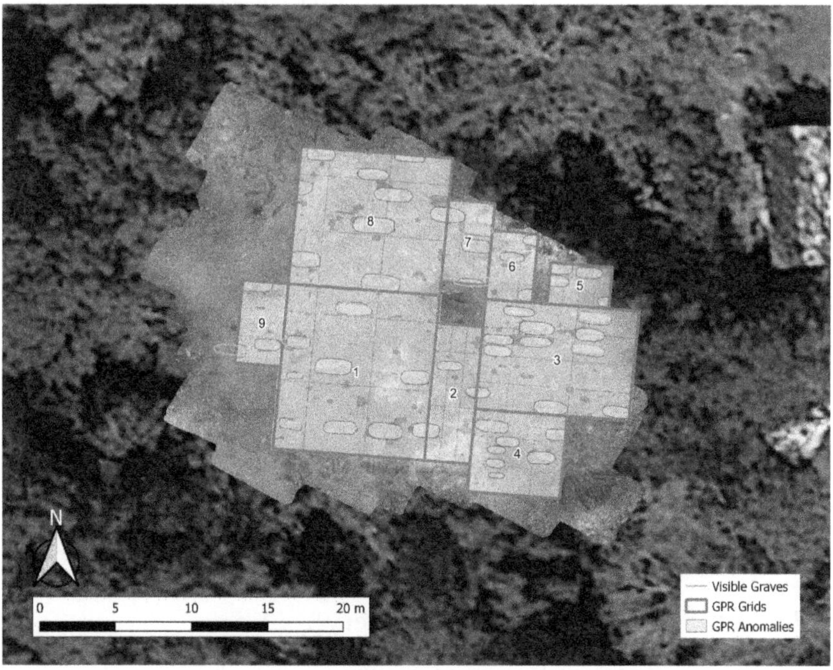

FIGURE 4.4 Map of the Rosewood cemetery. Image by author.

GPR is a geophysical method offering a non-invasive option for archaeological surveys. GPR uses electromagnetic waves generated from an antenna – which is pushed or pulled along the ground – from which reflective signals are collected, processed and interpreted. The theory of operation and applications for GPR in archaeology are presented in Conyers (2004, 2006a, b), Goodman et al. (2009) and Goodman and Piro (2013). In brief, a GPR unit records reflected radar energy and uses a lapse in travel time and the varying amplitude to create 2D transects, commonly referred to as radargrams or reflection profiles. Profiles can be compiled to create 2D and 3D imagery (Goodman et al. 2009). Data are collected in linear transects. Typically, GPR surveys are oriented perpendicular to the objects they hope to detect. In the case of graves, which are typically oriented east-west, transects are arranged north-south, perpendicular to the potential objects.

All marked and possible burials in Rosewood were oriented in this way, and a series of grids oriented north-south were created. Transects within the grids were spaced .5 m apart allowing for several returns per feature. As historic graves typically span 1–2 metres, this means they will appear in at least four to six transects. This survey was completed with a MALA X3M system, a 250 MHz antenna that has been extensively tested for simulated burials in Florida soils (Schultz and Martin 2011). The GPR data were processed and analyzed with GPRSoft and Radan GPR processing software. GPRSoft processing involved high/low pass filters to clean up the data, velocity analysis and migration to accentuate anomalies, and tweaks to gain to improve visual recognition. Each transect was then exported to the GSSI format (.dzt) for use in Radan. Final processing in Radan resulted in the creation of horizontal slices at varying depths, which interpolates 3D, volumetric data from the 2D data of the original slices. The GPR survey outlined an additional 30–40 anomalies that are likely unmarked graves.

To better contextualize the TDS and GPR survey data, images collected via unpiloted aerial vehicle (UAV) (in this case the DJI Phantom III Standard) provided images for the construction of low-altitude aerial imagery. The use of aerial imagery to assist with the identification, interpretation and preservation of cultural heritage has a long history (see Riley 1987 and Wilson 2000 for overviews). The advent of low-cost photogrammetry software has increased the use of low-altitude imagery in recent years (Wernke et al. 2014; Olson and Rouse 2018). Photogrammetry typically refers to the extraction of 3D points from a series of 2D images. Most uses of photogrammetry in cultural heritage make use of structure from motion (SfM), which is a technique for estimating spatially accurate points from a series of 2D images. Many photogrammetry programs also support the production of orthophotos, or 2D images with accurate geographic coordinates embedded in them.

An orthophoto – also known as orthophotograph or orthoimage – refers to an aerial or satellite image that has been orthorectified, or geometrically corrected and assigned geographic coordinates. An orthomosaic is built from mosaicking together different orthophotos. The orthomosaic for the Rosewood Cemetery was created using the 2D images collected via UAV, which embeds coordinates into each image's metadata with an onboard GPS. Images are collected in a grid across the site but may also be collected opportunistically depending on local environmental conditions (e.g., dense canopy). For this project, images were processed with the AgiSoft Metashape Professional software. The general steps involve (1) importing photos into Metashape, (2) aligning photos (requiring an overlap between photos so the software can match tens of thousands of points), (3) construction of a dense point cloud (which fills in the "gaps" created during the previous step), (4) creation of a mesh – a 3D model – from the dense point cloud, (5) production of a texture (an accurate image representing the surface of the mesh) and (6) exporting the orthomosaic. The resulting orthomosaic is also georeferenced, which allows it to be added to the project GIS to aid in mapping and visualizing the study area. Orthomosaics provide a low-cost method for delivering high-quality low-altitude aerial images in environments with a dense tree canopy. This was particularly the case at the Rosewood Cemetery site where a dense, low canopy required adjustment of the typical grid collection strategy with an opportunistic one. Figure 4.4 uses the resulting orthomosaic as a base map, illustrating these features.

Photogrammetry was also used to document the entire site as well as high-quality models of the three remaining grave markers at the Rosewood Cemetery. These features are threatened by natural processes, vandalism or both. The process to create a highly accurate 3D model from a series of 2D images is like that used for the creation of orthomosaics (see Douglass et al. 2015 and Porter et al. 2016 for a fuller description). However, instead of exporting an orthomosaic, the final step involves exporting high-quality 3D models complete with photorealistic textures. These 3D models can be used for public outreach, monitoring site processes (e.g., weathering of gravestones) and creating a 3D record for preservation purposes.

Additional data were required to create an interactive and immersive 3D virtual environment that successfully (and intuitively) translates the above research into a publicly accessible format. This began with the collection and processing of freely available LiDAR data, which provided an expanded ground surface for the virtual reconstruction. The LiDAR is freely available via the National Oceanic and Atmospheric Administration (NOAA) Data Access Viewer (https://coast.noaa.gov/dataviewer/#/). The LiDAR data for this project date to 2007, meaning it provides a good digital elevation model (DEM), but not fine scale enough to show depressions associated with unmarked graves. In order to show this level of detail, LiDAR was first subsampled using CloudCompare to remove all points except those classified as ground. The remaining ground points were interpolated into a digital elevation model using the Rasterize tool, and a 3D mesh was exported in .obj format for further processing in Blender. This data was then combined with a 3D model derived from UAV photos AgiSoft Metashape, which was also exported as a mesh and added to the LiDAR ground surface in Blender. These two data were merged into a single 3D object and the resulting

3D mesh retopologized to reduce the file size. The final, relatively lightweight ground surface 3D object was then given a realistic texture to simulate the site's sandy soil, complete with leaf litter, grass and other vegetation. Tutorials for all these steps can be found at www.youtube.com/anthroyeti.

The final steps involved further highlighting the location of graves and creating a more accurate representation of the site. GPR results were incorporated by aligning an image of the anomalies with the 3D surface. The ground surface was then edited to slightly exaggerate the location of visible graves as well as those identified by GPR. 3D models of three headstones were created via photogrammetry, retopologized and added to the virtual cemetery. Locations of these and other features were mapped by total station and recorded in the photogrammetry-based ground surface. Vegetation was then added to improve realism. Trees and shrub placement was informed by field mapping, photogrammetry and the orthomosaic (Figure 4.5).

The finished virtual cemetery was exported to Sketchfab via the Blender to Sketchfab exporter (https://github.com/sketchfab/blender-plugin/). Sketchfab offers a robust set of tools for annotating 3D models and virtual environments. Annotations are 3D locations embedded in the final virtual Sketchfab scene. Each annotation re-positions the viewer and includes notes explaining the unique aspects of objects or other features at each location. These can be followed one after the other to produce a virtual site tour. Ultimately, these and other features informed my decision to publish the model via Sketchfab instead of creating a standalone application. The site allows a broad segment of the world to interact with this content via the website or a mobile app. This makes virtual content available to a far wider range of people than publishing information via a webpage, interactive map or even a standalone virtual experience. Sketchfab also

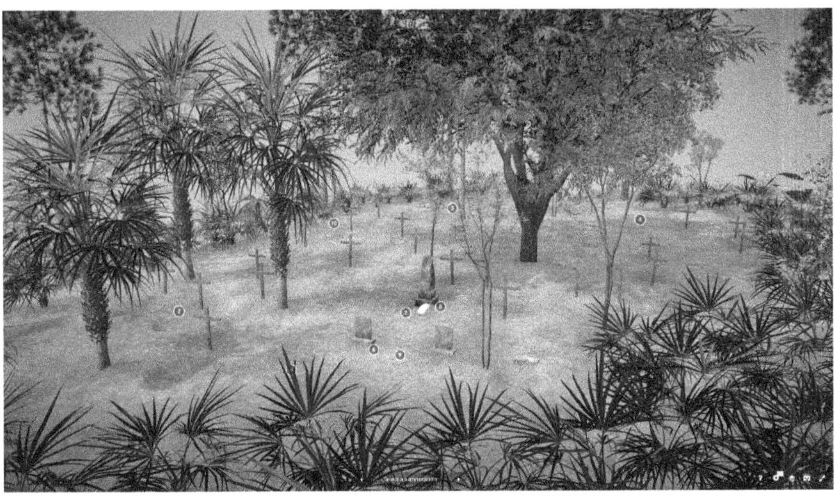

FIGURE 4.5 The virtual Rosewood cemetery. Image by author.

includes support for VR goggles and app-based augmented reality experiences, expanding the single output with immersive aspects.

The Virtual Rosewood Cemetery is an online, interactive reconstruction of Rosewood's Black burial ground. It is a spatially accurate reconstruction combining field mapping, GPR survey, LiDAR and photogrammetry data previously discussed. In brief, the steps to creating this reconstruction are (1) create and edit the ground surface; (2) add models representing grave markers to the ground surface; (3) add vegetation and other 3D objects for increased realism and (4) export to Sketchfab (https://sketchfab.com/). Readers can view an expanded discussion of the above steps and the finished 3D virtual environment at anthroyeti.net /2021/02/01/vrc_build/. Ultimately, this approach represents a low-cost, comprehensive method for documenting African American burial grounds, which represent long-neglected and often intentionally targeted heritage resources in the USA.

Discussion

The ability to use digital tools to collect, combine and interpret archaeological data provides new opportunities to develop important and unique insights. In many ways, working between these various data often supports a deeper familiarity than traditional analytical methods. This includes developing an experiential knowledge of the spatial aspects of a place, particularly when access to a location is restricted by ownership or distance. This may push the researcher to better understand how such sites relate to other historical data, such as aerial images or photographs. This has proven to be the case when seeking answers to a central – but largely neglected – question regarding the victims of the violence in 1923: Where are they buried? Like other researchers, I assumed these individuals were buried in Rosewood. However, there are no historical documents such as death certificates or burial records to confirm or counter this. Grave markers or other physical traces identifying the majority of those buried here are also absent from the site. Fortunately, the process of constructing the Virtual Rosewood Cemetery provided a deeper understanding of the site and resulted in a deeper understanding of previously unrecognized connections between these various data.

As previously mentioned, visitors to the physical site can see several long depressions, and depending on ground cover and training, most can identify ten or so graves by their depressions. The unmarked graves likely had ephemeral markers (e.g., wood) or their markers were vandalized and/or removed during the past century. Additional graves are identified via the GPR analysis. Even with all this information, the ability to assign names to individual graves lacking markers is impossible, even if the graves were to be exhumed, which I, the landowner, and descendants are against.

Fortunately, we can locate the names of many who are buried at the site. A combination of State of Florida Certificates of Death, oral histories and census records provides a lot of this information. A review of these sources reveals at least 44 individuals buried at the site (readers can access a full list by visiting https://virtualrosewood.com/rosewood-cemetery-records/). This number does not represent all burials, although it is much closer to the 50 or more graves revealed by the field mapping and GPR survey. Charting out the number of burials by year provides additional information (Figure 4.6). At first glance, several patterns seem to emerge but are potentially misleading. The absence of burials before 1900 and a large number of infant recorded deaths between 1917 and 1920 are two examples. It is likely that burials took place prior to 1900 but went unreported. This is possible as the State of Florida did not standardize and require death certificates until 1917. Many infant deaths between 1917 and 1920 are likely connected to the 1918 influenza pandemic. It may also be a result of the 1917 state reporting requirements and the fact that infant mortality in the past was far more common than we tend to acknowledge today. The fact that burials continue through 1922 is strong evidence that the 1923 Black victims are also buried here. Oral history accounts describe, for instance, how James Carrier was caught by a White mob while burying his mother (Sarah) and brother (Sylvester). Newspapers from the first week of 1923 also describe this, an important correspondence between oral history and historical documents.

Several newspapers also ran an image reportedly showing a group of Whites in Rosewood (or Sumner as the two communities were often conflated in these accounts) standing behind a line of graves reported to be African American burials. It is unlikely that local Whites would have buried Black victims of racial violence and/or taken the bodies 2–3 miles from Rosewood to bury at the White cemetery in neighbouring Sumner. Rural historical cemeteries were segregated along lines of race in Levy County, particularly between Black and White communities. Sometimes credited as being taken in Sumner, this image was likely taken in Rosewood following the killing and burial of James Carrier. Although the graves are mounded in the above photo, without constant re-mounding and other maintenance, such burials in Florida's sandy soil tend to "sink" and form (visible) depressions. This is partly due to the decomposition of the burials, and partly due to the nature of soil weathering in Florida. While extracting exact measurements from the image above is difficult, the positioning and distances between these three graves appear to match a line of graves along the western edge of Rosewood's cemetery. The spacing is similar and their placement next to a road suggests it may be the same place.

Understanding the final resting place of the victims of the 1923 Rosewood Massacre is perhaps more important today than ever. It provides closure for descendants. This is increasingly important as duplicitous researchers, more interested in self-aggrandizement than historical reality, seek to make "new" discoveries for the purpose of seeing their names attached to increasingly important sites (such as the 100th anniversary of Rosewood destruction in 2023). This has happened as recently as 2020 in Rosewood. The experience of investigating the Rosewood Cemetery reminds us that researchers must combine archaeology and

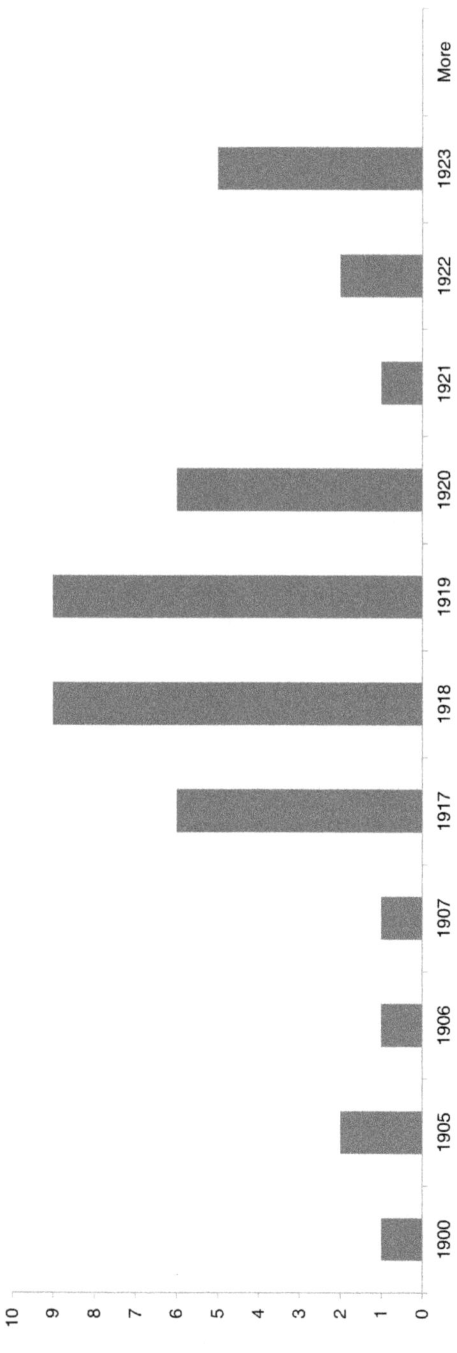

FIGURE 4.6 Rosewood cemetery burials by year. Image by author.

the fragmentary documentary record to craft a more complete interpretation of these important places. This includes accurately locating and possibly correcting erroneous or otherwise unreliable data (e.g., poorly labelled newspaper accounts from 1923). In the case of Rosewood, archaeology, census records, death certificates, historical newspapers and oral histories all combine to remind us of the importance even a small plot of land might have regarding larger patterns of violence in American history. Cemeteries remain important sites of memory and commemoration on the landscape (Baugher and Veit 2014), more so when they directly connect to histories of violent oppression. Experimenting with digital archaeology is not just good methodological practice; in Rosewood, it also represents a moral imperative for crafting an engaged archaeology that matters.

Conclusion

The application of digital technologies to difficult history provides a powerful approach for crafting a sustainable, engaged archaeology (Agbe-Davis 2010). It is an approach addressing the challenges often complicating this work and recognizes that achieving archaeology's true potential for revealing new truths about difficult histories is by no means obvious or self-evident (Morgan and Pallascio 2016). Digital archaeology offers two benefits supporting this work. First, they assist archaeologists in developing a deeply embedded understanding of our data (Eve 2012, 2014, 2017; Morgan and Eve 2012; González-Tennant and González-Tennant 2016). This deeper understanding supports answering difficult questions in data-driven and sensitive ways. Second, these methods provide a way of translating this scholarship into public knowledge, which is vital for achieving archaeology's potential in supporting public conversations on restorative justice (Franklin et al. 2020). The success of digital archaeology for these goals rests on our ability to address the rational and emotional aspects of difficult history. Ultimately, this is a creative process benefitting from long-term engagements with places of painful and shameful histories. The creativity required for this work in no way trivializes it. Rather, as digital archaeologists, we understand that such creativity is vital. Creative experimentation remains foundational to our engagement with technology and will continue to produce important insights and support progressive goals underscoring our shared humanity in the past, present and future.

References

Agbe-Davis, Anna S. 2010. "Concepts of Community in the Pursuit of an Inclusive Archaeology." *International Journal of Heritage Studies* 16 (6): 373–89.

Aufderheide, Patricia. 2007. *Documentary Film: A Very Short Introduction*. Oxford: Oxford University Press.

Baugher, Sherene, and Richard F. Veit. 2014. *The Archaeology of American Cemeteries and Gravemarkers*. Gainesville: University Press of Florida.

Colburn, David R. 1997. "Rosewood and America in the Early Twentieth Century." *The Florida Historical Quarterly* 76 (2): 175–92. http://www.jstor.org/stable/30146345.

Conyers, Lawrence B. 2006a. "Innovative Ground-penetrating Radar Methods for Archaeological Mapping." *Archaeological Prospection* 13 (2): 139–41.

Conyers, Lawrence B. 2006b. "Ground-Penetrating Radar Techniques to Discover and Map Historic Graves." *Historical Archaeology* 40 (3): 64–73.

Conyers, Lawrence B. 2004. *Ground-Penetrating Radar for Archaeology*. Walnut Creek, CA: AltaMira Press.

Deagan, Kathleen. 1982. "Avenues of Inquiry in Historical Archaeology." *Advances in Archaeological Method and Theory* 7 (1): 151–77.

Deetz, James. 1996. *In Small Things Forgotten: An Archaeology of Early American Life*. New York: Anchor Books.

D'Orso, Michael. 1996. *Like Judgment Day: The Ruin and Redemption of a Town Called Rosewood*. New York: G.P. Putnam's Sons.

Douglass, Matthew, Sam Lin, and Michael Chodoronek. 2015. "The Application of 3D Photogrammetry for In-Field Documentation of Archaeological Features." *Advances in Archaeological Practice* 3 (02): 136–52. https://doi.org/10.7183/2326-3768.3.2.136.

Dye, Thomas R. 1996. "Rosewood, Florida: The Destruction of an African American Community." *The Historian* 58 (3): 322–605.

Earley-Spadoni, Tiffany. 2017. "Spatial History, Deep Mapping and Digital Storytelling: Archaeology's Future Imagined through an Engagement with the Digital Humanities." *Journal of Archaeological Science* 84: 95–102. https://doi.org/10.1016/j.jas.2017.05.003.

Eve, Stuart. 2017. "The Embodied GIS: Using Mixed Reality to Explore Multi-Sensory Archaeological Landscapes." *Internet Archaeology* 44. https://intarch.ac.uk/journal/issue44/3/index.html

Eve, Stuart. 2014. *Dead Men's Eyes: Embodied GIS, Mixed Reality and Landscape Archaeology*. Oxford: Archaeopress.

Eve, Stuart. 2012. "Augmenting Phenomenology: Using Augmented Reality to Aid Archaeological Phenomenology in the Landscape." *Journal of Archaeological Method and Theory* 19 (4): 582–600.

Franklin, Maria, Justin P. Dunnavant, Ayana Omilade Flewellen, and Alicia Odewale. 2020. "The Future Is Now: Archaeology and the Eradication of Anti-Blackness." *International Journal of Historical Archaeology* 24 (4): 753–66.

González-Tennant, Edward. 2018. *The Rosewood Massacre: An Archaeology and History of Intersectional Violence*. Hardcover. Gainesville: University Press of Florida. https://upf.com/book.asp?id=9780813056784.

González-Tennant, Edward. 2014. "The "Color" of Heritage: Decolonizing Collaborative Archaeology in the Caribbean." *Journal of African Diaspora Archaeology and Heritage* 3 (1): 26–50.

González-Tennant, Edward. 2013. "New Heritage and Dark Tourism: A Mixed Methods Approach to Social Justice in Rosewood, Florida." *Heritage & Society* 6 (1): 62–88. https://doi.org/10.1179/2159032X13Z.0000000007.

González-Tennant, Edward, and Diana González-Tennant. 2016. "The Practice and Theory of New Heritage for Historical Archaeology." *Historical Archaeology* 50 (1): 187–204. https://doi.org/10.1007/BF03377184.

Goodman, Dean, and Salvatore Piro, eds. 2013. *GPR Remote Sensing in Archaeology*. New York: Springer.

Goodman, Dean, Salvatore Piro, Yasushi Nishimura, Kent Schneider, Hiromichi Hongo, Noriaki Higashi, John Steinberg, and Brian Damiata. 2009. "GPR Archaeometry." In *Ground Penetrating Radar: Theory and Applications*, edited by Harry M. Jol, 479–508. Amsterdam: Elsevier.

Hill, Austin Chad, Fred Limp, Jesse Casana, Elise Jakoby Laugier, and Malcolm Williamson. 2019. "A New Era in Spatial Data Recording: Low-Cost GNSS." *Advances in Archaeological Practice* 7 (2): 169–77.

Ifill, Sherrilyn A. 2007. *On the Courthouse Lawn: Confronting the Legacy of Lynching in the Twenty-First Century*. Boston: Beacon Press.

Jones, Maxine D. 1997. "The Rosewood Massacre and the Women Who Survived It." *The Florida Historical Quarterly* 76 (2): 193–208. http://www.jstor.org/stable/30146346.

Jones, Maxine Deloris, Larry E Rivers, David R Colburn, R Thomas Dye, and William R Rogers. 1993. *A Documented History of the Incident Which Occurred at Rosewood, Florida, in January 1923: Submitted to the Florida Board of Regents 22 December 1993*. Tallahassee: Board of Regents.

Lambert, Joe. 2009. *Digital Storytelling: Capturing Lives, Creating Community*. 2nd ed. Berkeley: Digital Diner Press.

Morgan, Colleen L. 2009. "(Re)Building Çatalhöyük: Changing Virtual Reality in Archaeology." *Archaeologies: Journal of World Archaeological Congress* 5 (3): 488–568.

Morgan, Colleen L, and Stuart Eve. 2012. "DIY and Digital Archaeology: What Are You Doing to Participate?" *World Archaeology* 44 (4): 521–237.

Morgan, Colleen L, and Pierre Marc Pallascio. 2016. "Digital Media, Participatory Culture, and Difficult Heritage: Online Remediation and the Trans-Atlantic Slave Trade." *Journal of African Diaspora Archaeology and Heritage* 4 (3): 160–78.

Nieves, Angel David. 2009. "Places of Pain as Tools for Social Justice in the "New" South Africa: Black Heritage Preservation in the "Rainbow" Nation's Townships." In *Places of Pain and Shame: Dealing with Difficult Heritage*, edited by William Logan and Keir Reeves. London: Routledge.

Olson, Kyle G, and Lynne M. Rouse. 2018. "A Beginner's Guide to Mesoscale Survey with Quadrotor-UAV Systems." *Advances in Archaeological Practice* 7: 1–15.

Porter, Samantha Thi, Morgan Roussel, and Marie Soressi. 2016. "A Simple Photogrammetry Rig for the Reliable Creation of 3D Artifact Models in the Field: Lithic Examples from the Early Upper Paleolithic Sequence of Les Cottés (France)." *Advances in Archaeological Practice* 4 (1): 71–86.

Riley, D N. 1987. *Air Photography and Archaeology*. Philadelphia: University of Pennsylvania Press.

Rose, Julia, ed. 2016. *Interpreting Difficult History at Museums and Historic Sites*. Lanham: Rowman & Littlefield.

Schultz, John J, and Michael M Martin. 2011. "Controlled GPR Grave Research: Comparison of Reflection Profiles between 500 and 250 MHz Antennae." *Forensic Science International* 209 (1–3): 64–69. https://doi.org/10.1016/J.FORSCIINT.2010.12.012.

Sluka, Jeffrey A. 1999. "Introduction: State Terror and Anthropology." In *Death Squad: The Anthropology of State Terror*, edited by Jeffrey A. Sluka, 1–45. Philadelphia: University of Pennsylvania Press.

Wernke, Steven A, Julie A Adams, and Eli R Hooten. 2014. "Capturing Complexity—Toward an Integrated Low-Altitude Photogrammetry and Mobile Geographic Information System Archaeological Registry System." "Digital Domains," Special issue, *Advances in Archaeological Practice* 2: 147–163.

Wilson, D R. 2000. *Air Photo Interpretation for Archaeologists 2nd Edition*. London: Tempus Publishing.

Wolf, Eric R. 1982. *Europe and the People without History*. Berkeley: University of California Press.

5

VR AS CRITICAL HISTORIOGRAPHY

The case of Wadi Salib in Haifa

Eytan Mann and Aaron Sprecher

Introduction

As a research tool, virtual reality (VR) is developing rapidly, with researchers of various disciplines calling for a better understanding of its potential. In the field of architecture, VR has been largely focused on exploring new possibilities of immersive visualization of architecture or simulating interactions with architectural space. In the context of architectural history, VR is still mostly limited to reconstructing sites that have been lost or are otherwise inaccessible. With VR, we can enter a Neolithic Tomb, walk through La Corbusier's villa or explore an unbuilt Hindu temple.[1] However, the use of VR in the context of architecture's broader concerns remains quite limited, the reasons being the lack of technological know-how, the limited reach of the technology in classroom settings and logistical difficulties. But beyond such "real-life" challenges that can surely be improved upon in the future, the general intellectual question of how VR can be used in the context of critical historiography of architecture, which aims to question and undermine stable representation of sites and their histories, remains in its infancy and is, in fact, hampered precisely by the technology's general promise of simple, faithful realism.

VR as a critical tool embraces the limitations of what can be understood as "real" within the VR platform but enables new engagement with actual sites and pasts. For us, employing VR to study the site of Wadi Salib, located in downtown Haifa, was not a tool that provides an additional layer of realism to what is being studied, but rather a medium that allows us to work between various epistemological registers to create something that is just as much a part of architecture as it is of a study of cultural significance within architecture. In other words, through the research presented here, we wanted to create something that is not just a personal statement but can be leveraged to become a working tool

DOI: 10.4324/9781003200659-6

to examine difficult pasts in their physical context and offer empathy and even some reconciliation. While attempting to do so, it is essential to discuss the new possibilities and caveats of using VR for critical historiography of built sites.

In this chapter, we discuss, first, the notion of critical historiography of contested places and the use of VR as a medium of such historiography. VR raises critical questions on the mediation of historiography: Can we be immersed in historiography? While we see examples of immersive history, such as in using VR to experience a Neolithic Tomb, or while playing historically based games, we are rarely immersed in the research setting, in which that same Neolithic Tomb is reconstructed, in the "behind the scenes" of its making.[2] The reason might be that historians tend to be suspicious of highly sensorial and impressionistic history. Impressions are the longtime adversaries of objective knowledge, and so the historian-scientist should work to remove the interference of subjective sensory impressions.[3] Immersion is a state of mind that encourages impression, and that is why it is often labelled as unscientific, as it can manipulate the mind rather than provide a clear and rational image of the past. Moreover, computer graphics employed to visualize built environments from the past often lack the required tools to identify their overall accuracy while simultaneously carrying a sense of truth. Borrowing from the concept of hyperreality introduced by Baudrillard, reconstructions intermingle the real and hypothetical without any means of distinguishing the two (Baudrillard 1983). At the same time, images carry a sense of realism and legitimacy that automatically leads users to believe them to be truthful.

As such, we ask if immersion in reconstructed environments allows a higher definition of historical facts, or rather, does it enable new modes of questioning the notion of facts. For this, we need first to frame historiography not in terms of factual reclamation but instead as an active construction, animation and recombination process of historical events and the locale of history – the site. In short, what does VR offer for critical historiography of sites, and what is at stake?

These epistemological questions are urgent as VR becomes more pervasive and permeates design fields and the humanities, including architecture schools. We suggest a methodology to explore the use of VR for critical investigation of contested sites while overcoming some of the caveats of using such a medium in this context. Using computation and digital technologies for historiography can potentially underline opportunities and problems in the process. The methodology was developed at the Material Topology Research Lab (MTRL)[4] and tested during a semester-long course at the Technion Israel Institute of Technology in Haifa, Israel. During the course, students studied Wadi Salib, a ruined neighbourhood in downtown Haifa that bears the scars of the whole region: Wars, displacement, nation-building and disillusion. Wadi Salib stores multiple narratives embedded within its streets and houses. Through the encounter with Wadi Salib, we developed the strategy of critically mediating the site and its history through fieldwork and archival research. The course outcomes were VR experiences that deal with different event spaces, generated using the methodological pipeline we assembled. As the investigation is ongoing, we have reached the assessment phase to review the work and discuss what is at stake in mediating history through immersive VR as a critical instrument to allow the voicing of multiple voices. Can we take advantage of the realistic illusionary capabilities of VR to teleport us in space and time while not losing touch with our role as critical thinkers?

Critical historiography

Historiography most often considers history an invisible phenomenon, something belonging to the past. The wars fought in the past, major decisions made to change the course of events and the inherited written documents from various periods of history could all fall into the oblivion of the invisible. And yet, writing (and visualizing) history in a particular time and place, George Simmel writes, contributes to our historical knowledge only when "it can be oriented in relation to other events". Access to history is through material conditions and the context of the historiographer. A book, a monument or an archival material differs from the historical event itself: They hold a presence that demands a different historiographical consideration. The event itself is not reducible to an empirical experience but unfolds through a representation of history. In this process of reproduction, the act of writing the past does not occur in a void; rather, it unfolds in its *present*. "The now of the present is imbued with the past", writes Hartoonian, while the present is neither seen as the continuum of the past nor separated from it (Hartoonian 2020, p. 1). Writing history in modernity considers the past to be a chain of events, the total of which is called progress. This approach sees the technology of historiography as an integral role in shaping the past. Technology shapes our perception of the past, as was claimed by Benjamin in *The Work of Art in the Age of Mechanical Reproduction*, where he unpacks the impact of technologies such as montage in film. Benjamin articulated the idea of "wish-images" in conjunction with the loss of aura; that is, the magical and ritualistic origin of the work of art where space and time are intermingled, and on the other hand, the new objectivity introduced by photography and film (Benjamin 1936). Benjamin describes a dialectic image between the desire of the subject and a new objective scientific image.

Critical historiography is a space of operating between the pulls of objectivity and subjectivity, especially productive in places of conflict histories and the question of their mediation (Jarzombek 1999). Jarzombek asks where the historian subject in the mediation of history is. To this question, there can be various answers, one of them is Dominic LaCapra's *Secondary Witnessing* – that mediating evidence of the past ought to include oneself as a second-order witness, an active agent of mediation. The opaqueness of the historian sheds light on the inherent problem of the historian's positionality when witnessing destruction and violence: As Dominic LaCapra articulates, "experience involves affect both in the observed and in the observer". For the observer, the experience problem leads to the role of empathy in historical understanding (LaCapra 2014). This critical stance invites us to write history actively. This position introduces new intimacy and sensitivity to history instead of absolute relativism that might cause a detached distancing from the materials and evidence of record (Jarzombek 1999).

Secondary Witnessing echoes poststructuralist history and overcoming the need for scientific objectivity; different communities value different pasts – not a monumental, national or global history, but a more personalized history that empowers the perspective of ordinary people (Lowenthal 2015). The work of the historian has never been merely the transliteration of a pre-existent past into a documentary medium. Instead, history is constituted by employing historical information into recognizable narratives and literary tropes (White 1978). Rather than getting caught up in dichotomous thinking such as "past as real" versus "past as constructed", we should focus on history as a continuum, identified through moments of mediation: The generation of documents, the collation of documents into an archive, the retrieval of facts from files and the construction of historical narrative (Trouillot 2015). Focusing on these moments is critical to understanding the intersection of power and knowledge and how history is written and how silences are created, to locate, contest and interpret archival materials made accessible and the gaps and underrepresentation of particular objects such as communities, locations or events. To locate such gaps, historians ought to adopt strategies that focus on key moments of historical mediation. In Trouillot's terms, historiography is implicated by technologies of *collection* of documents, their *structuring* into narratives and how *interfaces* of their dissemination culminate in a historical infrastructure, not always visible but very impactful on how heritage is formulated (Trouillot 2015). Following this poststructuralist position, we should look closely at the epistemological and institutional frameworks that produce history and heritage in contested sites. For example, we might ask how the institutional narratives of heritage have played a role in fossilizing some representations of the past while silencing others (Rajagopalan 2012). A critical investigation of history preservation practices, in writing or architectural design, is deeply embedded within and produced by complex power structures. According to this critical turn, history is not a "total fact" but is a constructed knowledge involving a selection of narratives, challenging the notion of ownership of heritage and the conditions for making the definitions. Such a critical approach calls for focus on media and mediation, on the technologies of historiography (Clark, 2004).

Technologies of historiography

Critical historiography foregrounds the mediation of history – the technologies by which we collect, organize and disseminate history. Along with mediations of the past, such as manuscripts, photographs and maps, historians can search for clues about how history is constructed and engaged through cultural products, memories, myths and politics. While historical uncertainty and disputation are sometimes viewed as the enemy of a respectful attitude towards the lived past, consensual histories run an even greater risk of becoming polite fables, the kind of cultural narratives that lead to rituals of remembrance rather than critical thinking and political agency (Zadeh 2016). Media theorist Steve Anderson invites us to consider the myriad "technologies of history" and how media practices broadly conceived help us think about the world, the past and our potential to act as historical and political agents (Anderson 2011).

Today, digital technology allows us to record and store architecture in digital form, and computational tools open new access to the analysis and organization of cultural heritage data. As we show here, the methodology we suggest deploys both computer graphics and natural language processing to establish new links between the site and stories. It is potentially a way to weave vast information about places and their histories and develop new modes of storytelling. The methodology presented here attempts to move towards a critical adaptation of what Anderson refers to as "database histories" – that is, "collections of infinitely retrievable fragments, situated within categories and organized according to predetermined associations, offer users, whether they are artists, gamers, or geeks, both the materials and structures by which the past may be conceived as fundamentally mutable and reconfigurable" (Anderson 2011, p. 122). Taking advantage of the logic of remix and computational culture and the kinds of repetitions and modifications built into video games, "database histories" projects rest along a continuum, moving from serious artworks to pop-culture hacks; however, they share a staunch refusal of the stability of a single "history" and instead offer us a relation to the past that is always already open to continual revision and reinterpretation. In practical terms, the implications of digital technology for archiving have primarily focused on technical questions of how to best preserve and disseminate historical data using rapidly expanding networks, notoriously transient file formats and unstable storage media.

The promise of "database histories" may lead to the false notion of a "total archive". The philosopher Arthur C. Danto coined the term "Ideal Chronicler" in 1965, describing a hypothetical model for history writing before the advent of computers (Danto 1982). In his view, a perfect historian would be able to account for every historical event, analyzing its significance from multiple perspectives at the moment they are being recorded. Though initially proposed to demonstrate the impossibility of an objectively perfect form of historiography, Danto's ideal of comprehensiveness, multiple perspectives and immediacy resonates with the promises of today's searchable databases and digital distribution networks. Historiography in the digital age seems destined to continually promise a direct and easy relationship to the past, awaiting only the technical apparatus capable of rendering it in its entirety. A critical conception of historiography we wish to adopt does not recover or preserve an objective factual history but instead engages actively in the conflicts and uncertainty of the past and present. Digital technologies' fragmentation of knowledge in the correct constellation can reinforce a critical historical study. Shifting from viewing "history" as a grand, totalizing narrative to a splintered conglomeration of subdisciplinary investigations, each emerging from, and self-consciously subjected to, their own rules of formation, as Foucault describes in *The Archaeology of Knowledge*. This shift entails a movement away from a single "history" towards fragmentary histories as an essential step towards acknowledging the chaos of the past and the unruliness of human thought. Discrete statements, Foucault argued, must always be analyzed within a field of discourse and considered in relation to disruptions, discontinuities, thresholds, mutations and limits (Foucault 1972, p. 5).

Works of history once understood to comprise an expanding field of collective historical knowledge are thereby repositioned as raw material in infinitely reconfigurable revision, remixing and recontextualization patterns. The work of the historian must now contend with the construction of open-source and accessible databases and the accretion of vast volumes of data referencing historical events, facts and images. The question of digital media's ultimate role in what we remember and how we view ourselves concerning the past remains the subject of an ongoing debate. This is because tools for visualizing history proliferate across platforms, networks, consoles and screens. While the materials of historiography are computationally stored, analyzed, segmented, tagged, rendered and processed into information, we see new, increasingly engaging digital interfaces through immersion.[5] Moving from "database histories" to immersive interfaces with such information entails moving from abstract information to increasingly spatialized historical materials, towards their becoming a virtually inhabitable space. As opposed to the striated world of the database, where knowledge is grouped into discrete data packets, the immersive and real-like representation of VR presents a *smoothness*, unified by the senses into a continuous world.[6]

Early VR theorists already spoke of the smooth quality of virtual environments, often referring to literary writing's capacity to create a coherent narrative that creates an illusion of immersion. Michael Heim, for example, claimed that "a world is not a collection of fragments, nor even an amalgam of pieces. It is a felt totality or whole". It is "not a collection of things but an active usage that relates things together, that links them ... World makes a web-like totality .... World is a total environment or surround-space" (Michael 2000, pp. 90–91). For Heim, moreover, worlds are existentially centred around a base we call home: "Home is the node from which we link to other places and other things .... Home is the point of action and node of linkage that becomes a thread weaving the multitude of things into a world" (Michael 2000, p. 92). In the context of historiography, the "web-like totality" that Heim suggests entails an augmentation of the database through sensibility and an ability to position ourselves within data. A world with an experiential quality that allows narratives to come forth. The craft of designing such event spaces is essentially architectural and complementary to historiography in designing such an inhabitable home.

Historical museums deal with such challenges: Weaving a multitude of things into a concrete spatial experience and designing an interface for historiography. The museum space demands a spatial order, direction, linearity and progression, all of which produce a "narrative landscape" (Ryan et al. 2016). Museum planners and designers arrange texts and stories along circulation paths that direct the movement of visitors and invest museum space with a sense of sequential, narrative order. Indeed, some contemporary museum buildings have been designed around the stories they intend to tell. This means that a museum's interior (and sometimes exterior) form provides an environment where the text "comes off the page" can be arranged in novel spatial configurations. Museums allow complex narratives to be told with the assistance of artefacts, texts (on inscriptions, labels and signs), reconstructions, audiovisual aids and human guides in a carefully controlled setting explicitly designed for this purpose. Notably, storytelling in museums is not constrained by linear time or continuous geography but allows spatiotemporal leaps through curation. VR, too, provides curation of event spaces.

The metaphor of the museum is not rare in digital heritage VR projects. As architects, we wish to push this metaphor further and imagine the design of a VR experience as a drawing plan for a museum without walls, defining an interactive environment to present historical materials as well as expose the manufacturing of political narratives. VR curation offers the opportunity to approach the site, and the archive about the site, with no apparent prioritization between their material presence and their non-material discursive mediation. In this materialist approach, both language and physical materials hold a reciprocal relationship in which "the symbol cannot exist without the substance, and the material reality of the substance holds a symbolic role" (Renfrew & Malafouris 2013, p. 59). Drawing inspiration from materialist thinkers such as Henri Bergson, Gilles Deleuze and Karen Barad, we embrace the idea that there are stratified epochs of revolution-based history, with new developments eradicating old systems. These approaches rethink how an archaeological object is conceived and suggest to:

> *record and represent the grain and patina of place through juxtapositions and interpenetrations of the historical and the contemporary, the political and the poetic, the discursive and the sensual; the conflation of oral testimony, anthology, memoir, biography, natural history and everything you might ever want to say about a place.*
> *(Pearson & Shanks 2001, pp. 68–69)*

To record everything, however, is, of course, impossible and futile. Nevertheless, capturing a flood of information can enable further "curation" in various ways, and the production of multiple presentations.

Wadi Salib

To examine a method of VR as critical historiography, we studied the site of Wadi Salib, a neighbourhood in downtown Haifa that tells a painful story of violence and destruction during the early years of the founding of the state of Israel. It is a landscape inflicted by wars and turmoil caused by grand ideologies of the first half of the 20th century that caused a displacement. First, during the Arab-Israel war of 1948, the Palestinian inhabitants fled the city in the name of the Palestinian "Nakba" (the displacement of the Palestinian population during the 1948 Arab-Israel War); then, during 1960–1980, a second displacement occurred when the state of Israel systemically "cleaned" the neighbourhood of its Moroccan Jewish inhabitants that settled in the abandoned Palestinian homes. Since the evacuation of Wadi Salib's last inhabitants, most of the neighbourhood's houses were levelled, with some still standing empty, as part of a strategic plan to "modernize the city".[7] Today, Wadi Salib stands in ruins empty amid Haifa. It is an urban-archaeological site stratified by narratives embedded within the dilapidated walls of houses. Slowly, several urban renewal projects are now underway.

In a semester-long course (spring 2021) for graduate architecture students at the Material Topology Research Lab at the Technion (Israel Institute of Technology), we sought to develop and test a methodology for critical historiography of Wadi Salib using VR. Following a series of preparatory lectures, ranging in topics from history, interactive design and real-time rendering techniques, we toured the neighbourhood of Wadi Salib extensively, accompanied by various guides, ex-habitants of Wadi Salib, who shared their stories about life there, now gone. A former inhabitant of Wadi Salib, who belonged to the second generation of residents, shared with the class his memories from his life at this place, mixed with historical anecdotes from multiple eras:

> When the shooting happened, I was standing right there at this very spot [he points towards the steps going uphill]. I heard the shot. By the way, this is just around the corner from where Haifa's mayor's son Ibrahim El Khalil was murdered twenty years before that (1939).

The guide opens his brown folder to show a photograph of Ibrahim El Khalil.

> Then, later, the Israeli prime minister came to visit the neighborhood of Wadi Salib before she gave the order to level the houses (1970). At first, there was an Arab family in this house; then we came in, then there was nothing. It's all gone now. Today, they preserve the buildings that remained; they want it to be an "old city center", to attract outsiders to come in.

This short story touches on several of Wadi Salib's difficult pasts: The Palestinian displacement in 1948, the shooting incident that triggered an uprising of Jewish-Mizrahis in 1959 and the gradual demolishing of Wadi Salib during the 1960s and 1970s by the state of Israel. More than other historical information sources, the tours provided uniquely contextual storytelling that was already immersive, as we were standing at the exact location of events. Such a guided tour triggers the imagination as it builds a "landscape narrative", constructing a story embedded in the site. The tour weaves a network of spaces and times into a spatial experience. We attempt to reproduce landscape narratives by using the immersive and interactive design of critical VR experiences. We aimed to design landscape narratives from a vast foundation of information using digital tools. A "database historiography" is mixed and remixed from a data repository that aims to move beyond a singular spatial experience and construct an engine capable of plotting multiple and diverse VR scenes.

Our work included footwork and archive research: Walking through the ruined houses of Wadi Salib and digging into public and private collections of historical materials. The simultaneous investigation of the actual site and its archive blurred our clear-boundary understanding of what is tangible and what is an intangible history of the site. The houses are empty and frozen in time; the stories and memories seem to cling to the remains. The conventional dichotomy of Tangible and Intangible Heritage, promoted by UNESCO, seems futile in Wadi Salib. "Tangible Cultural Heritage" refers to physical objects in varying scales – from monuments such as "architectural works, monumental sculpture and painting, elements or structures of an archaeological nature" to whole sites (UNESCO 1972). The various definitions provided by UNESCO and other organizations encompass material things as more concrete evidence and the presence of the past. UNESCO's "Intangible Cultural Heritage" refers to the "practices, representations, expressions, knowledge, skills that communities, groups, and, in some cases, individuals recognize as part of their cultural heritage" (UNESCO 2003). These definitions are manifested in the domains of "oral traditions and expressions, including language as a vehicle of the intangible cultural heritage; performing arts; social practices, rituals, and festive events; knowledge and practices; and traditional craftsmanship" (UNESCO 2003). Intangible heritage demands a participation component, an active way of knowing and an embodied experience. While tangible heritage practices closely examine concrete materials, intangible involves a tacit way of knowing by doing (Ingold 2013). The intangible entails a process rather than an object. Its appearance is temporal and often involves narratives.

To avoid too rigid conceptual compartmentalization of the materials we collected from the site itself and from archives, we suggest an in-between definition that lives in the liminal gap between these definitions, a "quasi-tangible" cultural heritage. By using the term "quasi", we echo Bruno Latour's conception of quasi-objects: Not static things to be preserved but "made to act by a large star-shaped web of mediators flowing in and out of it … [that] is made to exist by its many ties" (Latour 2005). Antonino Griffero, too, is drawn to the quasi-object as it is "responsible for one's feeling well (or not) in a space that is an 'in-between' – between perceiver and perceived" (Griffero 2016). A quasi-tangible cultural heritage model, then, acknowledges the agency of the perceiver as an active part of cultural heritage, Dominic LaCapra's *Secondary Witnessing*. Thus, the quasi-tangible follows a critical historiography approach by blurring boundaries between the tangible and intangible, object and subject, and fiction and fact and by undermining the modernist foray into irreconcilable binary oppositions (Ekbia 2009).

With this, we can capture the interaction between a spectator, a historian (ourselves as designers) and the place as a "landscape narrative". These are narratives organized "on the ground" that involve issues relating to the spatial form of text that is somewhat different from those involved in telling the story on the pages of a book, e-book or video screen. Configuring accounts in real-life settings can pose considerable challenges.

Methodology

As a first step, a digital model of the entire area was produced using drone photogrammetry. This model served not just as a "site" for the interpretations by the student teams but also as a type of portal for the students' projects. In each project, the site, its various interlocutors and its archival resources are all composed in the service of the narratives constructed by the students, through which Wadi Salib's complex histories can be seen anew. The efforts, which were then exhibited, provide epistemological and experiential cross-sections through the problematics of the site in the manner of critical historiography (Figure 5.1).

Students' work undertaken culminated in VR projects that posit a spectator inside a "site-archive": A virtual environment that synthesizes the site's built environment with archival materials is not unlike a guided tour. We attempted to design a data pipeline that generates these historiographical-synthetic VR environments. The methodology included (1) collecting data about and from the site of various types and media, which would then function as a foundation for further processing of the data. (2) We then employed computational methods (deploying Natural Language Processing to extract keywords and themes from text) to remix data, linking segments of texts and images into new narratives. (3) Finally, we rendered the newly composed narrative to a VR head-mounted display (HMD). Such a data pipeline, outputting experiential historiography,

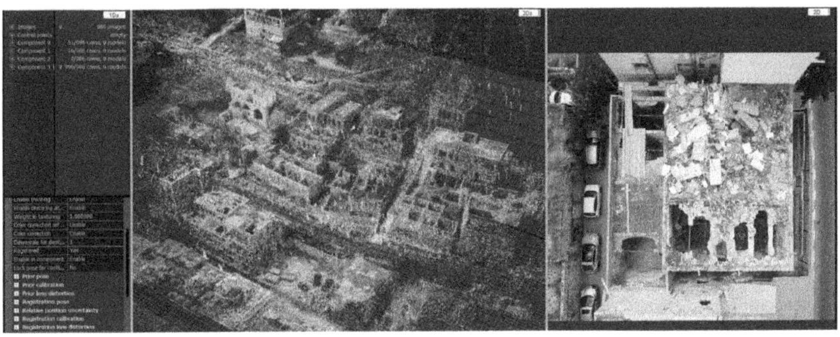

FIGURE 5.1 Drone photogrammetry model of Wadi Salib, produced during the course (MTRL 2021).

intends to unfold multiple, sometimes overlapping, spatial narratives – a collage image that includes architecture and oral or written stories about the site.

Data collection

Physical site

Direct collection included 3D scanning using drone and ground photogrammetry of the whole site laser scanning[8] for selected interior spaces, which produced a digital clone of the site on changing scale. The models were then implemented as a foundation layer for the design of VR scenes. Capturing the present state of ruination meant introducing a "present layer" to the VR projects that would curate past scenes.

Indirect collection entailed employing computational techniques to extract 3D spatial data about the site from archival materials, such as photos and film segments.[9] Unlike the direct collection, we attempted to use computational methods to extract space 3D information from historical photographs and reconstruct scenes. Transforming 2D photos into 3D space was proven limited using automated techniques since the photographs mostly lack the resolution and colour range to allow spatial reconstruction. We combined computational analysis with manual modelling to overcome reconstruction limitations (Figure 5.2).

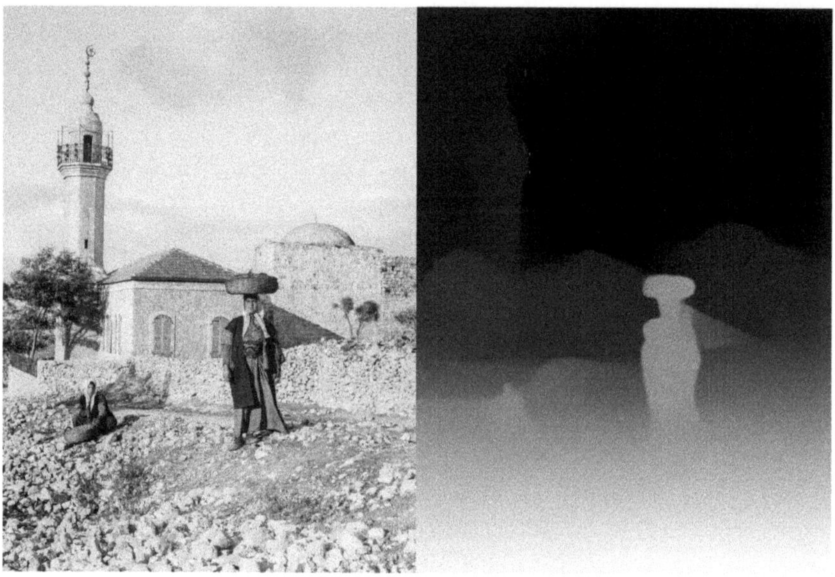

FIGURE 5.2 Reconstructing depth from 2D photograph, using monocular depth estimation.[a]
[a] Towards Robust Monocular Depth Estimation: Mixing Datasets for Zero-shot Cross-dataset Transfer. René Ranftl, Katrin Lasinger, David Hafner, Konrad Schindler and Vladlen Koltun https://arxiv.org/abs/1907.01341v3.

Stories

To collect oral and written history, we employed direct and indirect approaches:

Direct collection included interviewing individuals intimately acquainted with the site, such as former inhabitants and experts. The interviews included a series of questions about their memories and experience of the place: Who are you? When did you reside in Wadi Salib? What do you remember from this place? Can you recall the physical appearances of the houses?

We located former inhabitants through various networks, including Facebook groups. The interviewees included Jewish-Mizrahis, Palestinians and hobbyist urban historians who were all asked about their memories of Wadi Salib, their homes and the social life in the neighbourhood.

Indirect collection: Collection of archival oral and written stories from available archives and literature. Historian Yfaat Weiss's dense book *A Confiscated Memory: Wadi Salib and Haifa's lost Heritage* (24Weiss 1951) offered us an archival navigation map which we followed towards original documents such as "The Commission of Inquiry Into the Wadi Salib Events, the evidence of David Ben-Harush, July 26, 1959", and the "Provisional Arab Committee to the director of the Minorities Ministry, September 8, 1948", stored at the State Archive. We also assisted in Haifa Municipality's Department for Long-term Planning Archive.

Testimonies from reports, newspaper articles, films and other sources that recount events from various eras were collected as well. These are primarily organized around two main events – the 1948 Arab-Israel War and the 1959 Wadi Salib Riots of the Jewish-Mizrahi community were translated and added into the same database (Figure 5.3).

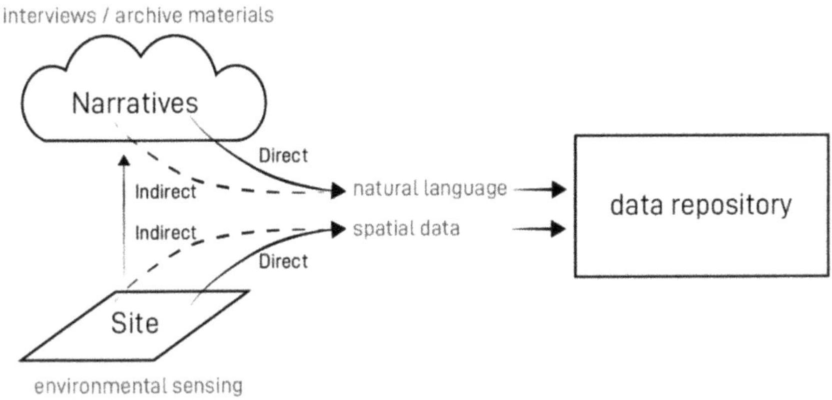

FIGURE 5.3 Simultaneous direct and indirect data collection and organization in a data repository allowed us to mix various data types, representing multiple epistemological registers.

Data analysis and remixing

The second phase of the methodology builds on the previous one and entails analyzing and remixing the data collected. We employed techniques to analyze natural language content (from interviews and literature) to identify and tag mentioning names of places, people and keywords. Working with spatial data produced by 3D scanning (geometry and point cloud file formats), we labelled segments of 3D digital models, to introduce metadata. Labelling both texts and 3D models allowed us to draw connections between textual descriptions to their physical locations within the site (Figure 5.4).

Immersive generative storytelling

The third phase of the method explored the plotting and rendering of the structured data to a VR HMD (Oculus Quest 2). For this, the students gained entry-level skills in designing interactive applications with Unity Game Engine, working with various media inside Unity, rendering in real time from a database to the screen and optimizing the projects for a VR render pipeline. The pipeline was designed to connect data segments according to various parameters – weaving together 3D models and components of text into a sequence of immersive scenes (Figure 5.5).

Breaking the work into these three phases, we planned the methodology to be a continuous sequence that aims to allow the content of the VR experience to evolve and transform, potentially closing a cycle between information and the site. This sequence was employed partially or fully in the students' projects.

For example, the project "60 Minutes" focused on the first defining event of Wadi Salib as a neighbourhood within the historical centre of Haifa. The 1948 Arab-Israeli War caused the evacuation of Wadi Salib from its Arab residences by Israel's armed forces of the "Hagana". In her book, historian Yfaat Weiss describes how Arab Haifa "faded instantly, in the blink of an eye, within just a few days in April (1947), no more" (Weiss 1951, p. 11). A curial moment occurred at noon on April 21, when the "Haganah" armed forces began their operation to take control of Haifa. Between April 21 and 22, a panic-stricken flight started on the Arab residents towards downtown Haifa and Wadi Salib. The fleeing crowd

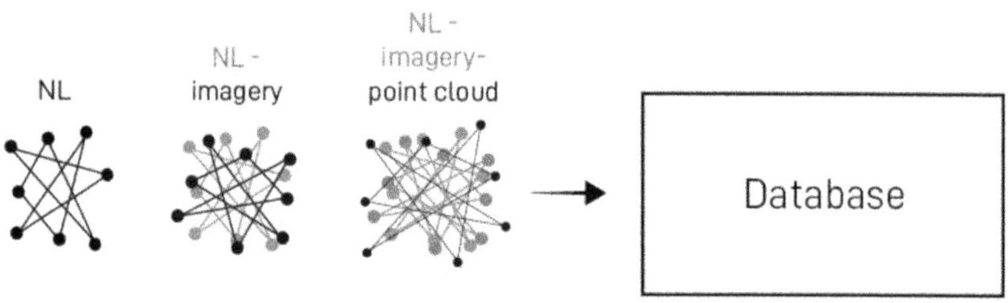

FIGURE 5.4 Labelling data prepared the materials for plotting new compositions.

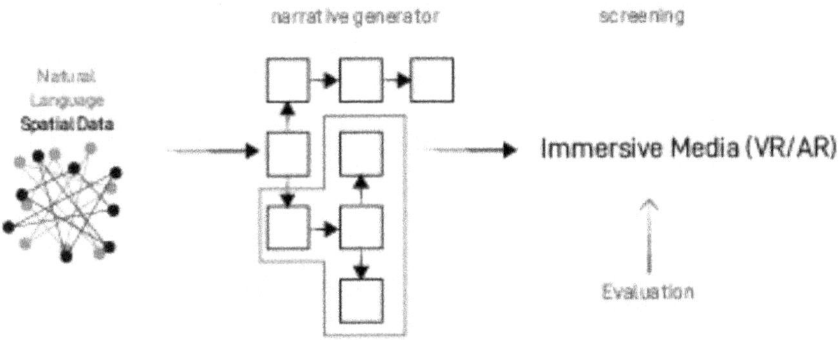

FIGURE 5.5 From data analysis to new data compositions rendered via VR HMD.

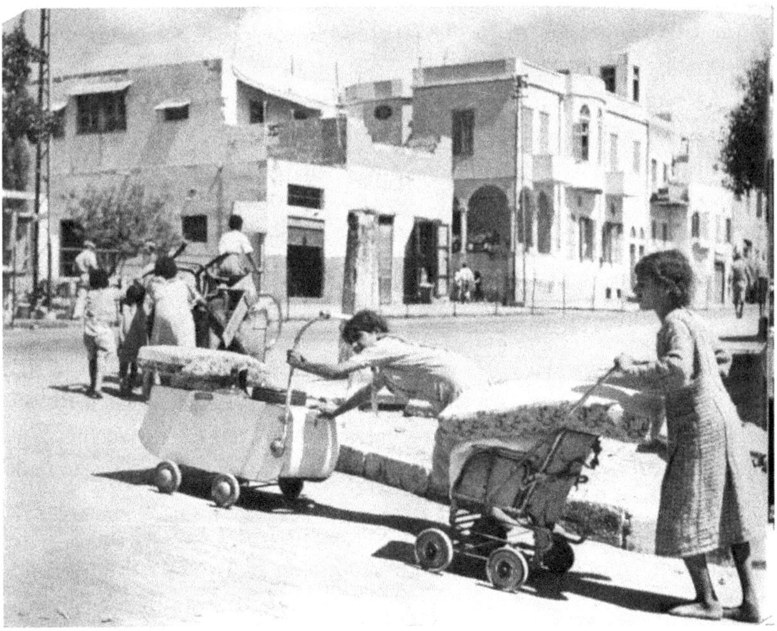

FIGURE 5.6 The Arab residents of Haifa fleeing the city during the 1948 war. Source: Hrant Nakashian, 1949 UN Archive.

infected residents with panic as it passed through the neighbourhood, and they joined in the escape. Arab delegation was convened to control the panic and decide whether to surrender or fight (Figure 5.6).

The VR project, designed and produced by David Keselman and Omer Ittah, both graduate architecture students, focused on these early events and followed the methodology above. First, the collection phase started with an archival investigation into the documents recording the events' hours before the fleeing, as recorded in the "Provisional Arab Committee to the director of the Minorities Ministry, September 8, 1948", at the "State Archive", and in historian Walid Khalidi's report from 1959, as referenced in Weiss's book (Weiss 1951, p. 20). Also, in the memoirs of the British observers, they noted that the position taken by the Jewish side was conciliatory and generally flexible. The meeting in the town hall between the Arabs and Jews lasted approximately an hour and a half, and upon its conclusion, the Arab representatives requested 24 hours for deliberation. This request was rejected, and they were asked to decide within an hour. The project focused on the 60 minutes in which the Arab delegation was assembled in a Khayyat's house in Wadi Salib, on what happened in that house during this time; an event spotted with uncertainty since there lacks a record of the negotiations, and historians' interpretations regarding this hour are divergent in their outlooks.[10]

The students first located the house that today stands in ruins. Over the years, the house's interior had become a shelter for the occasional homeless and a favourite location for graffiti artists. This ruined interior was 3D scanned using photogrammetry to produce a realistic simulation of its current state. The students then collected the available evidence on the occasion of the Arab delegations' discussions and transcoded the record from the conversation they could locate in which the two sides discussed the terms of surrender to the Israeli Hagana, some of which were disputed.

The 3D model outcomes from the scanning were then overlaid with sentences from the conversation, which were arranged in approximation to spatiotemporal order according to the house's rooms and order of occurrences. The scene was rendered to a VR HMD, allowing a user to walk through the ruined house and move between rooms while reading the segments of manuscripts from that night, that hour. Moving between the main room and the two adjacent rooms, the user can choose which discussion to participate in the Christian delegates sitting in the Northern room or the more militant Muslim representatives sitting in the Southern room.[11]

A full transcript of the events as they unfolded does not exist to our knowledge. The project embraced this gap by introducing indistinct talking sounds inside the VR experience that cannot be deciphered, hinting at missing pieces in the record. By allowing users to become "secondary witnesses" to the lost event space, to witness the discussions as well as the lack of record, the VR project employs a critical approach to historiography (Figure 5.7).

In another project titled "The Wadi Salib Riots", designed and produced by graduate architecture students Michal Orevi and Yael Leibovitch, the historical framing is of a later yet related event: The Wadi Salib Riots. Immediately after the fleeing of Wadi Salib's Arabs (1948), the new state of Israel directed newcomers – Jewish immigrants from Moroccans towards the empty houses of Wadi Salib. The transition of Wadi Salib from Arab to Jewish was swift.[12] When new residents – Jewish North-African immigrants – settled in the emptied Arab houses, it seemed that there was nothing left of the previous inhabitants. The former

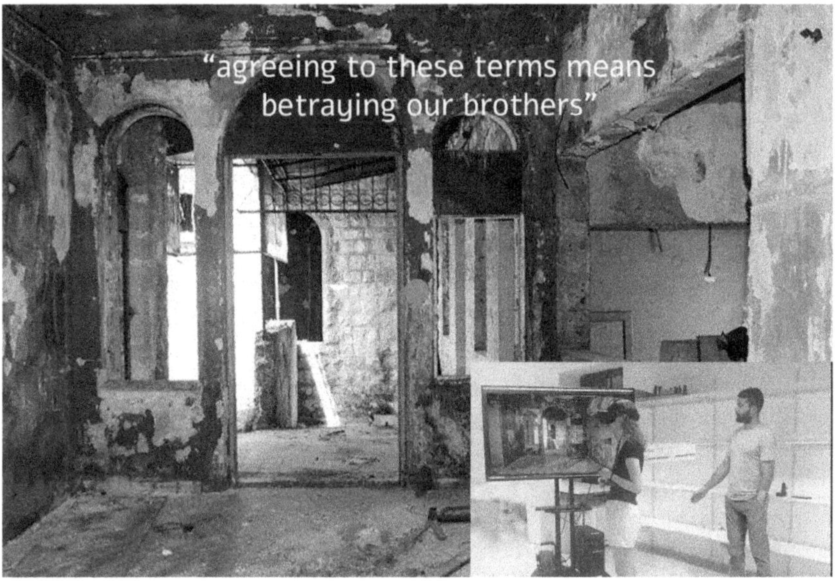

FIGURE 5.7 VR experience inserting a witness into the interior of a historic house, now abandoned. The transcription of negotiations of the Arab delegate is overlayed onto the rooms where they occurred. (David Keselman, Omer Ittah, Course:Virtual Real Environments, Instructor: Eytan Mann, MTRL, 2021).

Arab inhabitants were entirely forgotten (Weiss 1951, p. 11). What occurred in Wadi Salib after 1948 was compressed by historical memory into a single event, the "Wadi Salib Riots". These consisted of a chain of events during July and August of 1959, triggered by the tension between members of the North-African community residing in Wadi Salib and the Ashkenazi central government. The VR project focused on the event that triggered the riots: The shooting of a member of the Jewish-Mizrahi community by the Ashkenazi-controlled police on a summer evening of July 9, 1959. The shooting happened after the victim Ya'akob Akiva El-Karaiif, living in Wadi Salib at the time, entered one of the neighbourhood's coffee bars and asked for a glass of beer; the owner refused to sell him a beer, claiming he was already too drunk. Akiva responded by grabbing bottles and breaking them, which triggered a sequence of events. According to the report of the "Public Commission of Inquiry Into the Wadi Salib Shooting", after the bar brawl, a Jewish-Ashkenazi police Sargent Israel Walk felt under threat and shot Akiva in his stomach, leaving him disabled for the rest of his life. As the report recounts:

> Events unfolded rapidly. A policeman leaped from the patrol car while Akiva threw bottles at them, one after another, and hit, among other targets, the windshield of the patrol car. The police officers took cover behind

> the patrol vehicle, and then several shots were fired from Sergeant pistol through a hole in the windshield into the coffee bar. Akiva was hit and lay recumbent on the bar with a bleeding wound.[13]

Wadi Salib riots began the following day, triggered by this singular event, but propelled by years of systematic inequality and injustice against the Jewish-Mizrahi community of Wadi Salib, living in the emptied Palestinian houses. The Ashkenazi hegemony viewed the Mizrahim as passive recipients in Israel's then young Zionist state. In contrast, the Ashkenazim were seen as active contributors to creating the Zionist vision of a Jewish-national community in Israel. The demonstrators, members of this community, flood the streets in angry protest, waving black flags and placards with slogans such as "Where is justice?", "The police have killed an innocent man!", breaking windows of businesses in Haifa. The shooting incident sparked a wave of disturbances across the country and gave notice to the potential national repercussions of the local event (Figure 5.8).

The "Wadi Salib Riots" VR project collected available evidence about the shooting incident by directly interviewing individuals related to the events and identifying locations of the scenes, such as the bar where Akiva was shot and the city square to which the crowds assembled to protest that night. Simultaneously, the students engaged in archival work that included locating the original report on the event and viewing video interviews with witnesses.[14] The data was then segmented and tagged according to locations at the crime scene. Modelling the bar's interior where Akiva was shot and augmenting the model with superpositioned audio segments allowed a spatial narrative to be told in situ. Like in the previous project, gaps appeared in the story as "blind spots" in the archive. In

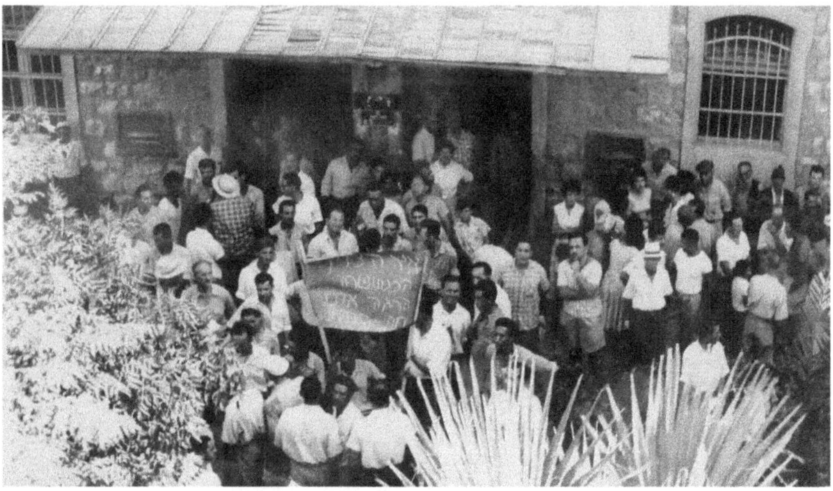

FIGURE 5.8 Wadi Salib Riots, 1959. Source: State Archive, photographed by Israeli Police, July 9, 1959.

such gaps, the design team manually produces a low-resolution model of the built environment – the street and houses' facades according to maps, intentionally presenting them in game-like graphics (Figure 5.9).

Finally, the VR experience was designed for a user to become a protagonist in the riots of the incident, to walk along the path of the marching men and women that day, supposedly on the night of July 9, 1959. As users walk inside the virtual reconstruction of the street, they witness a synthesized narration of the events from various sources. As they approach the shooting location, they are positioned inside a virtual environment made partly of a 3D scan of the current location and partially a white abstract model of the bar as it possibly was that night. As they hear a narration of the events, they are invited to reenact them, to become the protagonist as described in real time. During the scene, users are prompted to grab hold bottles behind the bar (using the VR hand controller) and follow the narration's pace as it recounts the events that evening when the victim of the shooting is upset and starts to throw bottles towards the street, smashing them on the pavement. In another scene, users are prompted to pick up a pistol from the pavement outside the bar, aim towards the bar and fire, this time inhabiting the character of the Sargent Israel Walk, who shot the victim. By encouraging participation in the events, the project attempts to transcend beyond witnessing and into the realm of reenactment of both the victim and the offensive police Sargent. The reenactment attempts to create new engagement and empathy with Ya'akob Akiva El-Karaiif, who got shot that night, allowing viewers who might not identify with the victim and renewed perspective. It aimed to provoke a sense of urgency and crisis visceral, allowing the user to "inhabit" the dry and laconic police reports. The possibility of assuming both opposing characters – Akiva inside the bar and the policeman standing outside – attempted to provoke a sense of Rashomon, not taking a clear ethical stance, but rather questioning a determinism, historical events that unfold in response to split-second decisions of individuals.

VR as critical historiography

Today, Wadi Salib stands mostly in ruins awaiting urban renewal. Here and there, new high-rise housing compounds are starting to appear instead of the ruined house. Digitally capturing the ruined historic houses and their histories is urgent in Wadi Salib since this landscape is on the cusp of changing. The methodology presented aims to go beyond digital preservation of the architectural ruins, develop a pipeline to collect archival data and link this data back to the site. By employing a computer-generated remix of the collected data, we attempt to produce a tool to generate multiple VR narratives that can alter and develop according to the parameters by which the information is organized. We created an engine for multiple, potentially endless narratives using this method, minimizing prioritization between historical periods or political identities. Overlaying a digital snapshot of a ruined site with historical materials echoes

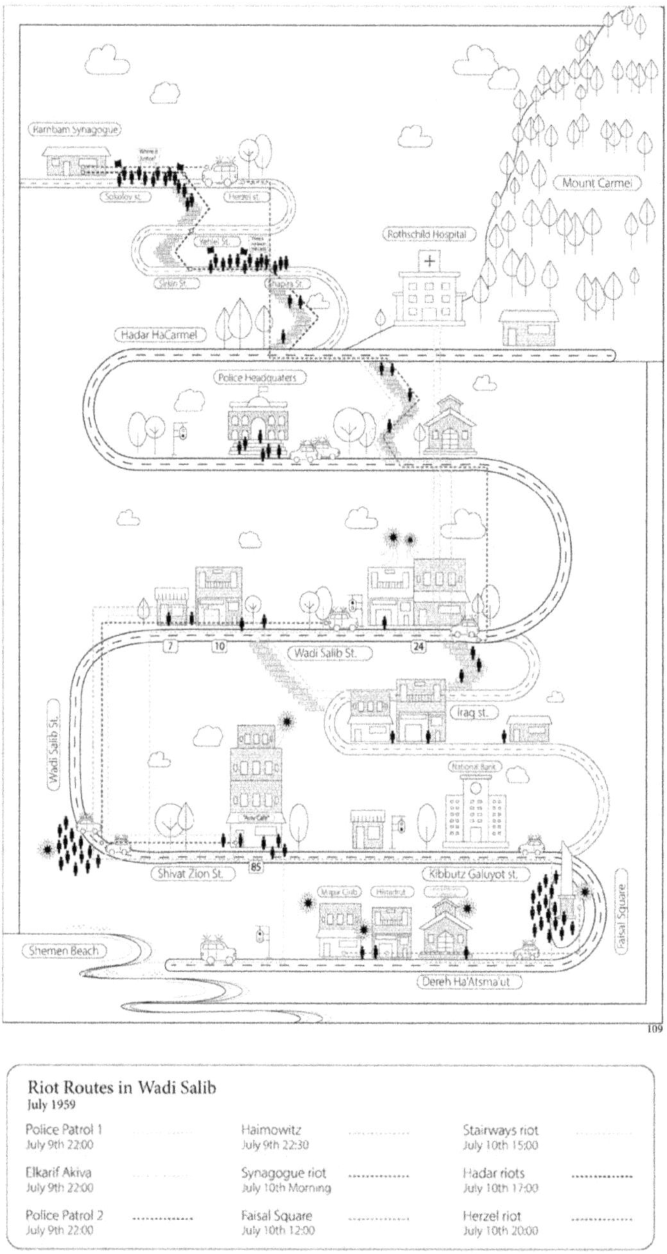

FIGURE 5.9 Diagram showing the reconstructed sequence of event spaces along the streets of the neighbourhood, localizing the record as depicted in "The Commission of Inquiry Into the Wadi Salib Events, the evidence of David Ben-Harush, July 26, 1959". (Yael Leibovitch, Michal Orevi, Course: Virtual Real Environments, Instructor: Eytan Mann, MTRL, 2021).

William Faulkner's character in the book *Requiem of a Nun*, proclaiming "the past is not dead, it's not even the past". This approach to historiography sees the past as not to be understood as severed from the present, so much as continually remade in the present through complex subjectivities. Society's relations to its past may be impoverished if they are confined to narrowly epistemic questions. Instead, VR as critical historiography aims to expand our understanding of the past through various entangled relationships that are political, aesthetic, material and emotional. Not history as fiction, but as sometimes fictional storytelling (Curthoys and Docker 2013).

For architecture students, the method deployed in Wadi Salib entails considering the site and the archive as materials of a landscape narrative while asking what is at stake when we act "inside" historiography. And how does VR help reconcile the difficult pasts of Wadi Salib? Inhabiting historiography entails what media historian William Uricchio defines as moving away from representation to active real-time and interactive simulation. Uricchio observes that the mediation opportunities through participation pose new and challenging questions about narrative authority. "What happens", he asked, "if we push the notion of mediation beyond language to the domain of game, enactment, or simulation? Does this allow us to slip out of the well-critiqued trap of representation? And if so, where does it land us?" (Uricchio 2005, p. 338).

The projects underline the affordance of VR as a medium to introduce a new participatory agency in the reading and writing of historical materials. To engage in a reenactment that constitutes a break with more traditional forms of historiography. Reenactment within a heritage context can demonstrate the uncanny, peculiar way we relate to the past and undermine the controlling and disciplining claims of an all-encompassing, authoritative historical mainstream. Reenactment as a motif, practice or genre is increasingly part of mainstream culture, from art with artists such as Carey Young, Marina Abramović and Jeremy Deller to music with the recent trend for musicians re-touring their seminal albums, from Sonic Youth to Primal Scream.

As a form of affective history – i.e., the historical representation that both takes affect as its object and attempts to elicit affect – reenactment is concerned with events and the individual's physical and psychological experience. This sort of affective history holds the potential to encourage sympathetic identification with the past, what Collingwood called the "precondition for historical understanding" (Nielsen, 1981).

As an offshoot of affective history, reenactment, specifically, seems to offer a framework within which multilayered and often contradicting narratives of contested sites, such as in the case of Wadi Salib, may be reduced to a comprehensible scale and historical grievances redressed in the present. Suppose critical VR historiography as a reenactment medium aims to gain legitimacy as a historical genre, it will be necessary to determine the extent to which affect can indeed be considered evidentiary. Reenactment tends to collapse temporalities, which implies forms of historical continuity that are potentially inaccurate and exploitable for ideological ends. Such risk will continue as long as reenactment ignores Walter Benjamin's insistence that historical empathy brings with it the question of perspective. Specifically, Benjamin's seventh thesis on the concept of history reminds us that empathizing with history's victors produces a corresponding kind of historical narrative.[15] If reenactment is to posit a genuinely new form of historical representation, it must remain open ended, allowing expressions of minor stories rather than grand narratives. VR as a medium of critical historiography can offer a common ground for historical empathy, inferring meaning in historical thoughts and actions based on evidence. Nonetheless, there is an inherent bias in a technique of historical inquiry due to the historian's position in the present and limited access to information about the past. Acknowledging that bias and exploring its impact on interpretation is key to engaging in historical empathy (VanSledright 2009).

Notes

1 For example, Lithodomos is a company founded by a team of archaeologists and artists that produced in 2018 a realistic reconstruction of ancient Jerusalem. This is a seamless depiction of Jerusalem in the time of King David (1010–970 BCE). The VR production "smooths" archaeological and historical speculation, often derived from political agenda, to appear as absolute reality. Lithodomos produces other urban environments such as London, Rome, Athens and other cities.

2 An exemplar project attempting to use the advantages of VR for representing contested sites while foregrounding the problem of representing narratives is a project by Georgios Artopoulos and Panayiotis Charalambous, showing the Paphos Gate in Nicosia. The medium of VR is used to visualize the historical palimpsest of the urban environment and engage users and local communities in the creative aspects of these environments' management. It shows a capacity of VR to enhance understanding of and engagement in architecture and its historical context, renewing cultural identity and fostering civic participation of diverse socio-cultural groups (Artopoulos 2019).

3 Plato is famous for a distinctive view of objective reality. He asserted roughly that the greatest reality was not in the ordinary physical objects we sense around us, but in what he calls Forms, or Ideas. Ordinary objects of our sense experience are real, but the Forms are a "higher reality", according to Plato. Having the greatest reality, they are the only truly objective reality, we could say. In epistemology, Plato accordingly distinguishes the highest knowledge as knowledge of the highest reality, the Forms. Our modern usage of the terms "objective knowledge" and "objective reality" seems to fit in reasonably well here. Aristotle, by contrast, identifies the ordinary objects of sense experience as the most objective reality. He calls them "primary substance." The forms of things he calls "secondary substance."". Hence, Aristotle's metaphysics seems to fit better than Plato's with our current understanding of objective reality.

4 The Material Topology Research Lab (MTRL) is a transdisciplinary research group, part of the Faculty of Architecture and Town Planning at the Technion (Israel Institute of Technology), working in the field of computational design, robotics and spatial simulation, exploring unique visualization, simulation and fabrication tools that are changing the way we imagine, make and inform our physical and cultural environments.

5 *September 1955 – A Virtual Documentary of the Istanbul Pogrom* shows some of the potential of VR storytelling, and the use of cutting-edge computational methods to offer new access to history through immersion. September 1955 is an 8-minute virtual-reality documentary of the Istanbul Pogrom, a government-initiated organized attack

on the minorities of Istanbul on September 6–7, 1955. This interactive installation places the viewer in a reconstructed photography studio in the midst of the pogrom, allowing one to witness the events from the perspective of a local shop-owner. The experience of the space induced by participating in the mundane activities of the photography studio aims to generate unique historical narratives that are reproduced and enacted by the viewer. See http://virtualxdesign.mit.edu/storm/76o0ihlgsph3n3iwtaniz7gttv01d0.

6 Deleuze and Guattari's smooth and striated architectures are adopted from biology: Smooth muscle consists of seemingly undifferentiated surfaces of single spindle-shaped cells whose contractions undulate and flow; striated muscles are regular, ordered and organized into strands of fibres forming a musculature which contracts and relaxes under voluntary control. Striated space, claim Deleuze and Guattari, consists predominantly of "closed intervals" and smooth space of "open intervals". Striated space "closes off surfaces"; smooth space consists of "distributed surfaces". These definitions promote architectural images, one being rigid and the other more dispersed, open-ended and free-formed (Deleuze, Gilles and Félix Guattari. *A Thousand Plateaus: Capitalism and Schizophrenia*. Bloomsbury Publishing, 1988. p. 500, quoted in: Buchanan, Ian and Gregg Lambert, eds. *Deleuze and Space*. University of Toronto Press, 2005).

7 Wadi Salib Strategic Plan, 1953, Ministry of Housing, State of Israel. Haifa Municipality Archive.

8 For drone photogrammetry, we used a DJI Mavic Pro, and for scanning the Trimble X7 scanner.

9 Techniques for extracting spatial information from images are: Photogrammetry reconstruction, depth mapping and available machine-learning models trained to identify architectural components in photographs.

10 The historical versions of this event are told by the Palestinian Walid Khalidi, son of Jerusalem, and the Jewish Ephraim Karsh, born in Haifa and generally identified with the right, are quite similar. Khalidi asserts that acceptance of the terms drafted by the Haganah would have relieved the English of their responsibility for the city's Arab residents. Were the local Palestinian representatives to have done so, they would in fact have put their fate in the hands of the Zionists. Karsh, on the other hand, maintains that since Haifa had been included in the territory of the future Jewish state according to the partition plan, acceptance of the terms in this city would in principle have denoted tacit acceptance of the principles of the partition plan, namely, acquiescence to Jewish sovereignty (Karsh 2001; Khalidi 1959).

11 According to historian Walid Khalidi's article "The Fall of Haifa", some 30 local residents, among the most prosperous in the city, reconvened in despondent mood at Khayyat's home in an attempt to formulate a policy with regard to the new situation that had arisen. They decided to dispatch a seven-man delegation to the town hall in the hope of ameliorating the conditions set by the Haganah. In his account, Walid Khalidi notes that British general Stockwell warned the Arab delegates that should they fail to sign the document, he would not be held accountable for the possible deaths of 300–400 more Arabs on the morrow. Khalidi goes on to relate that Khayyat replied: "What are you trying to do? We know Shabtai Levy, Ya'akov Salomon and all these people. We are old friends". Stockwell took this as an invitation to leave the room and to leave the two sides to themselves. When they failed to reach agreement, the Arab delegates were given a short extension of one hour. The Arab delegation returned to Khayyat's home, where the other committee members had been waiting all this time. In all probability this was the moment at which those present agreed upon a position, stating that they had no right to sign the terms of surrender.

12 One of the last to document the vanishing of the Arab Wadi Salib and the emergence of the Jewish neighbourhood was Binyamin Halfon, head of the Jewish Agency's Department of Jewish Affairs in the Middle East, upon being summoned towards the end of 1948 to visit the living quarters of the North African immigrants in the eastern

section of Haifa's downtown. Although the war had come to an end, its ravages were still evident in the city. These are Halfon's "impressions and observations of the visit":

> I left Haifa several weeks ago, and the old city was at the time a closed area that resembled a bubbling rubbish dump on which clumps of garbage, carcasses of pet animals, and remnants of unwanted articles were rotting at the mouth of the sewers. It was difficult to imagine that in these streets – between mounds of rubble no one knew when or how would be removed, in houses whose windows and floors had been ripped out, in buildings half of which were designated for demolition and the remainder still standing by some miracle – people would soon be living. But hither, in fact, immigrants were indeed sent, and it is these buildings that they, of their own accord, invade.
>
> *(Binyamin Halfon, the Jewish Agency for Palestine, the Department for Jewish Affairs in the Middle East, Visit to the North African Immigrants' Quarters [Haifa, End of December], Impressions and Observations of the Visit [in Hebrew], Central Zionist Archive (hereafter CZA), S20/10/41.)*

13 The Commission of Inquiry into the Events at Wadi Salib, evidence given by David Ben-Harush, July 26, 1959, State Archive, vol. 7253/1.

14 "People Are Everything", Israeli documentary TV series, 1990, interviews with witnesses of the riots (https://www.youtube.com/watch?v=sHUCRmZ0FnA&t=309s).

15 "There is no document of civilization which is not at the same time a document of barbarism. And just as such a document is not free of barbarism, barbarism taints also the manner in which it was transmitted from one owner to another. A historical materialist therefore dissociates himself from it as far as possible. He regards it as his task to brush history against the grain" (Benjamin 73).

References

Anderson, S. (2011). Technologies of History: Visual Media and the Eccentricity of the Past. In *Technologies of History: Visual Media and the Eccentricity of the Past* (pp. 122–201). UPNE.

Artopoulos, G. (2019). Virtual Environments as a Technological Interface Between Built Heritage and the Sustainable Development of the City. *IJEPR*, 8, 35–49.

Baudrillard, J. (1983). *Simulations*. MIT Press.

Benjamin, W. (1979). *One-Way Street*. New Left Books.

Benjamin, W. (1935). *The Work of Art in the Age of Mechanical Reproduction, 1936*. New Left Review Editions.

Clark, E. A. (2004). *History, Theory, Text: Historians and the Linguistic Turn*. Harvard University Press.

Curthoys, A., and Docker, J. (2013). The boundaries of history and fiction. In *The SAGE Handbook of Historical Theory*. SAGE Publications Ltd, pp. 202–220.

Danto, A. C. (1982). Narration and Knowledge. *Philosophy and Literature*, 6(1), 17–32.

Ekbia, H. (2009). Digital artifacts as quasi-objects: Qualification, mediation, and materiality. *Journal of the American Society for Information Science and Technology*, 60(12), 2554–2566.

Faulkner, W. (1919). *Requiem for a Nun*. Chatto & Windus.

Foucault, M. (1972). Archaeology of Knowledge. In *Archaeology of Knowledge*. Pantheon Books.

Griffero, T. (2016). Atmospheres: Aesthetics of emotional spaces. In *Atmospheres: Aesthetics of Emotional Spaces*. Taylor and Francis.

Hartoonian, G. (2020). *Time, History and Architecture : Essays on Critical Historiography.* Routledge.
Ingold, T. (2013). Making Anthropology, Archaeology, Art and Architecture. In *Making Anthropology, Archaeology, Art and Architecture.* Taylor and Francis.
Jarzombek, M. (1999). A Prolegomena to Critical Historiography. *Journal of Architectural Education*, 52(4), 197–206.
Karsh, E. (2001). Nakbat Haifa: Collapse and Dispersion of a Major Palestinian Community. *Middle Eastern Studies*, 37(4), 25–70.
Khalidi, W. (1959). *The Fall of Haifa*, 30–58. Middle East Forum.
LaCapra, D. (2014). *Writing History, Writing Trauma.* John Hopkins University Press.
Latour, B. (2005). *Reassembling the social: An introduction to actor-network theory.* Oxford University Press. P. 217
Lowenthal, D. (2015). *The Past Is a Foreign Country Revisited.* Cambridge University Press.
Michael, H. (2000). *Virtual Realism.* Oxford University Press.
Nielsen, M. H. (1981). Re-Enactment and Reconstruction in Collingwood's Philosophy of History. *History and Theory, 20*(1), 1.
Pearson, M., and Shanks, M. (2001). Theatre/Archaeology. In *Art and Archaeology: Collaborations, Conversations, Criticisms.* Routledge. https://doi.org/10.1007/978-1-4614-8990-0_14
Rajagopalan, M. (2012). Preservation and modernity: Competing perspectives, contested histories and the question of authenticity. *The SAGE Handbook of Architectural Theory.* SAGE Publications Ltd, 308.
Renfrew, C., and Malafouris, L. (2013). *How Things Shape the Mind: A Theory of Material Engagement.* MIT Press.
Ryan, M.-L., Foote, K. E., and Azaryahu, M. (2016). *Narrating Space/Spatializing Narrative : where narrative theory and geography meet.* Ohio State University Press.
Trouillot, M. (2015). *Silencing the Past: Power and the production of history.* Beacon Press.
Uricchio, W. (2005). Simulation, History, and Computer Games. In *Handbook of Computer Game Studies.* 327, 338
UNESCO (1972). Convention concerning the Protection of World Cultural and Natural Heritage was adopted by the General Conference of UNESCO on 16 November 1972.
UNESCO (2003) Convention for the Safeguarding of the Intangible Cultural Heritage, adopted by the UNESCO General Conference on 17 October 2003.
Vansledright, B. (2009). Thinking historically. *Journal of Curriculum Studies*, 41(3), 433–438.
Weiss, Y. (1951). *A Confiscated Memory: Wadi Salib and Haifa's Lost Heritage.* Columbia University Press.
White, H. (1978). *Tropics of Discourse Essays in Cultural Criticism.* Johns Hopkins University Press.
Zadeh, T. (2016). Uncertainty and the Archive. In *The Digital Humanities and Islamic & Middle East Studies.* Gruyter, pp. 11–64.

6

VIRTUAL HISTORY

VR, immersion and learning Holocaust history

Sara Pitcairn, Silvina Fernandez-Duque and Michael Haley Goldman

A visitor to the United States Holocaust Memorial Museum (USHMM) dons a Virtual Reality headset (VR).[1] The visitor sees a milk can that once held part of a secret archive from the Warsaw ghetto.[2] After a short time, the bare setting in which the milk can is displayed gives way to that of an office located in the Warsaw ghetto. Here, the visitor can explore documents and works of art collected in secret by ghetto residents. Finally, the visitor opens a door to a deserted scene of devastation in a Warsaw ghetto courtyard, hearing only a survivor's description of the ghetto after it was liquidated.

Emerging from the VR experience, the museum visitor tells a facilitator, "It felt surprisingly real. The 3D aspect was cool. I forgot there were people in the room and that I was at a museum … . Makes you feel more connected". This visitor's response speaks to the immersive, spatial, transportive and affective strengths of VR experiences. It also raises questions about what it means for a difficult or traumatic heritage to feel real, and for a visitor to have an embodied experience in a historical space or feel more connected to a difficult past. While these are not new questions, experiences that leverage new technologies can provide fresh insight.

Museums and cultural heritage sites have long employed immersive techniques to interpret the past. On a fundamental level, immersion can set a museum experience apart from the routines of everyday life. Practices that facilitate immersion include designing exhibit environments that, with varying degrees of accuracy, recreate historical settings offering opportunities for visitors to interact with spaces and objects beyond simply observing them and engaging multiple senses. These immersive techniques, among others, can provide a different perspective on the past and an individual's own relationship to it (Rymsza-Pawlowska 2017, 90–98).

DOI: 10.4324/9781003200659-7

Immersion in exhibitions

Even as technological developments enable new immersive possibilities, the function that immersion serves in current museum and public history practice is not new. Historian M.J. Rymsza-Pawlowska's analysis of historical interpretation around the 1976 U.S. Bicentennial illuminates strong parallels in the aims underpinning immersion nearly half a century ago and today. Through the recreation of historical settings, early examples of immersive museum experiences "fostered an experiential perception of history, ... worked to elicit in visitors the feeling of 'being there'" and "helped audiences both see and sense the past" (Rymsza-Pawlowska 2017, 90). Taken out of context, these descriptions of 1970s exhibitions could easily refer to VR experiences available today. Changes in perspectives and what individuals feel and sense remain key elements in immersive museum experiences.

Immersive exhibition experiences might be the last thing one expects from the history of the Holocaust. The graphic imagery and descriptions of traumatic events can be demanding and disturbing for visitors. The history of the Holocaust is unfamiliar for many who visit the United States Holocaust Memorial Museum, and they may find it difficult to understand how and why such a catastrophic event happened. Learning about the Holocaust can be uncomfortable, especially for young people, as it can challenge their worldview by exposing the extremes of human behaviour. In many ways, the main exhibition of the USHMM can be seen as an immersive environment to teach about the Holocaust. There are moments when the visitor moves from beyond a simple observer of artefacts to someone who becomes part of the story, such as when they receive an identification card[3] which describes one individual's experience during the Holocaust or when they opt to walk through a railcar in the exhibit about deportation to the concentration camps. In those moments, there is a deeper engagement with the perspective of the victim.

The main exhibition entitled *The Holocaust* begins with a large photo mural of American soldiers looking at burnt corpses on a pyre at the Ohrdruf concentration camp in 1945. The design of the space allows visitors to imagine themselves at that scene, to be standing opposite the soldiers and looking at the same bodies. A sense of immersion could begin even earlier, when the visitor steps into the main hall of the museum, where the design recalls train stations and industry and introduces asymmetry and hints at disequilibrium (Freed 1995, 104). The USHMM presents a factual, evidence-based history of the Holocaust, but as with many interactions with a difficult history, there is an emotional response that affects learning (Trofanenko 2011, 481–495). A typical visit to the USHMM is self-guided, and the visitor experiences a linear, chronological narrative documented through photographs, film, government documents, personal diaries and artefacts (Figure 6.1).

Immersion in museum experiences has alternately been viewed with promise, scepticism and controversy. Fundamental ideas about historical interpretation,

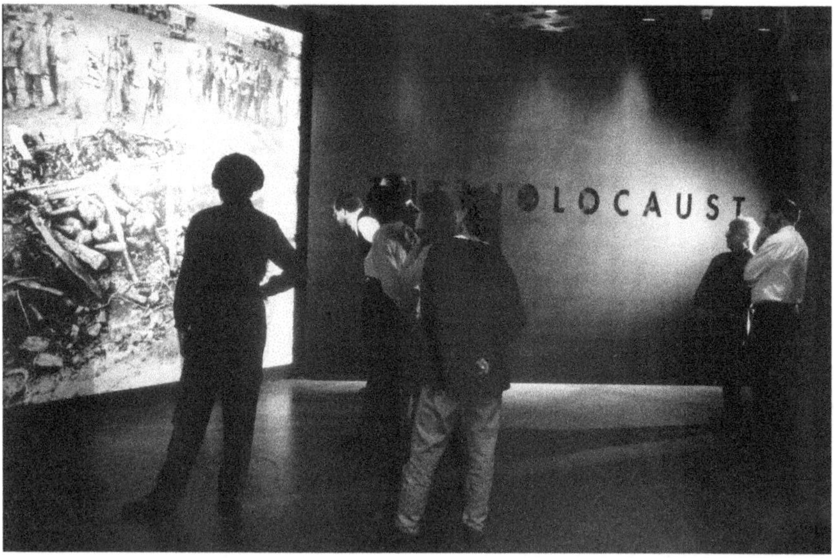

FIGURE 6.1 Visitors in the main exhibition of the United States Holocaust Memorial Museum. Copyright: United States Holocaust Memorial Museum.

authenticity and transparency have always been at play in these debates. Themes that frame contemporary discussions of immersive museum experiences emerge in earlier dialogue within the museum field about how objects should be displayed, the options an exhibition should provide for visitors to engage with those objects and the role of visitors within the museum setting (Rymsza-Pawlowska 2017, 90–98).

Immersive museum experiences invite visitors to play an active role in exploring the past and making meaning from it. Whether by encouraging different modes of participation, privileging a first-person perspective or fostering a more robust sense of place, immersion can make history feel more immediate. Emotion plays an important role in how individuals make meaning from museum experiences. John Falk and Lynn Dierking assert that museums evoke feelings of awe and reverence, as places where individuals encounter things that are out of the ordinary, including historically significant objects and narratives (Falk and Dierking 2016, 190–194). Immersion can also prompt visitors to draw connections between the past and present and reflect on relevance (Falk and Dierking 2016, 190–194). This meaning-making process is affective, informal and highly individual.

Immersive experiences, especially in evoking emotional responses and providing novelty, can be highly memorable. While factors that contribute to the memorability of a museum visit are not unique to immersive museum experiences, immersion may be particularly well suited to memory formation. The idea that memory and learning are inextricably linked is central to Falk and

Dierking's work on the evidence of learning in museums (Falk and Dierking 2016, 204–205, 214–216). The affective, participatory and novel aspects of immersive experiences can influence not only how individuals make meaning from museum experiences but also what individuals learn in museums (Falk and Dierking 2016, 204–205, 214–216).

It is important to acknowledge that visitors' varied affective responses to immersive experiences introduce a high degree of ambiguity for practitioners weighing the impressions, messages and lessons that visitors might take away from a museum or cultural heritage site. As Rymsza-Pawlowska asserts, "Appeals to emotion are wildly unstable and carry with them the potential for many kinds of readings" (Rymsza-Pawlowska 2017, 98). Museums and cultural heritage sites continue to grapple with the trepidation about immersion that springs from this ambiguity both in person and in virtual environments.

Visitors and difficult heritage

In developing programs and exhibitions that address difficult heritage, we must grapple with a range of visitor responses. Visitors may resist learning or exploring the stories and objects detailed in the exhibition because they are challenging; they may avoid reading labels or difficult imagery. Other visitors may develop empathy and form ideas about how the history is relevant to them today (Rose 2016, 34–48). And some visitors may think that all they need to know can be grasped in the course of their visit (Smith, Sullivan, Freeman and Alonso 2016, 382).

The idea of empathy or perspective taking is sometimes used as a tool for teaching history because it allows us to understand a situation from the perspective of another. Being emotionally engaged can also create opportunities for learning. Imagining a world other than our own and the context around people's behaviours and choices is key to understanding history and finding relevance in the past. Immersive experiences take advantage of these techniques. As we describe below, it is possible to create a simulated environment and allow one to take particular perspectives or play specific roles in an experience.

The affective, personal nature of how individuals perceive and make meaning from immersive museum experiences raises critical questions: How might the intent behind immersive techniques diverge from what visitors actually experience, remember and learn? What assumptions do audiences make about historical accuracy and authenticity in a museum setting? What is the role of transparency within an immersive environment? How might an immersive story about trauma affect a visitor's wellbeing and capacity for learning? Iterative design and audience research can help museums and cultural heritage sites navigate these questions.

There are risks when an immersive environment like VR recreates or simulates a traumatic history. While we may want visitors to the USHMM to identify with the victims of the Nazi regime and understand their persecution, it is not possible to know what they experienced. We've learned from classroom experiences that simulations of traumatic events and efforts to create empathy can be counterproductive. It risks trivializing and creating an unrealistic view of what happened, which simplifies the history and minimizes the experience of victims (Totten 2000, 165–171). Simulations can also risk a sense of over-identification with victims (Gubkin 2015, 103–120; Rose 2016, 36) and create a need for redemptive closure, which privileges redemptive narratives (Gubkin 2015). And one must be aware of the risk that the playful or novel aspect of an immersive environment will overshadow the substance of the history; immersive technologies should be in service of the story and objectives for an experience related to difficult heritage.

Virtual reality (VR) was famously described as "the ultimate empathy machine" by Chris Milk in a 2015 TED Talk (Milk 2015). But that characterization raises important questions about VR's appropriateness for creating immersive experiences about the Holocaust. Virtual reality experiences have been created to raise awareness of genocide and mass atrocities using 360-degree video, augmented reality (AR), volumetric VR and other virtual technologies. Using VR and immersive experiences to transport casual users to the centre of a victim's trauma risks exploiting their pain in the guise of empathy. There are many paths to generating empathy: books, films and first-person narratives all contribute to our understanding of a situation outside our own. We must question whether VR does this task efficiently or unfailingly. There is a power in finding yourself transported when you put on a VR headset, but the presumption that your simulated experience is equivalent to the actual experience is flawed. This flaw is particularly salient when dealing with sensitive subjects like war, genocide and the Holocaust. It is tempting to use the VR machine to take you immediately into someone else's shoes – to assume that you will gain knowledge this way – but it can be a trap. There is value in visualizing a spatial environment that cannot be gleaned from photos or written descriptions, but we can only enter that place of trauma from the perspective of an observer; the complexity and impossibility of knowing someone's traumatic situation should be at the forefront.

In using VR to teach the history of the Holocaust it is important to remember that the history is complex, with people making difficult choices and motivated by many different factors. Creating an experience where the role of the participant is appropriate is key to mitigating the risks of immersive environments. Our examination of VR interrogated what type of agency is appropriate for both learning and engagement.

Religion scholar Liora Gubkin's framework of "engaged witnessing" has influenced our thinking about creating immersive experiences related to Holocaust history. An experience where the participant takes on the role of a victim or perpetrator would not be appropriate nor achieve our goals. Gubkin's engaged witnessing offers a vision for grappling with difficult history that does not rely on identification or risk the trivialization of trauma; it also requires appropriate historical context – an emotional experience without an understanding of historical context is not meaningful learning. Engaged witnessing also describes multiple subject positions, which allows for an understanding of historical complexity and avoids simple narratives. It is also important to make more explicit how we know what we know, to examine the sources of information and to offer opportunities for reflection and dialogue (Gubkin 2015). All of these factors inform our approach to creating immersive experiences to mitigate any risks associated with affective responses, empathy and perspective taking.

Listening to audiences in immersion

Recent technological developments, such as readily available and affordable VR, have expanded the set of tools that museums and cultural heritage sites can use to create immersive experiences. While these tools afford some new and different opportunities, their affordances are part of the longer trajectory of spatial, participatory and multisensory techniques deployed in museums since the mid-20th century (Rymsza-Pawlowska 2017, 90–98). Therefore, longstanding questions about the benefits and dangers of immersion remain relevant today, especially for museums and heritage sites addressing difficult pasts.

Computer-generated realities offer museums a number of opportunities for immersive visitor experiences. VR headsets successfully fool the senses of the viewer so that they feel they are physically present in the space being displayed. Because the viewer feels physically immersed in a space, they also perceive themselves as able to act in that space, with a sense of agency. Within some VR experiences, the amount of agency given to the viewer can be quite extensive and allow actions akin to movement in real space. In addition to agency, spaces in VR are effectively limitless. The virtual space can adapt to the needs of the immersive experience by being as large or small as needed.

These three capabilities of VR – presence, agency and space – combine to provide opportunities for museum immersive experiences. Instead of showing a collection object in a display case, VR can place the object in its original setting. Instead of showing a scale model, these technologies can show the full size of objects that would never fit into a typical gallery. Historical settings can be recreated, microscopic environments grown to human scale, and imaginary spaces made real despite their failure to obey the laws of physics.

We imagined several ways that we could take advantage of VR technology to enhance teaching about the history of the Holocaust. Our approach to exploring immersive technologies has been three-fold: to understand the technology, to understand how to apply the technology with difficult history and to understand how our audiences experienced the technology.

Designing a successful experience relies on learning from our audience. It was important not only to test an experience as we built it to make sure that we were checking our assumptions but also to share authority by listening to and incorporating our audience's ideas. We learned through a variety of experiments, asking many questions about immersion and VR. These experiments allowed us to explore immersive technologies with our audience to understand how we could leverage them to teach about the Holocaust.

We began with viewing 360-degree videos in VR headsets. Initial experiments included the use of widely available video as well as staff-created productions that could be tested with the public. These projects gave us a greater appreciation for the importance of perspective and point of view in an immersive environment. In addition to 360-degree video, we tested a wide variety of virtual and spatial technologies with audiences and staff. Over the course of two years, we developed projects ranging from spatialized audio to projected 3D spaces to a variety of AR prototypes.

By working with audiences to understand these varied prototypes and programs, we learned about the affordances and spatial qualities of immersive technologies. The sense of presence offered by an immersive environment and the layering of storytelling within a spatial context allows for embodied learning that can have a lasting and affective impact on the user. We also gained a greater appreciation for how to approach difficult history in an immersive environment with nuance and respect. The perspective that a user takes on and the level of agency within an immersive experience is key to creating an experience that is respectful of both the subject matter and the user. Additionally, we developed tools and techniques for gathering quantitative and qualitative data to investigate affect and learning in an immersive environment.

We base our observations on the impact of VR and related technologies on our continual practice of exploratory, formative evaluation of simple prototypes. Prototyping allows our team to continually improve the experiences we create through an understanding of visitor experience. Using simple techniques including observation, open-ended questioning, AB testing and group interviews, we shape our products based on interactions with the audience. Formative testing is not a substitute for more formal summative evaluation but deepens our understanding of a new experience's potential and informs the questions we will ask.

Learning from a VR prototype

Through all of this exploration, data collection and analysis, we felt confident that we could create an immersive VR experience around difficult themes of the Holocaust that adhered to our values, did not traumatize the viewer and built on what we had learned. To explore how visitors might respond to a VR experience about the Holocaust, we looked at a significant but ordinary object in the main exhibition that has layers of meaning that are not immediately apparent. Our challenge was to see how we could help visitors understand the historical context of the milk can described at the start of this chapter. Could an immersive experience with a specific point of view and context help unlock the history and impact of this object?

In September 2019, we worked with an external partner, 371 Productions, to iteratively design, build and test a volumetric VR prototype. Our primary goal was to explore the potential power of VR as a medium for learning about Holocaust history. The prototype VR experience centred on stories from the Warsaw ghetto milk can on display in the museum's main exhibition. It included three distinct scenes with differing narrative approaches, levels of interactivity, completeness and media integration. Incorporating different types of scenes provided valuable points of comparison for our team and participants, yielding more varied learnings than we initially expected (Figure 6.2).

This exploration was structured as a two-week residency, which helped us not only gain a better understanding of the affordances of VR but also of the benefits of on-site, iterative, prototype development and the specific challenges and needs of VR production. Conveniently located in a flexible space within the museum, our team was able to reach both visitors and a significant number of USHMM affiliates, a group that included staff members, academic research fellows, contractors and volunteers. Each day, we invited visitors and USHMM affiliates to try the evolving VR experience. Observations and interviews with participants allowed for immediate feedback on the VR production, which raised important questions about usability, content and experience design. This formative prototype evaluation used open-ended, qualitative techniques to give us a thorough understanding of the experience including 86 interviews and observation sessions. The questions raised during the formative evaluation will be used to shape the summative evaluation once a final version of the experience is created in 2022 (Figure 6.3).

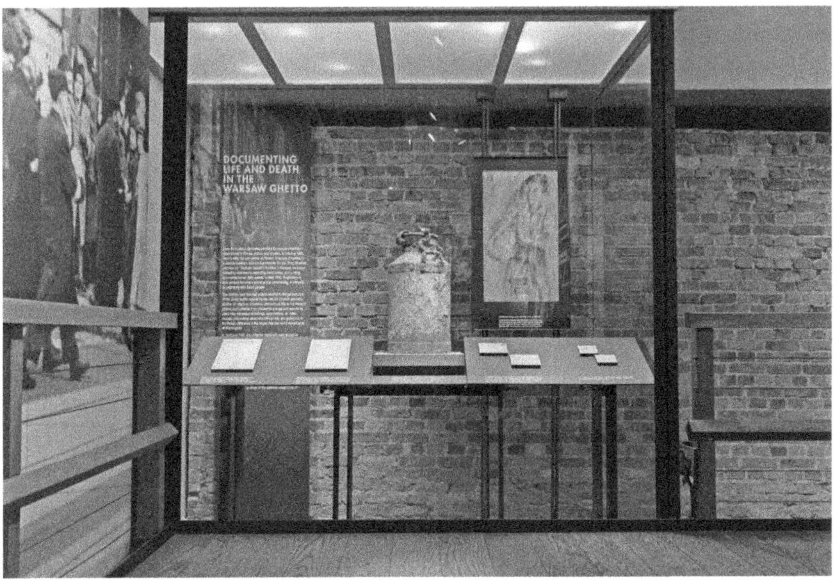

FIGURE 6.2 One of the milk cans used by Warsaw ghetto historian Emanuel Ringelblum on display in the main exhibition of the United States Holocaust Memorial Museum. Copyright: United States Holocaust Memorial Museum.

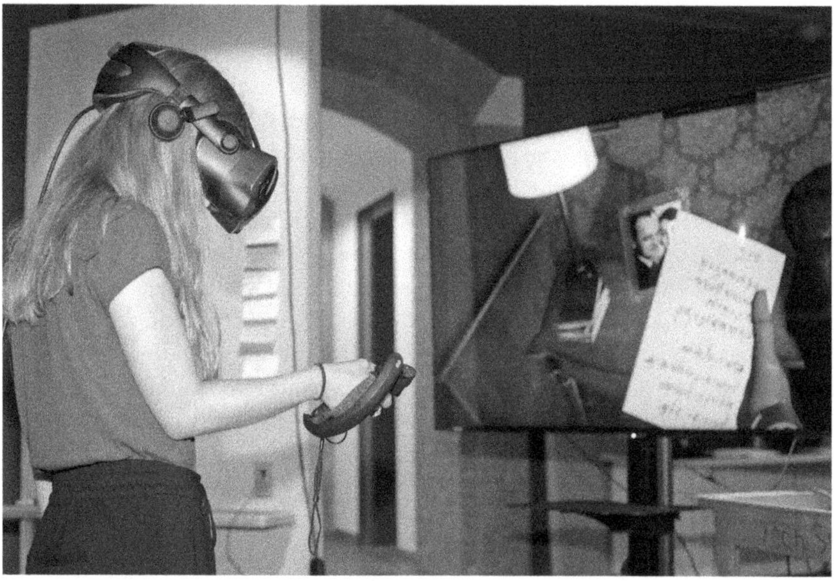

FIGURE 6.3 A participant wearing a VR headset and using hand controllers explores the virtual reality experience at the United States Holocaust Memorial Museum in 2019. Copyright: United States Holocaust Memorial Museum.

Based on feedback from visitors and USHMM affiliates, our external VR production partner continually made changes to the VR prototype for the duration of the residency. The interview questions we asked USHMM affiliates and visitors also evolved. We consistently asked participants about their impressions of the experience, which aspects of the VR experience stood out most to them, and whether the VR experience affected their perspective on Holocaust history. While the team ultimately collected data using three different sets of interview questions, the themes that emerged from participants' responses remained consistent throughout the VR residency. Instead of asking directly about respondents' sense of immersion or whether the VR experience prompted an emotional reaction, we posed open-ended interview questions to elicit a broad range of qualitative responses. The team then looked for themes and indicators of immersive and affective experiences emergent from participants' responses.

While focused on VR, this exploration provided insight into elements of storytelling and design that can inform the development of any immersive experience – regardless of format or medium. Our findings point to several key factors that influence how audiences understand and make meaning from difficult heritage in an immersive environment: context, perspective, agency and role. When working in the medium of VR, practical considerations around physical and emotional safety, production values and facilitation are also crucial.

Our understanding of context encompasses what participants experienced both within and outside a VR headset. We refer not only to the settings that participants explored within the VR experience but also to the logistics of where and how participants encountered the VR prototype and the introduction or preparation they received before trying it. Participant experiences within and outside a VR headset influence one another, especially when it comes to a sense of presence – the feeling of "being there".

To introduce historical context and prepare participants for the VR experience, we provided this brief overview for participants to read before donning the VR headset:

> In September 1939, Nazi forces invaded Poland. Soon after, Polish Jewish historian Emanuel Ringelblum began collecting documents, recording testimonies, and writing commentaries on daily events in Warsaw. The Jews trapped inside the Warsaw ghetto were subject to violence, starvation, and infectious disease. Ringelblum knew that the Nazi persecution of the Jews was unprecedented, and he was determined to leave a record for future historians.
>
> Ringelblum organised several dozen people to create a secret archive. This group sought to capture a wide range of voices and first-hand accounts of everyday life in the ghetto. To avoid any suspicion, they met on Saturdays, the Sabbath, and took the name Oneg Shabbat – "Joy of the Sabbath". The Oneg Shabbat asked contributors to keep their work secret for fear of what the Nazis would do if they found out.
>
> As the Nazis intensified deportations from the Warsaw ghetto to killing centers, there was a greater need to hide and preserve the archive. In 1942 and 1943, several members of the Oneg Shabbat packed the archive in metal containers, including three milk cans, and buried them.
>
> Surviving members of the Oneg Shabbat led a search team to recover the archive after the end of the war. This archive survived the Holocaust, even though many of its creators did not.
>
> In this VR experience, you will see one of the milk cans used to hide the archive, explore Emanuel Ringelblum's study, and hear survivor Rachel Auerbach's[4] description of the ghetto after it was liquidated.[5]

While this information was available to participants, we could not require them to read it. Based on participants' requests for more historical context during interviews, we learned that this type of background information should ideally be integrated into the VR experience itself or conveyed in a non-text format.

The VR experience prototype consists of three scenes – an introduction, an exploration of Ringelblum's study and a view after a deportation. In the introduction, users see the rusty milk can that is on display in the main exhibition of the USHMM. This short segment plays automatically and transitions the user to the next scene, the home office of Emanuel Ringelblum. Here the visitor can walk around the space and interact with primary documents such as a poem or a newspaper announcement. Users can use the hand controllers to pick up documents and hear a translation in English. The exploration in this scene is self-guided, and users can spend as much time as they want. When they are ready to move on, they open the door to transition to the third and final segment of the experience. In this last scene, the user stands in a courtyard alley surrounded by buildings and furniture strewn on the ground. The scene is quiet, and the user can walk around. A voiceover begins automatically, and the user hears a translation of Rachel Auerbach's letter describing the great deportation of the Warsaw ghetto in July 1942.

When encountering this VR experience within the context of a museum visit, participants made comments that reflect implicit trust or certainty that the prototype VR experience is an accurate and authentic representation of the past. Where one USHMM affiliate was explicit about an assumption of accuracy by stating, "The environments were nicely done. They seemed authoritatively researched", other participants used words like "real" and "actual" to refer to spaces within the VR experience.[6] Another USHMM affiliate remarked, "The office was the most impactful. This is a real space that existed, it isn't made up", while a visitor stated, "It was really impactful to be in the actual rooms and places". These comments reinforce the need for careful historical interpretation and transparency.

Unlike textual description, VR must contend with our often incomplete understanding of historical spaces. For historical spaces to be rendered in VR, there will be a need to fill in physical details that go beyond what can be found in available primary sources, which will force museums and cultural heritage sites to make and support historical interpretations of physical details. For example, many USHMM affiliates expressed concerns about the portrayal of Ringelblum's study in the VR experience, arguing that his personal space in the Warsaw ghetto would have been smaller and less refined. Creating spaces in VR requires cultural institutions to make careful historical interpretations and to be transparent about the sources and processes behind their interpretive decisions. Currently, there are no simple ways to indicate the level of research and certainty behind each element in a VR experience.

Considerations around accessibility, safety, production values and facilitation can have a major impact on how an individual perceives context, perspective, agency and role in VR. While our prototype did not address the need for accessibility, responsible creation of immersive experiences must also account for how well VR and other immersive technologies support access by people with disabilities. A 2017 survey by the Disability Visibility Project and Industrial Light and Magic's xLAB found a wide range of problems with VR devices and experiences, and little progress has been made in addressing these issues (Wong, Gillis and Peck n.d.; Philips 2020). Among these considerations, facilitation is the most adaptable. Practitioners can gain insight into how visitors are responding to an immersive experience and adjust their facilitation approach accordingly.

Facilitation can mitigate uncertainty while promoting greater familiarity with both a particular VR experience and VR as a medium.

Uncertainty and a lack of familiarity manifested in multiple ways in participants' responses. A lack of familiarity with the setting in which a person is placed when they put on a VR headset can cause hesitancy or even fear. It is important for practitioners to consider that these feelings may be more prevalent in the context of difficult heritage. One USHMM affiliate remarked, "I wasn't familiar with the space, so I was afraid to move around .... While it was beautiful, I wasn't sure where I could go". Another participant "really wasn't sure what was going to happen and didn't really feel prepared for what to do within each section". For this participant, uncertainty meant that they "felt a little lost" throughout the VR experience. In a similar vein, another participant talked about the negative affective impact of uncertainty: "It made me feel like I was doing something wrong when I couldn't pick up an object". This participant offered that "it would be nice to have some indication of what rooms and objects you can interact with and the ones you can't". As these comments suggest, effective facilitation may alleviate unease, apprehension, and other negative feelings by setting clear expectations for what participants will experience and be able to do when they put on a headset.

Still, it is reasonable for practitioners to expect that some people will be more comfortable than others with the ambiguity of what to do in an unfamiliar VR setting. One participant described becoming acquainted with the VR environment as "kind of trial and error. Eventually you figure out what you can and cannot interact with, especially in the office". Going further, another participant described a more experimental approach to testing the affordances of the VR environment:

> No, I've never done VR before. I got a bit of information prior, like that I couldn't open doors etc., but I still tried to do stuff I was told I couldn't do. I watched the screen when someone else was doing stuff and tried to learn the rules by watching. I was curious about the *rules* within that world.

While this comment speaks to the exploratory mindset of the participant, it also raises questions about whether they were more focused on discovering the "rules" of the VR experience than on the history it conveyed. Practitioners must weigh how the design of a VR experience can effectively balance setting explicit expectations and allowing for interactive discovery and exploration alongside storytelling that supports the overall goals of the experience.

Participants gave voice not only to their uncertainty but also to concerns about safety. One participant described how the experience was "immersive, but I had to remember not to trip over the wire too; I could tell I was getting close to the walls". The participant went on to describe that it was "cool to be placed somewhat inside of that history". The phrasing "somewhat inside" points to how concerns about safety can impede one's feeling of immersion. Concerns about safety can also constrain one's actions in VR, as one participant described, "I guess I didn't realise how much you could actually walk around. The cord was really awkward and restricted me. I didn't want to trip or unplug anything". Overall, these concerns may detract from a VR experience by creating a perception of limited possibilities for interaction and inhibiting the feeling of immersion. One participant described a negative experience beyond these detractions, stating, "In terms of the VR technology, I felt very anxious and claustrophobic. It felt unsafe just walking in the void, which made it hard for me to be immersed in the experience". It is important to recognize that, perhaps regardless of context, some may not feel comfortable or safe in VR.

Many participants commented on the distinction between the VR experience and traditional classroom, reading and museum experiences, due in part to greater interactivity and a sense of immersion. As expected, some participants compared the VR experience to other media with which they have greater familiarity, such as videos and digital games. According to one participant, "It reminded me of being in a video game. I was constantly asking what can and can't you do". One visitor contrasted the VR experience with other media they encountered within the museum itself, saying that they "expected something boring based on videos elsewhere in the museum but found this very interactive and engaging".

In our experience, the public frequently associates VR with gaming. Games are the most common application available for VR headsets. Many perceive games, and VR by association, as non-serious and thus questionable as a medium for exploring difficult subject matter such as genocide. Games, however, have long been used to examine difficult subjects and social change. The "Games for Change" and "Serious Play" conferences have brought together designers, activists, educators and others since 2004 and 2009, respectively, to explore the idea that games can address serious issues and ask important questions.

VR experiences take advantage of several important aspects of games, most importantly the sense of *agency* for the player. The ability of a player to make meaningful choices in games defines games for many in the field (Sharp and Thomas 2019, 151–177). The perception of choice in a VR experience contributes to the experience of virtual spaces as real or authentic, as discussed previously.

By offering a different perspective on history, the immediacy of VR immersion facilitates a learning experience that is qualitatively different from other ways of learning history. Several participants in the Warsaw ghetto VR remarked on being immersed in a 3D environment saying, for example, "The three-dimensionality is different. I think about the ways to take in information in the museum – the processed historical perspective, hearing someone describe their experiences – none are quite the same as experiencing something in 3D". Going further, USHMM affiliates articulated that this sense of immersion in a 3D space can afford a different perspective on history. One described how "standing in the courtyard, [you] get a sense you don't get from a photo … Can't get the sense of space from other materials". Another stated, "It had an impact on my feelings about VR. Just in terms of providing a sense of place – it does offer something really different than the other materials we have on the same subject". For another USHMM affiliate, immersion in a 3D environment offered "new images and experiences to associate with this history". These examples indicate that the perspective afforded by VR immersion offers something valuable for the study of history that other forms of media do not, including archival materials on their own.

Of course, many participants specifically described their emotional reaction to direct quotes and images from primary-source documentation. In answering what stood out most about the VR experience, one visitor detailed how the narration in the final scene combined powerfully with the embodied experience in VR. "The ghetto – the floating feathers. When she says that it came from the bed linens of dead people, I was like 'woah' because I had just reached out to touch one". The same visitor also commented on the digital representations of archival materials in the VR scene set in Emanuel Ringelblum's study: "Also the documents, the art. The woman wanted her art to survive so this never happens again. It's powerful". This affective response to the VR experience was typical of many participants' reactions.

Half of the participants we interviewed described how the affective impact of the VR experience contributed to emotional rather than intellectual understanding. Aside from using words like powerful or impactful, one participant summed up their affective response by describing the VR experience as "an interesting way to *feel* the history". A visitor spoke to the way in which VR immersion can enhance the connection one feels to the past, saying, "I feel a little more connected to it. I felt more personally connected *for sure*. It makes you feel it, and experience it emotionally rather than intellectually". Additionally, we learned that emotional impact can be different from one scene to the next, depending on a scene's interactivity, content and narrative approach. One visitor differentiated between two scenes by saying, "That was more like, kind of, getting information and hearing about it. The office gave background. As soon as I saw the liquidation, I was shocked. I felt a new wave of emotions".

Many VR experiences encourage active physical exploration of virtual spaces. Through the use of hand controllers, VR experiences can also encourage interaction with virtual objects. Participants responded positively to the active and interactive nature of the prototype VR experience. Each scene of the prototype VR experience allowed participants to experience a dynamic view in VR while walking around an empty space in the museum. Additionally, one scene in the VR experience centred on virtually picking up and examining archival materials.

In an interactive scene set in Emanuel Ringelblum's study, participants could pick up and examine virtual representations of documents from the Oneg Shabbat archive. Referring to the virtual hands that allowed participants to grasp documents of interest, one stated, "The movement of it was very realistic. The hand thing was … I don't know, it wasn't perfect, but gave a tactile understanding of the scene". This participant's experience indicates that interactivity, like perspective, can also contribute to a different type of historical understanding.

Through this interactive scene, the VR experience made archival materials available to visitors and USHMM affiliates in a way that few might otherwise access them. Participants' positive responses to interacting with documents in VR suggest that VR is another medium through which the museum can provide access to primary sources. Options for making a primary source's contents accessible in VR include reading the contents of documents aloud in voiceovers and/or adding readable text translations to virtual representations of documents.

VR affords a combination of agency and change in perspective that can serve as a platform to interrogate how participants perceive their identity and role when immersed in a historical setting. When considering their identity and role in the VR experience, participants seemed to make a distinction between feeling like one's self and feeling like a different person, and between having a passive or active role in the experience. While participants largely sensed that the scenes they were exploring were set in the past, some commented that the scene set in Emanuel Ringelblum's study felt like they were visiting a preserved space in the present.

A small number of participants perceived that, through VR, they were embodying a real person who lived the history firsthand, whether as Emanuel Ringelblum, Rachel Auerbach or someone else who experienced life in the Warsaw ghetto. Referring to the final scene in which a female voice narrates Rachel Auerbach's written account of the aftermath of liquidation, one visitor said, "thought I was the girl who was talking". When asked about the scene set in Emanuel Ringelblum's office, a USHMM affiliate stated, "I assumed it was my office and I was playing the role of Ringelblum". With less specificity, one visitor remarked, "I knew who I was – a refugee in a ghetto. Shocked by everything around me". Another participant described, "I kind of felt like I was someone else. Like a young kid realising that everything she knew was gone". Others perceived the experience through the perspective of a different person who had a more passive, rather than active or direct, role in the history. "I felt that I was a person who had discovered something that was disturbing and was trying to comprehend why this was so disturbing".

While these responses refer to a range of identities and roles, they demonstrate that immersion can create the perception of a first-person experience of history. Because we did not intend for participants to embody any particular historical identity or role, this insight was especially important for our team to learn. We would not have been able to understand the power of VR immersion to influence one's perception of identity and role in a historical setting without developing this prototype VR experience and talking to participants.

Most participants who discussed identity and role felt like themselves, having been transported to the past. There was some variation, however, in whether participants felt that they were playing an active or a passive role in the past. Perhaps due to a high level of interactivity, some participants felt that they were playing an active role in the past as themselves in the scene set in Emanuel Ringelblum's study. The following responses illustrate this response:

- "It was different, as if you've gone to visit someone, you've been invited into their home".
- "Actually, I definitely felt more like a visitor to the house – more like I was participating".
- "It felt like I was living back during this time. Felt so real".

The dominant perception about identity and role among participants was the feeling of one's self being transported to the past as a passive observer. The terms "time traveler" and "observer" were common, as in the following responses. "My point of view on the scene was that I was a visitor to the scene … almost like I was a time traveler". "I maintained an observer kind of status – without another 'human' to interact with, I was just transported there and observing". This response was common for both the scene set in Emanuel Ringelblum's study and the final scene in an outdoor space in the Warsaw ghetto after liquidation.

Technical limitations could also contribute to the audience's sense of self during a VR experience. Although constantly improving, VR creators still struggle to believably portray humans in a VR space. Because of this, many projects remove humans from the experience altogether. This decision to allow audiences to move through empty spaces that should be crowded often misrepresents historical spaces. For Holocaust history, for example, showing an empty ghetto in Poland misrepresents the historical experience of overcrowding. While technological advances might make realistic VR portrayals of humans more feasible, ethical questions about representing the historical reality of overcrowding in VR remain.

Unexpectedly, some participants indicated that the interactive scene set in Emanuel Ringelblum's study gave them the impression that they were visiting a historic site in the present. One participant said that the study "has a museum quality – like walking around a historic house". Another elaborated, "I felt I was just, almost like being in a place where you don't know the people but can see their lives and the things they have – like an antique show".

It is important to note that not every participant articulated a clear role that they embodied in the VR experience. Grappling with their role, one participant "assumed, whatever character was, was someone simply there – don't know if I was supposed to be a Jewish person". Another participant gave voice to their uncertainty by narrating the questions running through their mind. "I was thinking – Why am I standing there? When everyone has been deported? Did I survive? Am I a scavenger?" Participants' inability to articulate a clear identity and role highlights an important consideration for practitioners about how prescriptive a VR experience should be in order to achieve the objectives of a project and remain respectful of difficult histories.

Managing immersion for difficult history

Recognizing their inherent limitations as well as the potential of immersive experiences, how can the field best approach creating these experiences responsibly? Initially, museums and heritage institutions must address why immersive experiences serve as an appropriate and beneficial response to the needs of their audiences. What problem does an immersive experience solve for audiences trying to understand a difficult past? As suggested above, immersive experiences have the capacity to bring a sense of immediacy and connection to audiences. Do those capabilities align with the goals of the program?

However, even a clear alignment between the affordances of immersion with institutional goals cannot ensure that an immersive experience benefits audiences. Practitioners must also attend to the embedded values of the experience that shape the encounter. As explored in the interrogation of games, for example, implied values shape the experience and can have a detrimental impact on the outcomes of playing. Game projects often rely on explicit shared values for their creative teams. By developing a clear set of values to guide the project, creators can monitor the work for unintended impact on the audience. Similarly, establishing shared values for an immersive experience can help a project team stay true to its goals.

Another guardrail that keeps immersive experiences for difficult pasts on track is the development of an atmosphere of respect for all aspects of the project. This, of course, starts with respect for the subject matter itself. How does the immersion create the appropriate tone for the specific history? Can the project be transparent about the decisions being made to create the immersion? Project teams must make interpretive decisions while creating immersion, but clear statements of the historical work and reasoning behind these decisions create room for meaningful discussion of these choices.

Respect must also incorporate the communities surrounding the difficult history. What role does the community have in shaping their own narrative by participating in the creation of and commenting on the immersive experience? How can the project set clear expectations with the community about the nature of the project and how different voices and opinions will be accounted for? Members of a community often do not have a unified position, but an open, respectful review process can help make sure that the project's goals and values are shared with the community.

Finally, the creation of immersive experiences should respect the audience. The visitor's trust in cultural institutions demands that we reciprocate by creating safe virtual spaces in which they can learn about difficult history. The experience needs to meet them where they are and begin with their existing understanding of the subject. Can the project help facilitate their reflection on the experience? How can their synthesis of the experience be supported long after they have left the experience behind? Respecting the audience requires owning the introduction of difficult subjects and being ready to continue the conversation afterwards.

Ultimately, even with these elements – alignment, values and respect – immersive experiences represent a limited component of the larger work in understanding Holocaust history (in our case). On its own, an excellent experience visiting a museum, taking a class, or immersing in VR will neither ensure the continuation of Holocaust memory nor inoculate the public against extremist hate. Immersive experiences are by their nature ephemeral. By addressing the issues discussed above, the creation of thoughtful though imperfect experiences serves an important role in improving our understanding of the use of these experiences for audiences while simultaneously introducing audiences to the questions and problems of the history of the Holocaust. Immersive projects are a single step in the larger ongoing dialogue between educators, historians, curators and others on one hand and the general public on the other.

Reflective practices allow the creators of these experiences to improve their knowledge of the potential and pitfalls of immersive experiences while simultaneously continuing the discussion of the history itself. As creators, we must use each project as an opportunity to improve our understanding of practice. Audiences, meanwhile, are still adjusting to the vocabulary of digital immersive spaces. The growth of audience expectations and comfort in digital immersive environments will sharpen the use of these environments for educational and historical purposes.

Notes

1 The views expressed here are those of the authors and do not necessarily reflect those of the United States Holocaust Memorial Museum.
2 The milk can is an artefact on display in the USHMM's main exhibition and represents a story of Jewish resistance in the Warsaw ghetto during the Holocaust.
3 Each person visiting the USHMM's main exhibition receives an identification card that describes the experience of an individual who lived in Europe during World War II. Designed as small booklets to be carried throughout the exhibition, the personal stories help to humanize the scope and scale of the Holocaust.
4 Rachel Auerbach was one of three surviving members of the Oneg Shabbat group led by Emanuel Ringelblum. In the Warsaw ghetto, she ran the soup kitchen and also coordinated social welfare assistance. After the war, she spearheaded the search for the archive underneath the rubble of Warsaw and dedicated her life to collecting the testimonies of Holocaust survivors.
5 This text was adapted or pulled directly from several public-facing USHMM sources on this topic, including an exhibition text panel, social media post and podcast episode.
6 This and all subsequent interview quotes in the "Listening to Audiences in Immersion" section come from interviews of 86 participants who tried the VR experience in September 2019 at the USHMM.

Bibliography

Falk, John and Lynn Dierking. 2016. *The Museum Experience Revisited*. New York: Routledge.

Freed, James Ingo. 1995. "The United States Holocaust Memorial Museum: A Dialogue with Memory." *Curator: The Museum Journal* 38, no. 2 (June): 95–110.

Gubkin, Liora. 2015. "From Empathetic Understanding to Engaged Witnessing: Encountering Trauma in the Holocaust Classroom." *Teaching Theology & Religion* 18, no.2 (April): 103–120.

Milk, Chris. "How Virtual Reality Can Create the Ultimate Empathy Machine." Filmed March 2015 at TED2015, Vancouver, Canada, video, 10:25. https://www.ted.com/talks/chris_milk_how_virtual_reality_can_create_the_ultimate_empathy_machine

Phillips, Kaitlin Ugolik. 2020. "Virtual Reality Has an Accessibility Problem." *Scientific American*, January 29, 2020. https://blogs.scientificamerican.com/voices/virtual-reality-has-an-accessibility-problem/

Rose, Julia. 2016. *Interpreting Difficult History at Museums and Historic Sites* Lanham, MD: Rowman & Littlefield.

Rymsza-Pawlowska, M.J. 2017. *History Comes Alive: Public History and Popular Culture in the 1970s*. Chapel Hill: University of North Carolina Press.

Sharp, John and David Thomas. 2019. *Fun, Taste, & Games: An Aesthetics of the Idle, Unproductive, and Otherwise Playful*. Cambridge, MA: MIT Press.

Smith, Amy Fisher, C. R. Sullivan, Erin K. Freeman and Alyssa Alonso. 2016. "Ambivalent engagement: relational connection and depthful dwelling in a site of conscience." *Holocaust Studies* 22: 372–397.

Totten, Samuel. 2000. "Diminishing the Complexity and Horror of the Holocaust: Using Simulations in an Attempt to Convey Historical Experiences." *Social Education* 64, no.3 (April): 165–171.

Trofanenko, Brenda M. 2011 "On Difficult History Displayed: The Pedagogical Challenges of Interminable Learning." *Museum Management and Curatorship* 26, no. 5: 481–495.

Wong, Alice, Hannah Gillis, and Ben Peck. n.d. "VR Accessibility: Survey for People with Disabilities." *Disability Visibility Project and ILMxLAB*. Accessed March 1, 2021. https://drive.google.com/file/d/0B0VwTVwReMqLMFIzdzVVaVdaTFk/view?resourcekey=0-3X6VtbtDNvcbResutE_EVA

7

PRACTICES OF DIGITAL IMMERSION FOR THE STUDY OF BUILT HERITAGE AS A PROMOTER OF EQUITY IN URBAN SITES CHALLENGED BY DIFFICULT PASTS

Georgios Artopoulos

Today's fracturing identities and boundaries, exacerbated by global economic and political crises, intensifying migrations of people and consequent hostile tensions across borders internationally and within Europe, means that historic cities are facing acute cohesion challenges of physical, sociopolitical and/or cultural division. The integration of existing and new cultures, migrants and settlers in contemporary societies is arguably the most pressing challenge that Europe is facing in our era. A process of migration involves a change in space and environment, and the transformation of one's territory. People from various cultures meet in new "interface" sites, and this event intensifies their awareness of diversity (Mary Louise Pratt 2005). Individuals embody emergent practices that associate their original territories with the new ones, while at the same time they are bringing along their identities.

Part of this chapter's motivation owes to the current discourse on participatory methods in sustainable heritage (Gravagnuolo, Micheletti and Bosone 2021), as it aims to address everyday pressures on urban heritage sites from uncoordinated transformation through appropriation or incremental decay, and the subsequent structural and material failure of built heritage. This decay can be induced by the lack or inability of maintenance of a built construction due to scarcity of economic resources by its residents, inefficient governance and policy frameworks or challenges in social inclusion and often leads to the ghettoization of a neighbourhood that is left behind. In time, this condition can give rise to gentrification by means of well-documented processes of international capital investment, which more often than not has negative results on the social cohesion of the area (Butler and Robson 2001). This is particularly true in cases of the historic city centres of second- and third-tier cities in the European south (Giannakourou 2005), which were more exposed to the recent global economic crisis and regional conflicts than the rest of Europe. This condition brought to the fore new issues for these

DOI: 10.4324/9781003200659-8

cities due to weak policy frameworks, impact of climate change and population movement.

This chapter discusses a rare case of these conditions in the European territory, the historic core of Nicosia, Cyprus, the built environment of which is characterized by a dense palimpsest of historic structures – an urban terrain contested by bi-communal conflict (Calame and Charlesworth 2009). Specifically, the chapter will reflect on the capacity of practices of digital immersion for the contribution of positive everyday experiences to the inhabitants of historic neighbourhoods that are facing tensions due to their contested histories. Going beyond the relevant literature (Pilides and Alpha 2012), theoretical considerations will be raised through the analysis of a practice-led research about the fragmented, forgotten and threatened built heritage of Nicosia. Analysing and discovering the various elements comprising the palimpsest of urban life and city architecture can offer new ways of convergence between the various communities inhabiting Nicosia's past and present.

The war of 1974 and the subsequent division of its urban fabric has led the inhabitants of the centre to move away from the ever-present buffer zone that spatializes the conflict in the previously considered popular neighbourhoods (Zesimou 1998). The impact of this depopulation of the urban centre rendered these historic neighbourhoods that host the majority of Nicosia's built heritage of more than ten centuries empty of residents and prone to decay. This transformation through which one of the more significant assets of the city, i.e., its core which embodies the city's identity, has gradually undergone since the first violent incidents between the two communities in 1958 has had a negative impact on the function, experience and image of the city centre. This became even more evident after the introduction of the so-called green line by the British administration in 1960 which was later on consolidated as a hard border of the division with the events of 1974. This condition of the historic space has had multiple effects on future opportunities for the city's reactivation. Notably, as both its pre-conflict (Leventis 2005) and contemporary (as presented below) realities illustrate, this is a space where numerous traces of co-existing communities in the past can be identified that could function as a very compelling example of how a historic place can be approached as a promoter of multi-culturalism (Artopoulos and Bakirtzis 2016).

Historic Nicosia as a city-wide difficult heritage site

The historic city of Nicosia is a complex historic environment where, under the typical multiplicities of a contemporary urban landscape, lie both the political issue of division and the memory of a shared past. After the consolidation of the city's physical division in 1974, as a result of the invasion of Turkey to protect the Turkish-Cypriot community from an ill-conceived military coup organized by the dictators in Athens for the unification of the island with mainland Greece, the once shared urban landscape became a contested frontline between the

Greek-Cypriot (G/C) and Turkish-Cypriot (T/C) communities. This divided reality filtered the daily experience of the city directly influencing the ways heritage was perceived and interpreted, especially in regards to monuments and sites associated with the community that now lived on the other side of the dividing line. The cityscape of Nicosia contains many tensions and, as such, it comprises a particularly fruitful context to probe a series of inquiries concerning the perception, transformation and appropriation of heritage space.

Greater Nicosia is probably the only area in Cyprus to boast continuous habitation since the Bronze Age, 2500 BC (Michaelides 2012). Nicosia became the centre of administration and the island's capital between the 9th and the 10th century and served as the seat of the Byzantine governor of Cyprus. Nicosia became the Capital of the Lusignan Kingdom in 1192, to be conquered by the Venetians in 1474, and the Ottomans in 1570. The country was later included in the appendices of the British Empire in 1878, until the foundation of the Republic of Cyprus in 1959, only to experience civil and urban conflict for more than a decade, and the impact of an intercommunal war that led to its division in 1974. The city served as the island's capital from the Mediaeval period and has since been a centre of administrative and commercial activity. Its historic core is still defined by the iconic circular fortification system built by the Venetians in 1567–1569. The mediaeval core of Nicosia hosted all these historical events which have led to the complex overlay of built heritage and historical narratives that comprise its very rich, multi-layered architectural palimpsest.

The neighbourhoods of the historic core, instead of celebrating the city's long and important past, as captured by the Byzantine, Frankish, Venetian, Ottoman, colonial and modern architecture that comprises its built environment, they were, and to a certain degree still are, considered as the trauma of the city, a difficult heritage that is interpreted by both communities as the singularity of their conflict. This was provoked by the contested performance of space as the stage of conflicts that led to the separation of the urban fabric between north and south by the "green line" for peacekeeping, but also due to the ever-after omnipresent buffer zone, which became the symbol of loss and trouble for both sides of the Turkish Northern Cyprus and the Greek-Cypriot Republic of Cyprus, while the island remains divided to this day. In response to this condition, the inhabitants moved away from this area to expand and populate the suburbs of the city (Figure 7.1).

This rapid growth of the suburbs generated by the need for housing, in combination with the local planning regulations, evoked multiple urbanization issues for the authorities and inhabitants. In stark contrast with the spatial qualities of the old city, these built environments are characterized by the lack, or fragmentation, of public space, resulting in low levels of livability and vivacity (Patsavos and Pissourios 2018). At the same time, many historic neighbourhoods of the post-traumatic environment near and around the buffer zone are now populated and appropriated by migrant communities (Syrian, Nigerian, Bangladeshi, Filipino, Pakistani and others), who moved in since the 1990s (and furthermore

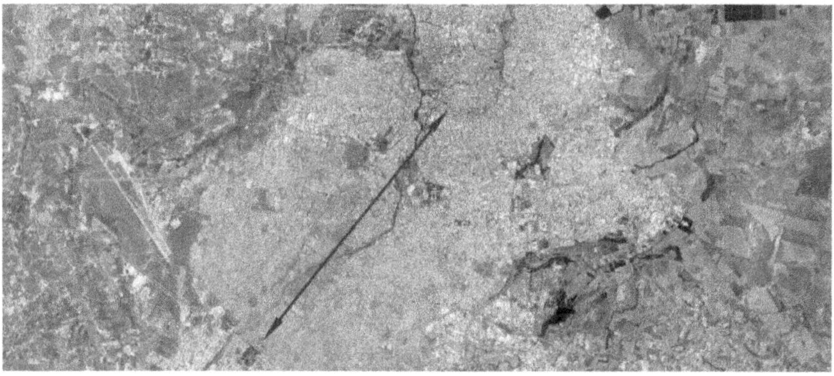

FIGURE 7.1 After 1974 Nicosia grew rapidly to the south, expanding its suburban areas as far as 15 km away from the old city core, occupying an area of 15 × 15 km, resulting in a built environment of very low density by EU standards. Image by Google Maps, processed by the author.

recently due to the migration crisis in the eastern Mediterranean and Middle East region) to occupy the abandoned building stock in the historic core, which is listed as heritage.

Recently the historic core of Nicosia is increasingly getting to be known once again for its ethnic multiplicity. In the past few decades, the city underwent rapid population change due to a high concentration of immigrants with official census statistics revealing that the percentage of Third Country Nationals has risen from 9% to over 15% (Population Census 2001 & 2011) and that immigrants have reached approximately 44% of the walled city population. This percentage is much higher today due to the thousands of refugees arriving on the island during the last few years. Nicosia Municipality has benefitted from EU Structural Funds, Solidarity and other funds and developed a range of social and cultural infrastructure and services to promote social inclusion and integration of immigrants in the local community (e.g., http://mingle.projectsgallery.eu). Migration and urban revitalization projects, such as the Eleftherias Square by Zaha Hadid Architects, the new City Hall, the creative industries neighbourhood by the buffer zone (a regenerative development project implemented by the Municipality, cf. Interregeurope 2020), and the pedestrianization of the main streets, are laying the grounds for the emergence of a new place identity, for the city to play a more international, contemporary role and be welcoming to innovation and tourism. There are no official stats to allow for any safe conclusions regarding the impact of these initiatives of the Municipality of Nicosia on the north part of the city, but as conveyed by the Municipality, its aim is to address also individuals and groups who are based in the T/C side of the city (RISE 2019). The old city is a testimony to the relationship between material heritage (e.g., historic buildings and monuments) and immaterial heritage from a traditional perspective; in a more contemporary perspective, the increasing multi-ethnic expression also creates new patrimonies-to-be.

In addition, Nicosia's complex built heritage that is populated by said social groups and communities, is largely threatened, as documented in United Nations Development Programme – Partnership For the Future and the bi-communal Technical Committee's reports (UNDP 2021). This vulnerability does not only concern the inaccessible built structures that lie in decay stuck in the buffer zone (Europa Nostra 2018) but also many buildings in the inhabited parts of the city. Laudable efforts are made by the Municipality to transform the centre into an attractive destination for young families and professionals in the creative industries by investing in renovating a select number of building facades and streetscapes in areas of special interest according to the strategic agenda of the local authorities, e.g., the conservation of heritage buildings in the area of the new City Hall adjacent to the Cultural and Creative Industries District (Constantinides 2017: 20). These interventions though are only driven by the authorities' agenda for the city's future (re)development, without a clear strategy for the mobilization and inclusion of the existing inhabitants of the historic neighbourhoods, a goal that instead several local non-governmental organizations (NGOs) are pursuing (https://www.sistemacyprus.com/). In parallel to the long-term strategy of the authorities for the historic core of the city, private initiatives driven by international investment capital are transforming the cityscape that surrounds the mediaeval core, investing in high-rise constructions around the mediaeval moat. These commingled spatial realities (Figure 7.2) grow within the existing built environment that was found "as is" by its current inhabitants and the communities who are re-appropriating today what is considered by its previous users as difficult heritage.

Studying this complex spatial reality with the aim of understanding how digital technology tools could contribute to the inclusion of the existing inhabitants in discussions about future developments and interventions in the historic city, in an attempt to lower the risk of gentrification, begs the following question. Whose heritage matters and for the inheritance of what artefacts, assets and values are we talking about? Can sites and their histories simultaneously belong to, and be shared by, more than one local community? Significantly, in the case of the old city of Nicosia, a high percentage of its current inhabitants is of different ethnic backgrounds from those groups who feel associated with the national and cultural identity of it, namely the G/C. Responding to this, the chapter considers the ways that these spatial practices of appropriation, which would allow for the "transformation of the properties" of fixed difficult narratives of the past, can be associated with current place-making activities by means of digital technologies.

The following sections present aspects of using digital tools, such as virtual reality (VR) and Information Communication Technology (ICT) interfaces, for the creation of the appropriate virtual *stage* to facilitate a dialogue between the relevant social groups and stakeholders, i.e., local inhabitants, social groups who appropriate the space and the local authorities. This virtual stage allows for the

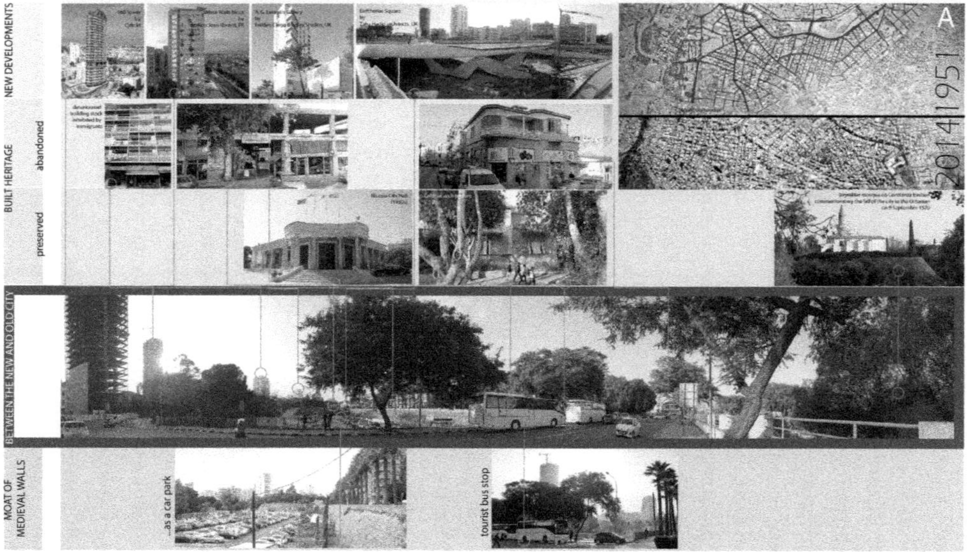

FIGURE 7.2 The many layers of past and present human activity as they co-exist in close proximity in the contested historic environment of Nicosia, impacting the spatial and visual identities of the place. From top to bottom: Numerous high-rise developments are built – more are currently under construction and in the planning permit stage; the significant built heritage of the old city is either preserved by the local authorities or completely abandoned to property owners and their tenants, who are in their majority low-income families of immigrants and in most cases cannot afford to renovate the properties. At the same time, the highly significant public space between the new and old parts of the city, that is, the moat of the mediaeval walls is occupied by bus and car parks, tennis courts and football fields, while the parts of the moat that are left to operate as open-air green spaces are highly popular destinations for the inhabitants of the old town. (A) 3D simulation of urban transformation of the area around the old city (1951–2014), based on data from the Land Survey Department of the Republic of Cyprus. Photographs and computer graphics by the author.

exploration of the role of built heritage in the contemporary city, as immersion and VR interfaces enable researchers to map and focus on those built heritage assets that each group of stakeholders identify themselves with, and interact with during their everyday activities.

Digital technologies and design thinking as good practices for active participation

In the case of the contested built heritage of Nicosia, challenges imposed by its difficult past can be overcome with the introduction of current approaches to driving urban transitions by means of participatory methodologies. Specifically, the research draws on a process that is motivated by the application of *design thinking* (Groat and Wang 2002) in the appropriation of historic sites. It is suggested that this can be further facilitated by the use of digital technologies in contributing new responses to current urban challenges, as identified by relevant European networks (Meyer and Hawlik 2021). This contribution aims to achieving livability and vivacity for all, safe, accessible and well-integrated spaces. This can be facilitated by enabling better models of governance by inviting all residents, inhabitants and citizens on board at an early stage of dialogue about urban transformation actions.

Any creative use of digital technologies is facing the challenge of simultaneously enabling the inclusivity of the many stakeholders and diversity of territories of application, as well as of bringing together the physical public space of a city, its digital representations and the digital networks of the social groups of said stakeholders (Broeckmann 2000). This chapter argues for new opportunities provided by the use of ICT-enabled co-creation methodologies, which under specific conditions can offer a virtual stage for stakeholder engagement with the present life of heritage sites (Artopoulos et al. 2018). Under the right conditions, the creation of dialectical interactions between stakeholders regarding the future of neglected historic sites, with a motivation to reactivate the public spaces of the relevant sites through the activities of their contemporary users, can enable processes that will allow for new spatial appropriations of these sites. Processes of appropriation can offer opportunities for multiple identities to co-exist, enhancing a sense of belonging for their users. Providing to people agency over the environment of a city can help in engaging them with the future use of the physical traces of past human activity.

This approach goes beyond typical heritage preservation strategies that focus on past identities; previously implemented heritage preservation strategies often aim at preserving memories of past users of these spaces and sites, in an attempt to re-instate the historical identity of the place and to promote its social or cultural significance – and therefore its value – as an example of heritage to be safeguarded (Pickard 2016). By trying to recognize those historical aspects that can be revisited through practical, design-driven (Avram, Ciolfi and Maye 2019) and non-binary enquiries (of *either* a Turkish-Cypriot *or* Greek-Cypriot identity), the present methodology aims at introducing bottom-up strategies of historic public space management in experimental stakeholder consultation processes, including workshops, virtual co-design sessions and design knowledge sharing.

Interpreting the multiplicity of heritage as an urban asset

The research is occupied with neglected historic spaces which host specific spatial characteristics that can render them relevant to contemporary inhabitants of the city in creative ways (Mortara et al. 2014), bringing together heritage aspects with the everyday needs and activities of the local communities. Expanding on the transformation of the ways culture is understood in the last century (Bennett 2015), the authors draw on Actor-Network Theory (Latour 2007), which is an approach to qualitatively analyze real-world conditions as networks of relationships between agents while being agnostic of the nature of these agents (e.g., human, inanimate object), or in other words, a set of conceptual mechanisms for exploring ethnography, cities, etc. as assemblages of associations. Through this framework, heritage is approached as a meshwork of meanings, associated identities and past human expressions that contemporary individuals and groups can adopt, adapt, appropriate, change, reuse and recognize with varying degrees. Heritage can be defined as a set of localized narratives that relate to a given group of people in a particular place, at a specific time (Dann 1994). Underlying the value of these places is the space in which they are hosted and rooted. In this context, heritage is considered an asset of the contemporary city that becomes an active space of its everyday life, rather than an agent of human activity that captures and tries to preserve a static image of the past in order to communicate a hegemonic narrative that is imposed (from the top-down) to characterize the identity of the place. Now heritage involves all types of culturally embedded commons of an urban environment, such as spaces associated with circulation networks and community support at the neighbourhood scale, including open-air sites, parks and local urban facilities.

Although there are several peer-reviewed studies addressing links between space, identity and territorial cohesion in contested heritage sites (Pullan and Baillie 2013), one notices a lack of research with regards to how digital technologies can contribute to the field of participatory heritage in terms of future possibilities of the spatial appropriation of these places. The presented experimental methodology was implemented in practice to respond to a real-world challenge, in order to explore spatial relations between these narrative-rich environments and the human activities that take place in them, as these are conveyed by individuals. The way people move in, respond to, look at, etc., public space is considered here a staged performance (Mahdzar 2008). Through walking, individuals interfere with physical obstructions, disruptions of movement, points of stasis and unpredictable situations in the urban landscape, moments that intensify sensual experience, an experimentation with spatial information available to them.

Literature in participatory design suggests that co-creation of public space is a way to increase opportunities for citizen engagement with the space of the city, but it is also a process that involves a wider range of city stakeholders, who influence the decision-making process, and embraces collective creativity (Sanches and Frankel 2010) for the production of new ideas. Building on the above, the presented research, by studying recordings of repetitive strings of actions that individuals pursue in their interaction with the built environment they use, proposes a more engaging and inclusive tool in participatory heritage than typical VR environments for delivering historical information to audiences. Further, it relies on the presented digital tools to engage both groups of local inhabitants and city stakeholders in the decision-making process.

Going beyond the use of VR for the representation of the historic evolution of the built environment in digital cultural heritage enquiries (Gonizzi Barsanti, Remondino and Visintini 2013), the presented research focuses on the way that the everyday users of the city would behave in space in order to learn from their own interpretation of the specific narratives that are embedded in contested spaces. Recent approaches to social sciences shed light on processes that augment the feeling of "belonging" and rootedness via the emergence of common identities and the establishment of lived experiences of the place (Hammack 2008: 222–247). Notably, as illustrated in Nicosia, new communities of city inhabitants, in their majority persons with a migratory background and long-term international business travellers, appropriate ephemerally historic built environments, which may be considered as heritage, that is, as culturally valuable assets, by their previous bearers. These historic built environments then are becoming associated with new emerging spatial identities, as their contemporary users assign new meanings to them through the everyday (inter)actions that are taking place in these spaces. However, if different local communities that are accessing the same public resources (e.g., heritage sites) express overlapping views about a heritage asset, then there is a greater possibility of identifying a shared approach to interpreting anew those spaces. These opportunities can be used to respond to the need for transforming peoples' tacit knowledge (i.e., urban heritage users as cultural bearers) into local awareness and capacity to make desirable and feasible user-driven changes in the way these neighbourhoods, which are left behind due to their difficult pasts, can be occupied and appropriated towards more resilient futures.

Based on the role of narrative in engaging people in interpretation processes (Weller 2007: 44), the research aims to contribute to the discussion about digital tools for elicitation (Collins et al. 2017) that offer opportunities for gaining a deeper understanding of participants' behaviours and the meanings of these behaviours (Brewer 2000) in spatial contexts. Drawing on the guidelines of the European Association for Heritage Interpretation (Interpret Europe[1]) for an inclusive understanding of processes of accessing, learning and engaging inhabitants, the research argues that spatial, rather than historical (which would require confrontation of individuals with the conflicts of the past), narratives can be used as a vehicle for engaging people in interpretation or meaning-making processes (Amin 2008). By focusing on space and the many ways this is appropriated by local communities, the research tries to capture how individuals inhabit a built environment that is considered "somebody else's" difficult heritage. Notably this condition affects the ability to understand the ways in which people appropriate space, as well as the way by which inhabitants and residents relate their actions and associate with a space that is characterized by specific (difficult) narratives. The research hypothesis is that communities and social groups may grow new relations with a given space by being involved in activities wherein they are asked to express their envisioned spatial transformations that would help them appropriate public space in their neighbourhood.

Below, preliminary tests of the presented methodology showed that it can facilitate participants in understanding the remaining traces of each heritage structure's construction phases in their urban context, a process of unfolding the palimpsest of the city's spatial narratives. This methodology, by offering an unmediated experience of the historic site to individuals who wander around in areas that are identified with difficult historic narratives, highlighted new directions for the future appropriation of the space. In doing so this approach to urban space rehabilitation contributes to practices of cultural rights and inclusion (Dodd and Sandell 2001). In support of this, Special Rapporteur K. Bennoune, in the publication of the final report to the Human Rights Council of the United Nations, recognized that the methodology developed by the authors for Nicosia can play a role in "promoting social resilience and fostering cultural rights in the city, by means of co-design practices and citizen engagement" (Bennoune 2017).

In practice, through this process the researchers were able to assess the following aspects:

- What are the relationships that current inhabitants of the city grow with the place?
- The spatial aspects and characteristics that play role in beneficiaries' (residents) engagement with space
- The connectivity of those territories which are used by beneficiaries with the rest of the urban fabric

This enquiry was evaluated by means of a co-creation activity conducted in the context of a COST Action Training School,[2] which brought together international experts with local stakeholders, representatives of authorities and communities (Artopoulos 2018).

In answering the above, the methodology operated at a city-wide level and at a neighbourhood scale. With regard to the former, a 3D interactive platform of Nicosia's historic core was created to enable the spatial understanding of the location and relations of key historic areas of the city, contextualized in their broader urban fabric. This accurate[3] virtual environment of Nicosia's historic core (https://youtu.be/bCrx_4SJpu0) is an accessible space for non-experts that hosts 33 important monuments and sites that span eight centuries (from Byzantine to Ottoman periods) within a unified (including both north and south parts of the city) representation of its fabric (Figure 7.3). This digital environment provides access to multiple narratives through different means of representation, including diagrammatic representation of urban zoning and building massing, use of photographs as two-dimensional billboards, modelling of vegetation and the street network, reality-captured three-dimensional reconstructions of heritage buildings of interest and two-dimensional user interface components.

This virtual environment is used by the authors as a platform for discussion, engagement and deliberation of future planning (Figure 7.4, panel 2), as it has a great outreach capacity targeted at raising public awareness of the historic city's shared urban landscape. The virtual environment captures more parameters and aspects of the spatial configuration of areas of historical narratives – and of their development and transformation in time, it enables reflections on their identity and presence today – and the differences between the current state of appropriation of these sites, and by doing so it can raise public awareness better than typical cultural heritage methods of representation. These capacities and qualities of this virtual environment are exploited and further developed currently, as a Local Time Machine (https://www.timemachine.eu/ltm-projects/interactive-visualization-of-historic-nicosia/) that is onboarded on the TIME MACHINE EU initiative, while they are evaluated as part of the permanent collection of the Leventis Municipal Museum, cf. Heritage in Motion gallery

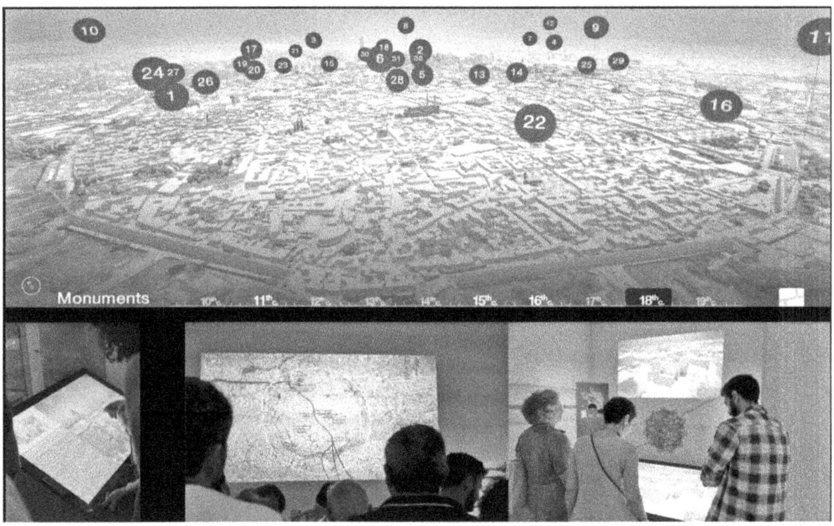

FIGURE 7.3 (Top) Time machine of the historic core of Nicosia spanning from 10th to 19th century. (Bottom) The permanent installation of the time machine in the Leventis Municipal Museum. Photographs by the author.

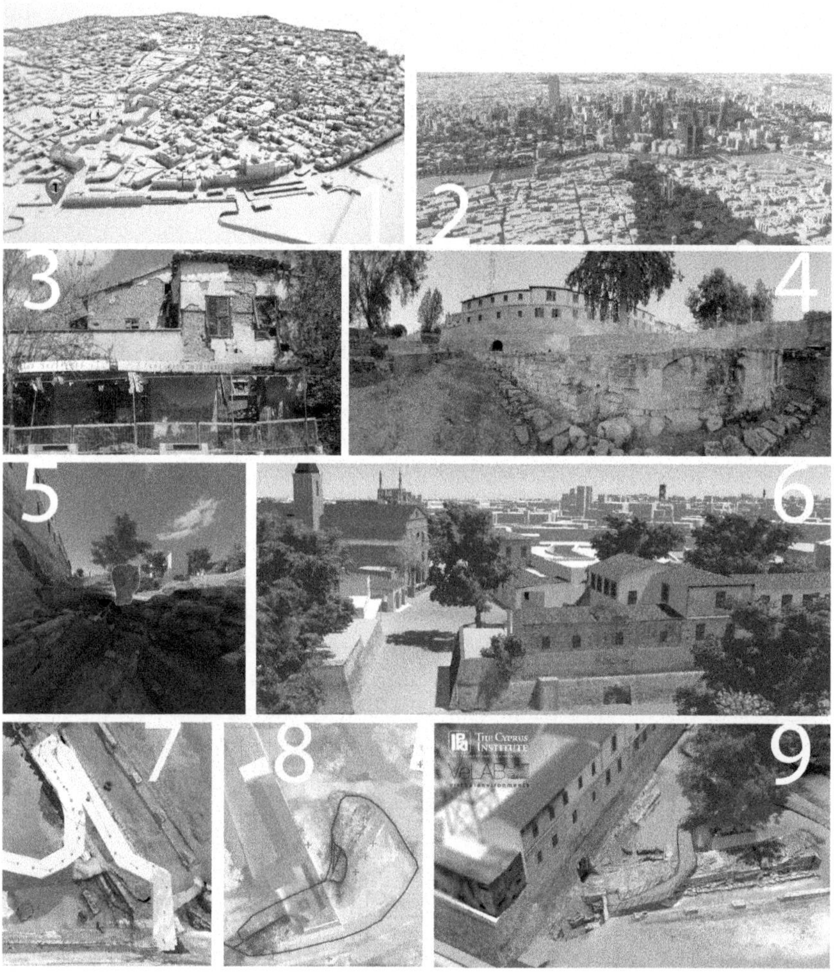

FIGURE 7.4 The co-design VR interface involves a mobile app for the users to draw schematically proposed routes in and around the site. A walking path can be registered on the touch screen of a portable device by moving around the dots which function as the control points of the route. These routes are then automatically mapped in the virtual environment, in order for their "co-creators" and others to walk on them in the real-time 3D Virtual Environment with the use of stereoscopic goggles for evaluating qualitatively the experience of a site visit. Images by the author; panel 7 by Colter Wehmeier.

(https://heritageinmotion.eu/). The latter is used by the authors to collect feedback on visitors' preferences of monuments, historical periods, etc., through the automated generation by the software application of metadata regarding the selection of buildings to be viewed, the choice of language, the duration of interaction and the number of sessions.

A site-specific practice: A neighbourhood with difficult past and present realities

Part of this interactive digital twin of the city is an experiment conducted with VR-enabled design tools focused on the reactivation of a site located in one of the most contested parts of the historic city, characterized here as an example of difficult heritage. This experiment was created to function as a testbed for developing and assessing the capacity of the presented methodology for stakeholder engagement in participatory processes. Since 1974 and the physical separation of Nicosia, one of the three mediaeval gates of the city, the Pafos gate has become an iconic symbol of division, as it is virtually located in the infamous "Green Line". Pafos gate's historical continuity spans from the Middle Ages until today, as the gate operated without interruption during the Venetian, Ottoman period and British rule.

The spatial context of the site comprises several historical structures characterized by a multiplicity of narratives: The buffer zone running through the site at its thinnest width (Figure 7.4, panel 1); the Holy Cross Catholic Church of Nicosia that is visited by a majority of migrant families; the moat that runs around the mediaeval walls encircling the old city which is considered as urban commons contributing to the spatial identity of the historic core; a United Nations station that overlooks the site; and the Kastelliotisa hall, formerly a female convent and originally part of the Lusignan palace (13th–14th century). The police headquarters was built on top of the gate and has completely changed the structure and form of the Pafos gate, while the carcass of the Spitfire coffee shop across the road from the Pafos gate, popular among British soldiers and locals in the 1950s, is a reminiscent of the intercommunal conflict, as it was used as a checkpoint before the war. Tension in the neighbourhood is present even today, as recently captured (2020[4]) by the incident that took place in the thin line of the buffer zone that crosses the site. Turkish army members were mobilized by the presence of Municipality of Nicosia workers who tried to install external scaffolding on the ruins of the building façade of the Spitfire coffee shop that lies on the Greek-Cypriot side of the buffer zone to support it as it was falling down after heavy rains in the winter (Figure 7.4, panel 3).

Significantly, the neighbourhood is home to numerous NGOs and community groups, such as the Hope for Children CRC Policy Centre, who support migrants' children from Syria and African countries, and unaccompanied refugee children; the Holy Cross Catholic Church dating back to 1900 but built on the site of an older church (1642) dedicated to the Holy Cross. The neighbourhood is identified by its large Maronite community, who facilitated the foundation and operation of the Centre for the Safeguarding of Maronite Language (today recognized as an endangered language), and importantly this is the city area where Caritas Cyprus is located, which provides a place for migrants and refugees to socialize, to access legal, healthcare and psycho-social support, to learn languages and, if necessary, to access food, clothing and other humanitarian services. Between 2013 and 2014, the part of the moat outside the Pafos gate that was used as a car park was excavated in an effort led by the Cyprus Department of Antiquities and the Municipality of Nicosia not only to preserve the history of the area and the mediaeval fortifications (Figure 7.4, panel 4) but also to develop and reactivate the neighbourhood which was in decay since the 1980s, a condition that has resulted by the embodiment of difficult narratives in this locale.

Furthermore, this is one of a couple of areas across the Nicosia buffer zone considered by bi-communal initiatives as candidate sites to open as a checkpoint for the public to cross the cities. This was yet another very convincing reason behind the selection of this site by the authors as a testbed. In the likelihood of opening the crossing, this area will become a popular tourist destination, which together with the thousands of inhabitants of both sides of Nicosia (Turkish-Cypriot and Greek-Cypriot) who will be walking across – as it currently happens in the existing checkpoint at Ledras Street – will put a lot of stress on the circulation infrastructure. In the likelihood of this event, the design and organization of the public space in the area would be required to be pedestrian-friendly. These considerations influenced the scope and motivation of the research, as this was developed to lay the grounds for a practical tool that would be useful to planners and policymakers of the Municipality who would thus be enabled to engage stakeholders and the local communities in the dialogue and public consultation that should precede the implementation of any urban interventions on the site.

Eventually, the virtual co-design methodology developed by the authors achieved tacit results and enabled the transformation of the physical space of the city. Specifically, the responsible authorities, i.e., the Ministry of Public Works, the Department of Antiquities and the Municipality, decided to change the initially approved management plan of the Pafos gate excavation and, instead of a controlled archaeological site, to build the architectural intervention that was produced through the VR-enabled experiments presented here (Figure 7.4, panel 9) (expected completion of construction works in 2022).

Using an immersive environment for co-creation, or learning from the crowds

Aiming to study the everyday experiences of the site, this neighbourhood-scale virtual environment was developed to allow researchers and stakeholders of the process to:

- Identify spaces of historical continuity and fragmentation: Visualize the historical context of the site in the immersive environment (Figure 7.4, panels 5 and 6).
- Map observations of the pedestrian circulation around the site of interest (Figure 7.4, panel 8).
- Identify spaces of interaction between communities, as well as spatial issues that challenge the image and experience of visiting the site, e.g., obstructions,

visual noise, poor signage, barriers to pedestrian movement, unwelcoming environment for the elderly and physically disabled.
- Identify neglected spaces and reflect on the relation of the moat with the mediaeval city Walls: By enabling users to draw their own walking path through the site (Figure 7.4, panel 7).

The co-design process included the following steps, with participants:

- Exploring the site physically through visits guided by experts (historians of architecture, archaeologists, architects)
- Learning about destroyed and removed assets from the site through the interface of an Augmented Reality mobile app
- Virtually exploring reconstructions of earlier phases of the site and its neighbourhood, as in a time machine, to better understand the historical transformations of the space and interpret the history of the complex structures that define the architectural palimpsest they encounter in the present day
- Registering user-defined routes (walking paths) through the site which are then automatically mapped in the virtual environment (Figure 7.4, panel 8)
- Virtually visiting the site with their movement being limited on the walking paths they had previously suggested
- Finally, being asked to assess the opportunities for interesting walking experiences that their proposed route would offer

The routes suggested by the individuals who participated in the process informed the architectural design of the proposed intervention for the post-excavation management of the archaeological site (Figure 7.4, panel 9). As mentioned above, this methodology was applied in practice through an H2020 COST Action Training School, as well as in VR theatre evaluation sessions at the Cyprus Productivity Centre, to engage local key stakeholders, including some of the NGOs that are operating in the area, international experts and inhabitants of the city in the management of the archaeological site of the moat of the mediaeval city of Nicosia. The results of these experiments were later disseminated internationally.[5]

These evaluation sessions with a targeted group of 23 participants in total provided insights that supported the development of the methodology. As these were participants of the Training School, they were acquainted with the challenges, pressing needs and current discourse in the field of urban and heritage studies. In addition to this characteristic of the group, the combination of various ages, disciplines and expertise, the inclusion of both practitioners and academics, as well as the participation of visitors (of European origin) and local inhabitants of the city, provided the necessary plurality of the targeted group to the evaluation tests. In the tests conducted, the gender composition of the respondents was about 57% male and 43% female. The average age was about 35 years, with the youngest user group being 18–24 years old and the oldest between 45 and

51. The respondents were from eight countries, higher participation was from Cyprus (six respondents) and then Greece, Italy, the UK, Portugal, Lithuania, Hungary and Brazil. Their knowledge base is informed by eight academic disciplines, ranging from architecture, urban planning and landscape architecture to information technology, humanities (archaeology and art history) and social science subjects (sociology and economics). Half of the participants were local residents (50%) while the rest were foreigners, and this parameter was important as the testing required that participants should memorize and recall specific historical content that was spatially distributed. Half of them visit or pass-by heritage sites in their everyday route from home to work. Thirty-seven per cent consider these sites as major attractions of the city, while 18% live nearby historic sites and monuments. This parameter was significant because the testing aimed at understanding the impact of adding alternative walking paths for circulation through and around the archaeological site. Eighty-one point two per cent strongly agreed, or agreed, that the "projected space and objects looked real", and 87.5% "had the impression that they could explore the space easily and convincingly and travel in time" to understand the spatial complexity of the site through the analysis of the historical palimpsest of the neighbourhood. Most importantly, the qualitative feedback collected through questionnaires and the unstructured conversation was then combined with quantitatively analyzed information (i.e., data of visitor movement and preferences with the virtual environment plotted on maps) (Figure 7.4, panel 8).

This methodology offered insights that facilitated steering the planning and site management process towards the right direction since all distinct groups of inhabitants should be offered opportunities to grow links with a historic space of the city. These opportunities emerge out of the co-development of common visions for their neighbourhood and the public spaces they appropriate in their every day, their familiarization with social and cultural conditions, the topography of a place and the current needs for integration in the contemporary life of the city.

As supported by the findings of qualitative methods like semi-structured interviews with open-ended questions (Batista and Žemaitaitienė 2018) that complemented the presented digital methodology for the validation of results, the area is popular among its current users, occupants and passers-by, while the locals recognize its potential to advance their quality of life. However the interviewees noticed that improvements are required to make the space attractive and in line with their everyday needs and expectations, including the lack of signage, the fragmented experience of the space and the lack of public consultation regarding the management of the place. According to UN-Habitat Charter of Public Space (2016), resilient public open spaces are "an integral and meaningful part of the urban architecture and landscape, with a determinant role in the overall image of the city" (point 14.g). Respecting this criterion for the future function of the site under study, the proposed methodology aimed at facilitating the co-design of a walking path through the archaeological site of the Pafos gate that would contribute to its integration in the neighbourhood by promoting the complex palimpsest of historical narratives of the architectural remains (e.g., Frankish, Venetian, Ottoman) as the overarching identity of the place. It was understood by the authors through the user-testing sessions that this multicultural character of the site was perceived as the most relevant and attractive spatial identity by the locals, passers-by as well as stakeholders from the authorities. This consideration of the participants was in stark contrast with their sensitive and biased responses to questions regarding the value of the most recent structures on site, e.g., the Spitfire coffee shop, from where UN soldiers would check the crossing of people between city sectors after the first intercommunal conflicts in 1963–1964 (Figure 7.4, panel 3) or the concrete bunker situated on top of the Pafos gate, which is associated with the difficult hi(stories) of conflict between the T/C and G/C communities, as these were framed by the sociopolitical context of the post-colonial period of Cyprus. Hence the co-designed route of the walking platform across the site was spatially organized to provide views of significant finds such as a city aqueduct from the Ottoman period, architectural parts of the Lusignan palace discovered in secondary use, a unique in the city gothic era bridge and the foundations of the Venetian walls (Figure 7.4, panel 4) while also being aligned with the entrance of the gate tunnel, following the inclination of the terrain and turning around the only tree in the site to provide shaded views of the landscape (Figure 7.4, panel 9).

Conclusions and future considerations

Today, in many (often, second- and third-tier) European cities, social and spatial segregation has created a vicious circle of neglect for some historic areas in which marginalized and vulnerable groups have found refuge – and in parallel, they have led to the gentrification of others. Public space in cities is of high priority for the EU, also highlighted by UN-Habitat in its *Global Public Space Toolkit: From Global Principles to Local Policies and Practice*,[6] which argues that if cities want to expand the prosperity of their inhabitants and become resilient, they need to consolidate rights to the "commons" for all, and particularly the residents most in need. Approaching heritage sites as urban commons though poses new challenges, as built heritage inherently entangles issues of identity and history that evolved on top of layered social structures in time and through competition, and thus heritage is much more dynamic and fragile as a common resource than the public open space of the city. In the context of the discourse about inclusive public space, this chapter was occupied with a discussion about a specific example of difficult heritage, and it presented a methodology to approach this as an asset of urban space to be used for the implementation of an inclusive practice of co-creation. It was presented how the built environment of Pafos gate, a historic neighbourhood of Nicosia located near the buffer zone, is conditioned by many contested narratives.

This place is interpreted by locals as difficult heritage, a condition which results in the area being largely appropriated by migrant communities. However today, far from being an ethnic specific enclave, the old city started attracting not only migrants but also young families, artists and people seeking a different way of life to the suburban condition that the city offers in other areas, a diversity which is reflected in the uses of the land (retail, artisan shops, etc.), as well as in the way that the street space is appropriated. Moreover, the historic core of Nicosia is undergoing a phase of transformation at various levels, beyond the interventions implemented according to the official regeneration strategy of the local authorities. This presents a unique opportunity for the stakeholders of the city to explore new approaches of urban reactivation that take into consideration not only the valuable historic identities and narratives of the place but also the limitations posed by its difficult past, as well as the new opportunities that arise from its current appropriation by a very diverse and rich community of different social groups.

Responding to this consideration, the research was conducted on the premise that technological interfaces of immersion can contribute to new methods of participatory heritage which through co-creation can offer a dynamic stage of dialogue for inhabitants and local users of heritage sites. By doing so, these methods can strengthen the connection between heritage and the everyday life of contemporary communities of users, making heritage a part of their agency and consequently enabling inhabitants to valorize it, on the grounds of its meaningful presence in their daily and communal activities. Through this practice of inclusion and engagement, historic places that are facing challenges due to their difficult pasts can be approached through a different lens, one of smart governance, that is essentially a user-driven process rather than a place identity-driven process (wherein the focus lies in questions of cultural ownership and historical identity).

Instead of a conclusion, it is worth noting that the building on top of the Pafos gate, which served as barracks for the Ottoman and the British rulers of the island aiming at the control of this sensitive entryway, is attracting the interest of the city authorities for a renovation and reuse. At the beginning of the 20th century part of the walls adjacent to the gate was demolished to effectively free the city and allow its development beyond its fortified limits. The building constructed next to this city entryway is listed today and represents a unique example of the heritage of Cyprus' colonial architecture. As in the case of the surrounding spaces, the building has undergone many transformations over time. During Ottoman Empire, the space was used as army barracks; under British administration, the police station of Nicosia was hosted with the construction of new building structures; in the 1960s, the premises were used to house the Police HQ of the Republic of Cyprus, with new additions; and in 1963, a concrete bunker was built in the north side, together with a UN control tower on the other side of the street to monitor the movement of individuals during the intracommunal conflict and was in operation until 2014. The Ministry of Justice and Public Order, with the agreement of the Department of Antiquities (responsible for the listed building as a monument), intends to renovate the building to host a Museum, with the aim to create a space that will be open to the local communities of inhabitants. It is expected that this decision of the public authorities will strengthen the confidence of the inhabitants that this area no longer exists as a traditional "division and frontier" site of the city, but, in spite of its violent separation, it can be reactivated in a positive way. For this research, such an opportunity would allow for further development to extend its capacity in engaging local communities in more intensive design decisions of smaller scale than the presented application, which was occupied with an intervention at the urban scale, and will complement the assessment of the methodology for participatory processes at the architectural scale.

Acknowledgements

This work was supported in part by the European Union's Horizon 2020 research and innovation program, the project Virtual Research Environment for Regional Interdisciplinary Collaboration in Southeast Europe and Eastern Mediterranean VI-SEEM (675121). This chapter draws from research conducted at the Cyprus Institute by G. Artopoulos and N. Bakirtzis with S. Hermon, in collaboration with the National Center for Supercomputing Applications at the University of Illinois at Urbana-Champaign (United States) and Colter Wehmeier; part of the groundwork for the simulation and analysis work has been done by P. Charalambous in close collaboration with Inria, France, and the University of Cyprus. The authors also want to acknowledge the close collaboration of the Cyprus Department of Antiquities, in particular the director M. Solomidou-Ieronymidou and archaeological officer P. Christophi, as well as the support of A. Petridou and A. Papadopoulou from the Municipality of Nicosia.

Notes

1 http://www.interpret-europe.net/top/news/singlepage-news/news/why-we-need-a-clear-stance-in-interpretation/.
2 http://cyberparks-project.eu/training-schools.
3 This interactive platform relies heavily on unstructured 3D spatial data and was generated through a semi-supervised photogrammetric documentation pipeline and a manually created baseline model of the urban fabric of the city, including an accurate digital terrain model based on ordinance data provided by the Land Survey Department.
4 https://in-cyprus.philenews.com/nicosia-municipality-suspends-spitfire-cafe-building-works-due-to-turkish-harassment/.
5 This methodology was selected by external expert panel as one of the two Best International Practices of public space co-creation by means of playful applications of ICT and is showcased in both the Online State of the Art Catalogue and the Book, Public Play Space Initiatives (https://www.publicplayspace.eu/state-of-the-art-catalogue/).
6 https://unhabitat.org/global-public-space-toolkit-from-global-principles-to-local-policies-and-practice.

References

Amin, A. (2008). 'Collective Culture and Urban Public Space', *City Journal*, 12 (1), 5–24.

Artopoulos, G. (Ed.) (2018). *Hybrid Heritagescapes as Urban Commons in Mediterranean Cities: Articles on Accessing the Deep-rooted Spatial Interfaces of Cities*, Cyprus, Nicosia: The Cyprus Institute. ISBN 978-1981237173.

Artopoulos, G. and Bakirtzis, N. (2016). 'Post-Digital Approaches to Mapping Memory, Heritage and Identity in the City', in *Digital Futures and the City of Today*, 139–156, UK, Bristol: Intellect Books.

Artopoulos, G., Synnes, K., Bahillo, A., Smaniotto C. C., Rebernik, N. (2018). 'Use of Data Analytics for Enriching Public Spaces with Unique Experiences of Localised Cultural Heritage Content', in *Kultur and Informatik: Hybrid Systems*, edited by Carsten Busch, Chrisitan Kassung and Jürgen Sieck, 99–112, Glückstadt: VWG. ISBN 978-3-86488-128-2.

Avram, G., Ciolfi, L. and Maye, L. (2019). 'Creating Tangible Interactions with Cultural Heritage: Lessons Learned from a Large Scale, Long Term Co-design Project', *CoDesign*, 16(3), 251–266. https://doi.org/10.1080/15710882.2019.1596288.

Batista J.S. and Žemaitaitienė, G. (2018). 'The Moat of Nicosia: Uniting or Dividing Space?' in Artopoulos, G. (Ed.), *Hybrid Heritagescapes as Urban Commons in Mediterranean Cities: Articles on Accessing the Deep-rooted Spatial Interfaces of Cities*, 137–142. Cyprus, Nicosia: The Cyprus Institute.

Bennett, T. (2015). 'Cultural Studies and the Culture Concept', *Cultural Studies*, 29 (4), 546–568.

Bennoune, K. (2017). *Report of the Special Rapporteur in the field of cultural rights on her mission to Cyprus*, 12. http://spinternet.ohchr.org/_Layouts/SpecialProceduresInternet/Download.aspx?SymbolNo=A%2fHRC%2f34%2f56%2fadd.1&Lang=en. Retrieved from: http://spinternet.ohchr.org/_Layouts/SpecialProceduresInternet/ViewCountryVisits.aspx?Lang=en

Brewer, J.D. (2000). *Ethnography*. Buckingham: Open University Press.

Broeckmann, A. (2000). 'Expressing Connection: Relational Architecture' in *Vectorial Elevation: Relational Architecture* no. 4, Mexico, edited by Lozano-Hemmer, R.. Mexico City: Conaculta and Ediciones San Jorge.

Butler, T. and Robson, G (2001). 'Social Capital, Gentrification, and Neighborhood Change in London: A Comparison of Three South London Neighbourhoods', *Urban Studies*, 38, 2145–2162.

Calame, J. and E. Charlesworth (2009). *Divided Cities*. Belfast, Beirut, Jerusalem, Mostar and Nicosia: University of Pennsylvania Press.

Collins, S.G., Durington, M., Favero, P., Harper, K., Kenner, A. and O'Donnell C. (2017). 'Ethnographic Apps/Apps as Ethnography', *Anthropology Now*, 9 (1), 102–118.

Constantinides, G. (2017). 'Urban Planning for Environments in Crises', Seminar Organized by the Scientific and Technical Chamber of Cyprus for the International Day of Urban Planning. Retrieved from: https://docplayer.gr/8199287-Poleodomia-se-perivallon-krisis-kai-me-poia-ergaleia-seminario-sypok-etek-pagkosmia-imera-poleodomias.html

Dann, G. (1994). 'Tourism: The Nostalgia Industry of the Future', in *Global Tourism: The Next Decade*, edited by Theobald, W., 55–67. Oxford: Butterworth-Heine-mann.

Dodd, J. and Sandell, R. (2001). *Including Museums: Perspectives on Museums, Galleries and Social Inclusion*. Leicester, UK: Research Centre for Museums and Galleries.

Europa Nostra (2018). *Europa Nostra appeal to two Leaders of Cyprus: "Save the Endangered Heritage in the Buffer Zone of Nicosia"* https://www.europanostra.org/europa-nostra

-appeal-to-two-leaders-of-cyprus-save-the-endangered-heritage-in-the-buffer-zone-of-nicosia/. Accessed 15 June 2020.
Giannakourou, G. (2005). 'Transforming Spatial Planning Policy in the Mediterranean Countries: Europeanization and Domestic Change', *European Planning Studies* 12 (2), 319–331. https://doi.org/10.1080/0365431042000321857
Gonizzi Barsanti, S., Remondino, F., Visintini, D. (2013). '3D Surveying and Modeling of Archaeological Sites. Some Critical Issues', *ISPRS Annals of the Photogrammetry, Remote Sensing and Spatial Information Sciences*, II-5/W1, 145–150.
Gravagnuolo, A., Micheletti, S., Bosone, M. (2021). 'A Participatory Approach for "Circular" Adaptive Reuse of Cultural Heritage. Building a Heritage Community in Salerno, Italy', *Sustainability*, 13. https://doi.org/10.3390/su13094812
Groat, L., Wang, D. (2002). *Architectural Research Methods*. New York: J. Wiley.
Hammack, P.L. (2008). 'Narrative and the Cultural Psychology of Identity', *Pers. Soc. Psychol. Rev.* August (12).
Interregeurope (2020). Online. https://www.interregeurope.eu/fileadmin/user_upload/tx_tevprojects/library/file_1587938114.pdf. Accessed 12 October 2021.
Latour, B. (2007). *Reassembling the Social: An Introduction to Actor-Network-Theory*. Oxford and New York: Oxford University Press.
Leventis, P. (2005). *Twelve Times in Nicosia. Nicosia, Cyprus, 1192–1570: Topography, Architecture and Urban Experience in a Diversified Capital City*. Cyprus: Nicosia.
Mahdzar, S.S.B.S. (2008). *Sociability vs Accessibility Urban Street Life*. Doctoral thesis, University of London.
Meyer, S. and Hawlik, R. (2021). 'City engagement in the Joint Programming Initiative Urban Europe and the role of intermediary organizations in R&I policies for urban transition', Retrieved from: https://link.springer.com/content/pdf/10.1007/978-3-030-57764-3_19.pdf
Michaelides, D. (2012). *Historic Nicosia*. Nicosia, Cyprus: Rimal Publications.
Mortara, M., Catalano, C.E., Bellotti, F., Fiucci, G., Houry-Panchetti, M. and Petridis, P. (2014). 'Learning Cultural Heritage by Serious Games', *Journal of Cultural Heritage*, 15, 318–325.
Patsavos, N. and Pissourios, I., (eds) (2018). *The Cypriot City Paradigm: Urbanity Issues in Design and Planning*. Athens: DOMES Publications.
Pickard, R. (2016). 'Management strategies for historic towns in Europe', in Labadi, S., Logan, W. (eds.), *Urban Heritage, Development and Sustainability. International frameworks, national and local governance*. London-New York: Routledge, 151–174.
Pilides, D. and Alpha, E., eds. (2012). *Fortified Cities: Past, Present and Future*. Nicosia: Bank of Cyprus Cultural Foundation.
Pratt, M.L. (2005). 'Arts of the Contact Zones,' in *Profession 91*. New York: Modern Language Association.
Pullan, W. and Baillie, B. (2013). *Locating Urban Conflicts: Ethnicity, Nationalism and the Everyday*. Houndmills, Basingstoke, Hampshire: Palgrave Macmillan.
RISE, Research centre on Interactive media, Smart systems and Emerging Technologies (2019). Online http://teaming.rise.org.cy/en-gb/home/. Accessed 19 May 2021.
Sanches, M.G. and Frankel, L. (2010). 'Co-design in Public Spaces: an Interdisciplinary Approach to Street Furniture Development', Retrieved from: http://www.drs2010.umontreal.ca/data/PDF/105.pdf
UNDP United Nations Development Programme (2021). *Study of Cultural Heritage*. https://www.cy.undp.org/content/cyprus/en/home/operations/projects/partnershipforthefuture/study-of-cultural-heritage-in-the-northern-part-of-cyprus.html. Accessed 15 May 2021.

United Nations Programme on Human Settlements (UN-Habitat) (2016). 'Charter of Public Space', The Third Conference United Nations on Human Settlements. Online http://www.inu.it/wp-content/uploads/Inglese_CHARTER_OF_PUBLIC_SPACE.pdf. Accessed 12 October 2018.

Weller, M. (2007). *Virtual Learning Environments: Using, Choosing and Developing your VLE*. Oxford, UK: Routledge.

Zesimou, S. (1998). 'Seeing beyond the Walls: Maps, Power and Ideology in Nicosia', *Journal of Mediterranean Studies*, 8 (2), 252–283.

8

FIRST-PERSON INTERACTIVE EXPERIENCE OF A CONCENTRATION CAMP

The case of Block 15

Agiatis Benardou, Anna Maria Droumpouki and Georgios Papaioannou

Introduction

The German occupation of Greece from October 1943–1944 claimed more victims in relation to the total population than in any other non-Slavic country (Figure 8.1). Although its effects can still be felt today in the Greek culture of remembrance, and despite the considerable amount of research concerning World War II and the German occupation in Greece, very little is still known about Greece. The Balkans and especially Greece are literally absent from the European map of occupation terror and are completely unknown to a broader European public.

With regard to World War II, the Greek historical culture is an absolutely special case. The way of coming to terms with the past in Greece differs greatly from that in other formerly occupied countries due to the civil war. During the three and a half years of the brutal occupation, the resistance of the Greeks was active and extensive. The National Liberation Front (EAM), which was mainly influenced by the communist party, was by far the largest resistance organization. But the end of the war brought the afflicted people no peace as a positive point of reference – especially since internal disputes from the occupation continued to smoulder. In a bloody civil war lasting more than three years (1946–1949), a centre-right coalition, which was dominated by an extremely national-conservative or monarchist wing, was victorious in 1949 with massive British and American help. The outcome of the civil war also revised the official memory of the Occupation: For both phases, the communists were declared the main enemy and traitors, dangerous elements for the nation and social order. The resistance of the EAM was reduced to its negative aspects, which made it easier to justify the ex-collaborators and to reintegrate them into the victorious "national" camp. Three and a half years of occupation seemed obliterated (Fleischer 2010: 222).

DOI: 10.4324/9781003200659-9

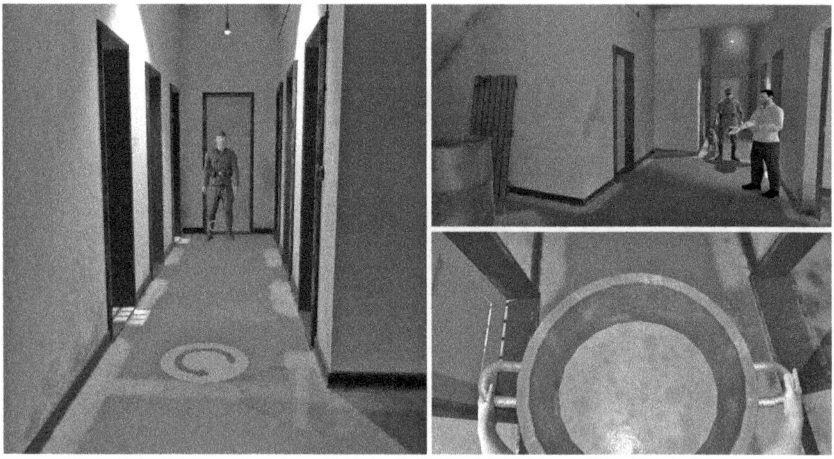

FIGURE 8.1 Screenshots from the VR production demo.

According to the historian Constantin Goschler, there was no common "anti-fascist culture of remembrance" in Greece, such as in Eastern Europe, or a "patriotic culture of remembrance", such as in France or Italy, which included the left resistance (Goschler 2015: 164). As a result, there was no shared memory of the 1940s in post-war Greece, but only a divided memory, which can be traced back to the conflict between the right and left political camps. Only in 1974 with the collapse of the military dictatorship and the legalization of the Communist Party did cracks appear in this narrative. In 1982 the first socialist government officially recognized the EAM and its affiliated organizations as structures of national resistance. When the Holocaust finally became a topic in the rest of Western Europe, in Greece the historiographical analysis of the resistance just began.

Despite the growing interest of both scholars and the public in highlighting sites of memory, there has been no effort to understand the spatiality of the wartime period in Greece, due, in large part, to difficulties of access, or absence of knowledge, around sites at all scales, from killing sites to concentration camps. There is no comprehensive study of the German concentration camps in Greece; even statistical data or relevant archival material hardly exist. Almost only memoir literature as well as oral and public history are available for research. Of the presumably 36 (and not further specified) concentration camps set up by the Germans – with over 100,000 prisoners and 48,000 executed – Haidari in Attika and Pavlos Melas in Thessaloniki are among the worst.

Concentration camps are the fundamental instrument of control and punishment for the occupation policy across Europe. The enormous social and cultural impact of the camp experience has meant that smaller places of internment, such as forced labour camps, transit camps, prisons and jail houses, which played no smaller role in the vast system of repression within which they were integrated, have, nevertheless, been largely overlooked. A burgeoning historical interest in the "concentration camp" is reflected, increasingly, in the appearance of works that move beyond structural and functional analyses to capture socio-spatial categories such as "place", "space" and "void" (Wachsmann 2015). This perspective prioritizes the connection between place (and space) and those various aspects of genocide, collaboration and complicity (Aleksiun and Kubátová 2021; Cole 2020; Meng 2011). It enables consideration of myriad processes of transformation and the creation of an archaeology of space which captures the diachronic perspective: The "before" and "after" of a site. Commemoration and musealization, negligence and abandonment, preservation or adaptation of space continuation or discontinuation of the original use, are all affirmations of a troubled past, than those in the post-war era tried so desperately to make sense of.

In her discussion of Auschwitz-Birkenau and the challenges of heritage management during the Cold War, Katie Young notes that

> it is a critical time for the camps as the memory of the Cold War fades and can no longer be used as an excuse for the deteriorating state of the camps today. The camp buildings and artefacts stand desperately in need of protection as their deterioration is further compounded by an endless stream of visitors and inadequate funds for upkeep. Despite these limitations the camps' significance remains unquestionable.
>
> *(Young 2009:50)*

A number of studies have taken the transformations of these sites of memory as a *topos* and particularly so within the fields of memory studies and commemoration (Skribeleit 2005; Young 1993). Camps provide a very tangible frame of reference for reflection on the experience of suffering; they can coherently frame trauma and can be visited in ways that evoke understanding and raise awareness of past injustice now embedded within contemporary discourse (Hubbel 2020: 3). Memorials exist, alternatively, to provide a physical focus for an often remote, or unlocated, traumatic event.

Greece is a country obsessed with the preservation of the past. This obsession, however, is focused, almost without exception, on Ancient Greece and Classical antiquity. As recognized by Stratos Dordanas, very little research has been undertaken on the concentration camps of Occupation Era Greece, and few structures built that serve to memorialize the loss and trauma implicitly associated with them.[1] Indeed, the history and transformation of concentration camps and prisons during the Occupation Era, both Italian and German, remains an intriguing but rarely researched subject. The former concentration camps of Haidari in Athens, Pavlos Melas in Thessaloniki and the Italian and German concentration camps in Larissa exemplify the problematic materiality of memory in heritage. In all three cases, site deterioration is due to neglect. These camps have not been declared "heritage sites" as other similar sites have been elsewhere in Europe. There has been no "memory boom" in Greece of the type that has characterized renewed interest in the materiality of World War II in Europe. According to Mark Mazower,

> The Second World War remains invisible for the visitors who flow into Greece during the summer, relaxing on the sunny beaches or becoming accustomed with the ancient temples in ruins and theaters. But for those who know where to seek, behind the fences of the old abandoned Jewish villas in Thessaloniki, or at Chaidari, where the new block of flats hides the view to the so called "Bastille of Greece", the scars from the wounds of the Nazi Occupation era still exist.
>
> *(Mazower 1994: 407)*

Indeed, World War II remains inaccessible to those attempting to connect with the period through surviving ruins, while memorial sites of the 1941–1944 period exist, largely, in a state of decay, crowning the silence which characterizes the memory culture of the 1940s in Greece more widely. The study of sites of "Difficult Heritage" in Greece is inevitably a study of the same collective oblivion, a mild form of "damnatio memoriae" which, according to Aleida Assmann, constitutes a fundamental characteristic of all nations (Assmann 2006: 104).

The concentration camp of Haidari is 9 kilometres west of the capital Athens. The Haidari camp in the sparsely populated suburb of Haidari (1940 with 5,868 inhabitants) was built in 1937 during the Metaxas dictatorship and served as a training centre for the Greek army. However, the construction was not completed. The site is located at the foothills of Pikilio Hill north of the Athens-Corinth road. In the beginning, the camp functioned as a branch of Averof Prison on Alexandras Street. After the outbreak of the Greco-Italian War, it was "inaugurated" on September 3, 1943, as a concentration camp with the transport of 590 prisoners from the Italian Larissa camp, which was to be closed. Among the 590 prisoners counted by the camp doctor Antonis Flountzis, there were 243 communists from Akronafplia prison, 20 prisoners from the island Anafi as well as another 327 prisoners of the Italians. Among these first prisoners was Flountzis himself, which means that his information can be assessed as relatively credible. The Haidari camp was primarily a transit camp for the prisoners on their transport to the concentration camps in Germany or Poland, and the same conditions and rules prevailed as are known from all other types of horror during the Nazi regime (Flountzis 1976: 21).

On September 10, 1943, after the Italian surrender, the Sicherheitsdienst (security service) took over the former barracks to "concentrate" suspects who had been arrested in connection with resistance actions or raids. Haidari also became a transit station for thousands of Jews who were deported to Auschwitz. The facilities of Haidari extended over approximately 50 hectares. In the whole camp there were about 20 block buildings or barracks, as well as larger and smaller barracks, each of which served different purposes. The block buildings were divided into two parts, each with its own entrance. There were three prisoner categories: The first category was placed in the so-called "free camp", the next in "light solitary confinement" in the cellars of Block 4, while the last category in Block 15 was subjected to complete isolation. The Germans had set up sewing and wood workshops as well as a shoe and equipment production facility in the camp, in which prisoners with the appropriate skills were employed. There they repaired furnishings that had been confiscated in Greek private houses and made shoes and civilian clothes from materials that had been stolen from various cloth and leather warehouses in Athens. The articles produced were intended for the various SS services or were sent directly to Germany. The inmates of the Haidari concentration camp were also sent to other "work" outside the camp, such as following the bombing of Piraeus. There were also accommodations for guards, administration barracks, a kitchen and storage sheds. There were hardly any washing facilities, so the hygienic conditions in the camp were unsustainable. It is known from testimony that many of the prisoners went blind due to poor living conditions and the lack of vitamins. For example, the sewage pits were deliberately rarely emptied, which meant that the prisoners had to relieve themselves in the corridors and stairs of the block. The toilets in Block 15 were full of faeces and the sick collapsed in the midst of the excrement. In one case, a prison guard was reported to have been forced to pick up excrement and bring it to a nearby pit with his hands (Chatzipateras and Fafaliou-Dragona 2003: 154).

An estimated 20,000–25,000 people were imprisoned: Men and women, prisoners of war, partisans, members and officials of the Communist Party of Greece, Jews, hostages arrested in purges, political leaders such as the leader of the Liberal Party and later Prime Minister Themistoklis Sofoulis or the ministers and former premiers Stylianos Gonatas and Georgios Kafantaris (Flountzis 1976: 749). Some well-known personalities from the intellectual and cultural life of Greece were also imprisoned in Block 15, including the actress Rena Dor, Professor Emmanuel Kriaras and his wife, the composer Nikos Skalkotas and, for three months, the actor Giorgos Oikonomidis. Professor Emmanuel Kriaras, then-director of the Medieval Archives of the Academy of Athens, was detained in Block 15 for three days. His brief testimony describes life in prison and isolation (Chatzipateras and Fafaliou-Dragona 2003: 153–154).

Since the beginning of 1944, Chaidari was an internment place for various groups of people, so for members of the EAM and the conservative partisan organization EDES, for members of espionage networks and British services, for trade unionists, students, workers, high officials, in individual cases even for members of the collaborating Greek Security battalions and members of German services who had been charged with contacts with the Allies or criminal offences. In November 1944, the *New York Times* reported that Chaidari was one of the largest Nazi camps in occupied Europe, which shows that the camp had achieved dubious fame well beyond the Greek border.[2]

The fate of the prisoners was extremely tragic. A life-threatening workload, constant malnutrition, a lack of medical care, fatal living conditions, lack of water, constant harassment and arbitrary murders characterized their everyday lives. Unfortunately there are no death registers left, which makes a general balance of the victims of the Haidari concentration camp impossible.

The immersive experience on Block 15

"Block 15" (2020–2023) is an R&D project hosted by the Department of Informatics, Athens University of Economics and Business, focusing on the infamous Block 15 of the Haidari concentration camp in Western Athens, the largest and most notorious German concentration camp in wartime Greece. The project, so far the first and only of its kind in Greece and SE Europe, makes the building, currently an endangered one, accessible to audiences and communities of diverse backgrounds through the use of immersive technologies. "Block 15" is co-funded by the German Federal Foreign Office through funds of the Greek-German Future Fund and the Hellenic Ministry of Culture.

The project aims to create an impact on different levels:

- Enhancing the understanding of and engagement in the functions of the building and the historical context
- Renewing the cultural identity of the region of Athens
- Fostering civic participation of diverse socio-cultural groups

Through an original interactive scenario based on primary and multimedia archival sources and with the employment of digital storytelling, the immersive virtual reality experience under development does not only bring back to life the actual monument that is Block 15 but also functions as a reminder of the horrors and torture inflicted by the Nazis on prisoners, in an attempt to reintroduce a historically and politically contested site to heterogeneous audiences.

"Block 15" is supported by the Municipality of Haidari, the Central Board of Jewish Communities in Greece (KIS) and the Jewish Community of Athens.

What makes Haidari and Block 15 difficult to process for digital narrative and 3D visualization?

As part of an operational military facility, Block 15 and the surrounding spaces associated with the production narrative are not open to the public. As such, special permits apply to visit the site, and most digital content captured cannot be directly published or be part of a digital production. Both facts significantly hindered our work and limited the digitized visual resources we could introduce to the production.

Perhaps our biggest challenge was that, for the production of a predominately visual experience, most resources were either recorded testimonies of captives or scattered and heterogeneous non-visual data (e.g. rough sketches, Red Cross register entries). Coupled with the extensive renovation of the military camp and the Block 15 building due to the change of function of the spaces, this left us with little hard evidence to work with for the visualization of the site during the reference period. Although basic structural information remains mostly intact (particularly for the Block 15 building), interior details such as electric cabling, as well as the function of particular rooms and the appearance of other utility buildings now demolished, can only be extrapolated from similar military camps of this era.

Since the intended audience of the production includes youngsters but also people with varying tolerance levels to violent content, we had to avoid blunt brutality and offending visuals, without however suppressing facts and diminishing the grim atmosphere, inhuman procedures and desperate psyche of the prisoners. Violence had to be "felt" rather than "seen".

Methodology

Scenario

In terms of narrative, script and interaction scenario, there were two major limiting factors: The (user) point of view, i.e., *who* is the user, and the exact time frame of the scenario. The first was actually very problematic since the identity of the user's avatar directly affects the clearance to access parts of the camp, one's ability to freely explore the site and the available interactions. The time frame had to be carefully chosen according to the historical information so as to maximize the convergence of events impacting or referenced by the scenario without artificially stretching the virtual reality (VR) experience time or altering factual information for the sake of narrative.

In the scenario we developed, the user takes the role of a cook's male assistant. This is no person of any significance or historical reference, whose identity can be easily attached to any user, regardless of age. Second, although not free to roam the camp site, the prisoners tasked to provide food for the other captives followed an itinerary that allowed them escorted access to several buildings. We could therefore develop a story, which takes the user through many typical everyday scenes in the camp and Block 15's isolation ward and allows one to partake in or glimpse events unfolding either as part of the story or in the background.

The scenario of the virtual reality production has been developed as a dramaturgical narrative, which, however, is based on thorough historical research and is truthful to historical sources and events, in accordance with their actual timeline. The narrative revolves around the experience of a prisoner in Block 15 of the Haidari concentration camp during a 24-hour period: From the morning of the 9th to the morning of the 10th of August 1944.

The user of the virtual experience is the protagonist of the narrative (in the "role" of the prisoner), who has just been transferred to the Haidari concentration camp from the *mploko* (blockade) of Vyronas and is appointed to the kitchens. Thus, the eyes of the user and the newly arrived prisoner coincide – initially "virginal" and unsuspecting, then gradually becoming aware of the grim reality of the camp. Soon enough, the user/prisoner takes on a "mission": To deliver a note from the women's block to another prisoner in solitary confinement within Block 15. The user is assigned a partner who will help with the game mechanics, but who also guides or queries the user with regards to historical events taking place during their stay in the concentration camp.

With the action unfolding in ten scenes, taking place in different parts of the Haidari concentration camp and Block 15 (men's detention block, courtyard, kitchens, camp gate, women's block, cells and chamber 18 of Block 15), the user interacts with other prisoners as well as with German officers and soldiers and becomes a witness of events significant to camp life. Among them, the morning roll call; the selection of the 50 prisoners to be executed in Mandra, Attica, on August 9, 1944; the strenuous efforts of the prisoners' mothers to see them from afar; the forced labour and tortures of prisoners carrying heavy stones in the courtyard under the whip of German soldiers; the distribution of food and other essentials by the International Committee of the Red Cross; the tortuous arrival of the Jews of Rhodes; the ration distribution in the chambers and everyday life of prisoners; the arrival of hundreds of prisoners from the *mploko* of Dourgouti and Katsipodi escorted by the Security Battalions; and the isolation and the horrors afflicted on prisoners in Block 15.

Featured in the script as characters are also actual persons, such as the prisoners Eleni Georganta and Antonis Flountzis – the camp doctor – but also German military personnel, such as the camp commander Fischer, the interpreter Wassenhoven and the guards Kovac and Suneric. The user can choose to interact with people (testimony) and objects (object interaction) and thus obtain additional information on certain aspects of camp life.

The narrative is preceded and followed by a brief presentation of additional historical data about the Haidari concentration camp and Block 15, enriching the provided information and, at the same time, strengthening the user experience.

Block 15 aims at heterogeneous audiences with diverse ages, personality traits and cognitive, academic and professional statuses. The educational value of storytelling aside, it is essential to underline that the central character, who is the mainstay of the narrative, is utterly transformed through and after the experience. In the way the interactive scenario is designed, each challenge carries implications and emotional gravitas. The central character becomes an agent who takes on an active role. In his work on the mechanics, dynamics and aesthetics (MDA) framework for enterprise gamification, Umar Ruhi introduces three types of narratives in immersive gamification: "Integrated narratives", "emergent narratives" and "interpreted narratives".[3] These narrative layers are related to various elements of each production. "Integrated" narratives are connected to the mechanics and are recommendations of the designers. "Emergent" narratives are associated with the actions and dynamics of the players-participants: "they are created by players during their interaction with the gamification application in a dynamic fashion as they perform different activities".[4] "Interpreted" narratives are related to aesthetics and perceived as "the desirable emotional responses evoked in the users when they interact with the gamified system".[5] Ruhi ascertains that (2015) for an immersive experience to be successful it must show coherence between all three styles of narratives. In Block 15, we sought to combine all three types of narrative to trigger empathy and optimize the user experience.

Technological and aesthetic approach

Early on in the pre-production phase, we faced the dilemma of whether a 360-degree stereoscopic video production or an interactive (3D-modelled) VR application would be more appropriate and effective. Both approaches have their merits and shortcomings, and we carefully weighed all of them, after compiling a short tech demo for each one. The 360-degree video is much more captivating when focusing on specific characters and their convincing and dramatic acting. However, it is far more limited in terms of interactive opportunities, and more importantly, its creation process is practically monolithic and inflexible. On the other hand, the full 3D production allows for more creative freedom, great reuse and adaptability of assets (3D models, animations, interaction scripts) as well as the ability to tweak and modify every aspect of the production for corrections and scenario modifications.

We have chosen the second approach for our VR production and therefore focused the scenario accordingly, distancing the user from face-to-face interactions and dialogues, capturing wider-field actions and focusing on the user's ability to move more freely and interact with the environment, instead. The VR production is based on the Unity game engine. Particular attention has been given to atmospheric lighting to establish the desired mood, a fast-paced yet grim scenario and optional interaction opportunities that reveal additional historical information and open up new dialogues. That said, the dramatic potential of a cinematographic 360 production was compelling enough to motivate us for a separate side project that would be more passive in terms of interactivity yet more emotionally intense.

Production

Conversing with and following the cook around the camp to enter Block 15, we see through the assistant's eyes various parts of the camp, including the kitchen rooms, part of the courtyard in front cell blocks, where the roll call used to take place, and, of course, the Block 15 building and its interior. For the 3D modelling of the latter, the original building still stands, albeit renovated and modified. Since plans for the historical building do not exist and any sketches were scarce and unreliable, we had to take on-site measurements and photos from which we eventually reconstructed enough structural and functional information to reconstruct the spaces visited in the VR production (see Figure 8.2). No digitally

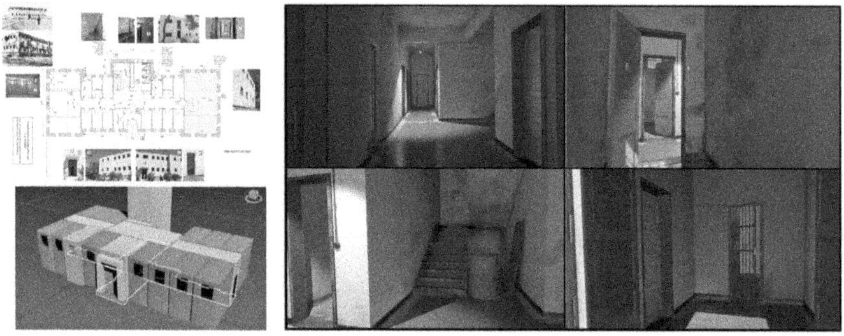

FIGURE 8.2 Reconstruction of the Block 15 ground floor from measurements, photographic evidence and prisoners' descriptions and sketches.

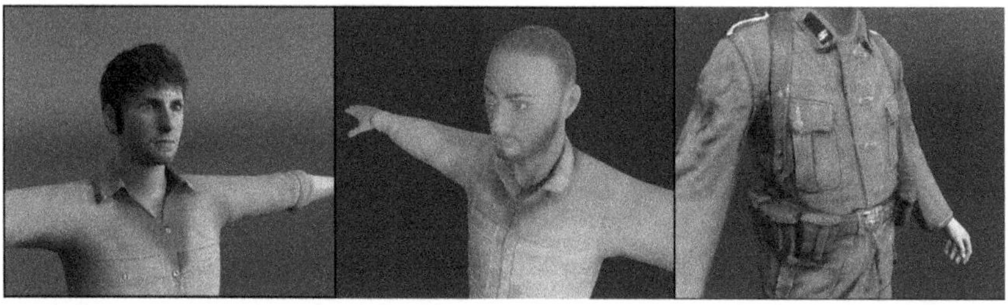

FIGURE 8.3 Character examples and details from the VR production demo.

captured data could be used directly as they would (a) clash with military regulations and (b) not reflect the function and conditions of the building in the timeframe of interest. Instead, all models and textures were created by hand, respecting the measurements and photographic evidence, where available. For the interior, although most elements are preserved (ground floor general structure, some doors, window grills, etc.), we had to use cross references from other similar-era Nazi concentration camps and military facilities for certain details that would not have survived the repeated renovation (e.g. electrical systems, wall and floor colours and markings).

Although for several notable characters, both prisoners and German officers, we have evidence of their presence at the camp in the specific period of the production, we did not focus the narrative on them, since the medium would not allow for detailed close-up facial reconstruction or convincing virtual acting. Instead, we modelled several neutral characters to bear the principal roles associated with close interaction. Figure 8.3 shows examples of such generic 3D character models and their details, as used in our production.

The scenario and the scene implemented in the demo VR application place the user in various outdoor and indoor parts of the camp, where scenes of violence take place as the story unfolds. Brutality, torture and demeaning

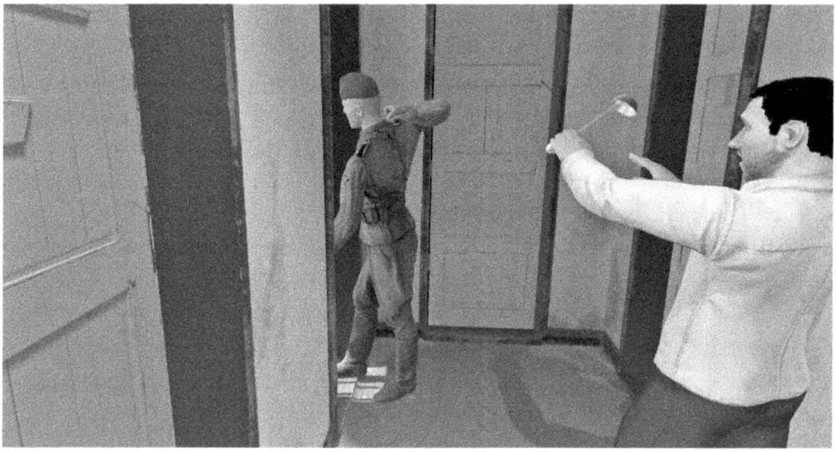

FIGURE 8.4 Brutality is either implied or hidden from the camera to avoid the presentation of excess violence.

treatment were everyday occurrences, and although a realistic and uncensored production must not hold back such evidence, exposure of all audiences to potentially shocking content would not be a good practice. Instead of avoiding the presentation of sensitive content to certain user groups, we opted for a different approach, often followed in cinematography: Violence is hidden in plain sight, by preventing direct exposure to it but rather either implying it or choosing less offensive channels to communicate it. For example, in the scene of Figure 8.4, the soldier opens the holding cell and aggressively beats the prisoner. The user only glimpses the incident by watching the partly obscured figure of the soldier, but not the begging and bleeding inmate. On the other hand, the proximity of the event and the vulgarity and desperation conveyed by the accompanying audio, more than compensating for the lack of visual presentation of the brutal encounter.

Preliminary results: Conclusion

The virtual reality production on Block 15 is due to be refined and completed by the end of 2023; however, iterations in design have enabled us to carry out several user assessment sessions. The sessions, predominantly focused on Athens University of Economics and Business students, included observation of user experience, short interviews and a brief questionnaire.[6]

Participants' familiarity with immersive experiences varied from experienced gamers to absolute beginners. Overall, their impressions about the Block 15 production were very positive. Despite some initial concerns about the scope of the production and some reservations expressed on the actual subject of the project, all participants were intrigued on a perceptual and emotional level.

The scene inside Block 15, a narrow and quite claustrophobic building, caused uneasiness, which was expected and in part deliberate, albeit unavoidable. On the contrary the scene in the kitchen, a larger room in itself, was perceived by some as impressive, while others found it somewhat dull. Most participants were in awe at the outside view of Block 15, which is revealed in all its grimness when the user exits the kitchen and looks slightly to the right.

While violence was perceived not as glorified or as traumatic, observation revealed that some participants tended to react to the scenes with sounds or gestures. It remains to be confirmed whether younger demographics will respond similarly.

Although not all triggers were identified as such and therefore not activated, measurements of the questionnaire administered illustrated that the educational aspect of the production was successful: Most participants answered questions on historical details alluded to in the production correctly.

Notes

1 Interview for the Arolsen Archives International Center on Nazi Persecution Website: https://arolsen-archives.org/news/keiner-hat-bislang-damit-gearbeitet/.
2 "Haidari Prison Outside Athens ranks high among Nazi horrors", *New York Times*, 2.11.1944.
3 Umar Ruhi, Level Up Your Strategy: Towards a Descriptive Framework for Meaningful Enterprise Gamification. *Technology Innovation Management Review*, 5(8), 2005, p. 8
4 Ibid.
5 Ibid.
6 The user assessment design was based on the work conducted in the context of the Scottish heritage Partnership initiative (Murray Pittock 2018).

Bibliography

Adamopoulou, Areti, "Simultaneous Equations: Early Cold War Cultural Politics and the History of Art in Greece," in *Making Art History in Europe After 1945*, edited by, Jesús Carrillo Castillo, Noemi de Haro Garcia, Patricia Mayayo Bost, Routledge, New York 2020, pp. 149–166

Aleksiun, Natalia, Kubátová Hana (Eds.), *Places, Spaces, and Voids in the Holocaust*, Wallstein Verlag, Göttingen 2021

Assmann, Aleida, *Der lange Schatten der Vergangenheit. Erinnerungskultur und Geschichtspolitik*, C. H. Beck, Munich 2006

Cole, Tim, "Geographies of the Holocaust," in *A Companion to the Holocaust*, edited by Simone Gigliotti, Hilary Earl, John Wiley & Sons, Hoboken 2020, pp. 333–38

Cole, Tim, Knowles Anne Kelly, "Thinking Spatially about the Holocaust," in *Places, Spaces, and Voids in the Holocaust*, edited by Natalia Aleksiun, Hana Kubátová, Wallstein Verlag, Göttingen 2021, pp. 291–299

Distel, Barbara, Benz Wolfgang (Eds.), *Der Ort des Terrors*, 9 vols, C. H. Beck, Munich 2005–2009

Dordanas, Stratos, Kalogrias Vaios, "Das nationalsozialistische Polizeihaftlager Pavlos Melas in Thessaloniki. Geschichte und Wahrnehmung," in Alexandra Klei-Katrin,

Annika Wienert-Stoll (Eds.), *Die Transformation der Lager. Annaherungen an die Orte nationalsozialistischer Verbrechen*, Transcript Verlag, Bielefeld 2011, pp. 289–308

Droumpouki, Anna Maria, *Monuments of Oblivion. Traces of Second World War in Greece and Europe*, Polis, Athens 2014

Droumpouki, Anna Maria, "Contemporary Greek History in Abandonment: Second World War Memory Sites and the Use of Memory in Public History," in *Making Sense, Crafting History. Practices of Producing Historical Meaning*, edited by Waaldijk Berteke, Salvaterra Carla, Agardi Izabella, Edizioni Plus, Pisa 2011, pp. 75–91

Fings, Karola, "Slaves for the 'Home Front': War Society and Concentration Camps," in *Germany and the Second World War*, edited by Jörg Echternkamp, Vol. IX/I, German Wartime Society 1939–1945: Politicization, Disintegration, and the Struggle for Survival, Oxford University Press, Oxford, pp. 207–283

Fleischer, Hagen, "»Endlösung« der Kriegsverbrecherfrage. Die verhinderte Ahndung deutscher Kriegsverbrechen in Griechenland," in *Transnationale Vergangenheitspolitik. Der Umgang mit deutschen Kriegsverbrechern in Europa nach dem Zweiten Weltkrieg*, edited by Norbert Frei, Wallstein Verlag, Göttingen 2006, pp. 474–534

Fleischer, Hagen, *Wars of Memory. Second World War in Public History*, Nefeli, Athens 2009 [*Οι Πόλεμοι της Μνήμης. Ο Δεύτερος Παγκόσμιος Πόλεμος στη Δημόσια Ιστορία*, Νεφέλη, Αθήνα 2009]

Fleischer, Hagen, "The Past Beneath the Present, The Resurgence of World War II Public History After the Collapse of Communism: A Stroll Through the International Press," *Historein*, 4, 2003–4, pp. 45–130

Fonzi, Paolo, "Beyond the Myth of the "Good Italian". Recent Trends in the Study of the Italian Occupation of Southeastern Europe during the Second World War," *Südosteuropa* 65, no. 2, 2017, pp. 239–259

Halbwachs, Maurice, *On Collective Memory*, University of Chicago Press, Chicago 1992 [*Les Cadres Sociaux de la Mémoire*, Presses Universitaires de France, Paris, 1941]

Huang, Shu-Mei, Lee Hyun Kyung, *Heritage, Memory, and Punishment. Remembering Colonial Prisons in East Asia*, Routledge, Abingdon and New York 2020

Hubbell, Amy L., Rojas-Lizana Sol, Akagawa Natsuko, Pohlman Annie, "Acknowledging Trauma in a Global Context: Narrative, Memory and Place," in *Places of Traumatic Memory: A Global Context*, edited by Hubbell Amy L., Rojas-Lizana Sol, Akagawa Natsuko, Pohlman Annie, Palgrave Macmillan, London 2020, p. 1–12

Hubbell, Amy L., Akagawa Natsuko, Rojas-Lizana Sol, Pohlman Annie (Eds.), *Places of Traumatic Memory. A Global Context*, Palgrave Macmillan, London 2020

Klei, Alexandra, Stoll Katrin, Wienert Annika (Eds.) *Die Transformation der Lager. Annäherungen an die Orte nationalsozialistischer Verbrechen*, transcript Verlag, Bielefeld 2011

Knowles Anne, Kelly, Cole Tim, Giordano Alberto (Eds). *Geographies of the Holocaust*, Indiana University Press, Bloomington & Indianapolis 2014

Králová, Kateřina, *Das Vermächtnis der Besatzung. Deutsch-griechische Beziehungen seit 1940*, Böhlau, Köln 2016

Kokkinos, Giorgos, Lemonidou Elli, Agtzidis Vlassis, *Trauma and Politics of Memory*, Taxideftis, Athens 2010 [Γιώργος Κόκκινος / Έλλη Λεμονίδου / Βλάσης Αγτζίδης, *Το τραύμα και οι πολιτικές της μνήμης. Ενδεικτικές όψεις των συμβολικών πολέμων για την Ιστορία και τη Μνήμη*]

Liakos, Antonis, "Rebels and Gangs in Academic Amphitheaters," in *Greece '36 - '49. From Dictatorship to Civil War. Sections and Sequels*, edited by Fleischer Hagen, Kastaniotis, Athens 2003, p. 25–37

Macdonald, Sharon, *Difficult Heritage. Negotiating the Nazi Past in Nuremberg and Beyond*, Routledge, London and New York 2009

Macdonald, Sharon, *Memorylands. Heritage and Identity in Europe Today*, Routledge, London and New York 2013

Pittock, M. (2018) *The Scottish Heritage Partnership Immersive Experiences: Policy Report. Project Report*. University of Glasgow, Glasgow.

William, Logan, Keir Reeves, *Places of Pain and Shame: Dealing with 'Difficult Heritage'*, Routledge, London and New York 2009

Mazower, Mark, *Inside Hitler's Greece. The Experience of Occupation, 1941–1944*, Alexandreia, Athens 1994

Mazower, Mark, "The Cold War and the Appropriation of Memory: Greece after Liberation," in István Deán, Jan Gross, Tony Judt (Eds.) *The Politics of Retribution in Europe, World War II and Its Aftermath*, Princeton University Press, Princeton 2000, pp. 212–232

Meng, Michael, *Shattered Spaces: Encountering Jewish Ruins in Postwar Germany and Poland*, Harvard University Press, Cambridge 2011

Morsch, Gunter (Ed.), *Von der Erinnerung zum Monument. Die Entstehungsgeschichte der Nationalen Mahn- und Gedenkstatte Sachsenhausen*, Oranienburg 1996

Nora, Pierre, "Between Memory and History: Les Lieux de Mémoire," *Representations*, 26, 1989, pp. 7–24

Rosenfeld, Gavriel, "A Looming Crash or a Soft Landing? Forecasting the Future of the Memory Industry'," *The Journal of Modern History*, 81, no. 1, 2009, p. 122–158

Ruhi, U., "Level Up Your Strategy: Towards a Descriptive Framework for Meaningful Enterprise Gamification," *Technology Innovation Management Review*, 5, no. 8, 5–16. https://dφoi.org/10.22215/timreview/918

Skribeleit, Jorg, "'Orte des Schreckens'. Dimensionen verraumlichter Erinnerung," in *Der Nationalsozialismus im Spiegel des offentlichen Gedachtnisses*, edited by Petra Fank, Stefan Hordler, Metropol, Berlin 2005, pp. 205–220

Teneketzis, Alexandros, *Monuments of the Second World War in Europe 1945–1975*, Asini, Athens 2020 [*Τα μνημεία για τον Β 'Παγκόσμιο Πόλεμο στην Ευρώπη (1945–1975)*, Ασίνη, Αθήνα 2020]

Tsiara, Syrago, *Sites of National Memory*, Kleidarithmos, Athens 2004 [*Τοπία της εθνικής μνήμης*, Κλειδαριθμος, Αθήνα 2004]

Voglis, Polymeris, Nioutsikos Ioannis, "The Greek Historiography of the 1940s. A Reassessment," *Südosteuropa*, 65, no. 2, 2017, pp. 316–333. https://doi.org/10.1515/soeu-2017-0020

Voglis, Polymeris, "The Memories of the 1940s as an Object of Historical Analysis: Methodological Proposals," in *Memories and Oblivion of the Greek Civil War*, edited by Van Bushhoten Riki, Vervenioti Tassoula et al. Epikentro, Thessaloniki 2008, p. 61–80

Wachsmann, Nikolaus, *KL: A History of the Concentration Camps*, Little Brown, London 2015

Whitehead, Christopher, Bozoğlu Gönül, Daugbjerg Mads, "Remapping European Heritage and Memory. Positions, Inspirations, Approaches," in Whitehead Christopher, Eckersley Susannah, Daugbjerg Mads, Bozoğlu Gönül (Eds.), *Dimensions of Heritage and Memory. Multiple Europes and the Politics of Crisis*, Routledge, London/New York 2019, p. 26–50

Winter, Jay, Sivan Emmanuel (Eds.), *War and Remembrance in the Twentieth Century*, Cambridge University Press, Cambridge 2009

Young, James E., *The Texture of Memory. Holocaust, Memorials and Meaning*, Yale University Press, New Haven/London 1993

Young, James E., *At Memory's Edge: After Images of the Holocaust in Contemporary Art and Architecture*, Yale University Press, New Haven 2000
Young, Katie, "Auschwitz-Birkenau. The challenges of heritage management following the Cold War," in *Places of Pain and Shame. Dealing with 'Difficult Heritage'*, edited by William Logan, and Keir Reeves. Routledge, London and New York 2009, p. 50–68

INDEX

For Product Safety Concerns and Information please contact our EU representative GPSR@taylorandfrancis.com
Taylor & Francis Verlag GmbH, Kaufingerstraße 24, 80331 München, Germany

www.ingramcontent.com/pod-product-compliance
Ingram Content Group UK Ltd.
Pitfield, Milton Keynes, MK11 3LW, UK
UKHW020205200926
475702UK00004B/621
* 9 7 8 1 0 3 2 0 6 0 8 5 9 *